ROGER STEVENSON
FEB. 16, 1990

P9-CRO-854

SELLING BY MAIL

Also by Susan K. Jones

TIME-MANAGEMENT FOR EXECUTIVES (co-author)

SELLING BY MAIL

An Entrepreneurial Guide to Direct Marketing

John W. Graham
Susan K. Jones

CHARLES SCRIBNER'S SONS NEW YORK

Copyright © 1985 John W. Graham and Susan K. Jones

Library of Congress Cataloging in Publication Data

Graham, John W.
  Selling by mail.

  Includes index.
  1. Mail-order business. 2. Direct marketing.
I. Jones, Susan K. II. Title.
HF5466.G67   1985   658.8'4   85-14267
ISBN 0-684-18215-7

Published simultaneously in Canada by Collier
Macmillan Canada, Inc.—Copyright under
the Berne Convention.

All rights reserved. No part of this book
may be reproduced in any form without
the permission of Charles Scribner's Sons.

1 3 5 7 9 11 13 15 17 19   F/C   20 18 16 14 12 10 8 6 4 2

Printed in the United States of America.

For Joe and Danielle

CONTENTS

Acknowledgments ix

Introduction 1

SECTION ONE

1. The Basics of Direct Marketing 3
2. Corporate Strategy: A Direct
    Response Perspective 8
3. A Word to Retailers about the Direct Response Field 13

SECTION TWO

4. The Direct Response Buyer 24
5. The Offer 32
6. Direct Mail Formats 60
7. Catalogs 85
8. Mailing Lists: The Vital Customer Link 113
9. Direct Marketing Testing 121
10. Print Media: Strategy and Execution 125
11. Telephone Direct Marketing 135
12. Broadcast Media 140
13. Public Relations for the Direct Response Marketer 146
14. Fulfillment: An Operations Overview 161
15. Back-End Marketing 168

SECTION THREE

16. The Mathematics of Direct Marketing   188
17. Working with Agencies and Doing In-House
    Staffing for Direct Response Promotions   193
18. Scheduling and Critical Dates for Direct Mail
    and Space   205
19. Postal and Lettershop Coordination   211
20. Legal Concerns of the Direct Marketer   219
21. Art/Layout/Design   223
22. Copy/Working with Copywriters   238
23. Print Production   253

    Appendix I: The Direct Marketing Plan   266
    Appendix II: A Glossary of Direct Marketing Terms   271
    Appendix III: Periodicals   286
    Appendix IV: Books and Monographs   289
    Appendix V: Associations and Clubs   293
    Appendix VI: Seminars   295
    Appendix VII: A Word about Ethics and Regulation   297

    Index   303

ACKNOWLEDGMENTS

The knowledge imparted in this book largely reflects my experiences with a number of fine people in diverse environments. William C. Brown, Glenn T. Matthews, and James P. Smith, Jr., have each played a major role in shaping my professional development. I hope each will be honored by this documentation of the knowledge they so unselfishly shared with me. To J. P., I offer my heartfelt thanks for your confidence, friendship, and loyalty.

To my contemporaries Ronald G. Gregory, Thomas L. Jones, and Robert Nash, I say thank you for the times spent thinking and churning over new concepts and approaches. May we continue to learn together in this exciting field.

To Joe and Mary—thanks for a loving environment and for helping me to understand the adventure of life.

Finally, I warmly acknowledge my co-author, Susan K. Jones, for her contribution to direct response education as the primary author for chapters on the direct response buyer, the offer, formats, catalogs, telephone, broadcast, public relations, back end, working with agencies, scheduling, postal/lettershop, art, copy, and print production.

John W. Graham
Jacksonville, Florida

My thanks for help with this book extend back far beyond the creation of the manuscript. I would like to thank the people who opened the world of writing and advertising to me: teachers and professors, including the late Dr. Steuart Henderson Britt, Mr. and Mrs. Park W. Lenhart, Dr. John Maloney, Dr. Jack Sissors, and Professor Edward Stephens.

My sincere thanks go as well to the people whom I consider my mentors in the direct response field. Generous with their explanations and help, they taught as much by example as by instruction. They are Tom Brady, Gene Colin, John Hugunin, Lauren Januz, Herb Krug, Jim Schmidt, and J. P. Smith.

I also thank C. C. Bestwina, René Cudahy, Helene Dunne, Ron Gregory, Randy Howell, and Diane (Carnevale) Jones for their professional support, loyalty, and friendship.

I thank my mother, Janet Kraus, and my sister, Nancy Cundiff, for their love, help, and understanding.

Finally, I warmly acknowledge the contributions of my co-author, John W. Graham, whose diverse experience has greatly enriched this presentation. John Graham is the primary author of chapters on the basics of direct marketing, corporate strategy, lists, print media, fulfillment, direct response math, legal concerns, and testing.

Susan K. Jones
Winnetka, Illinois

INTRODUCTION

Most direct response books available today are aimed at the direct marketing professional. They serve as handbooks for the working ad man or woman who already has a general knowledge of direct response basics. A few other volumes—some bordering on sensationalism—are aimed at the kitchen table marketer who hopes to parlay a good product into a part-time business and eventually a career.

But until now, no direct response book has specifically addressed the general business community—the nondirect response marketer who wants to learn how to take advantage of the ripe profit opportunities direct marketing offers today. This manager could be an entrepreneur who sees direct marketing as a way to begin or expand a new business. He or she might be a small-business person or a department head within a larger firm—charged with implementing a direct response program for lead generation or sales to consumers or business. The manager might own a retail store and wish to improve traffic or to establish a second profit center by means of catalogs or other mailings.

This book may well be of great help to the direct response professional, but it is not meant for the "kitchen table moonlighter." It assumes the reader can afford to sink at least $20,000 to $50,000 into an initial marketing effort. But of course, wherever possible, suggestions are given for inexpensive means of testing, obtaining customers, and maximizing the use of available assets.

The book is written for novices; no prior direct marketing experience is assumed. It will teach small-business people how to start an in-house direct marketing operation or to find and work with a suitable agency. The reader will learn how to select other outside sources, how to evaluate the work they do, how to set up a testing program and evaluate results, how to budget, and much more. It is a handbook for the novice, smaller-budget direct marketer who hopes to learn from others' successes rather than from his or her own trial and error.

HOW TO USE THIS BOOK

Some aspects of direct marketing are of near-equal importance to all marketing people—whether the target audience is consumers, retail store customers, or business establishments. But many of the how-to's of direct marketing depend a great deal on the target market and on the product. And so this book comprises three main sections, arranged so that readers may gain all the basic and general information they will need in sections one and three while skipping some of the material in section two that may be of little interest for their particular target markets.

Section one provides an introduction to today's direct marketing field and to the opportunities it offers for various types of firms. It covers the basics of direct marketing: what types of businesses should use it, and how direct marketing fits into overall marketing concepts.

Section two covers consumer, retail, and business applications. These include the mail-order buyer, the offer, formats, catalogs, telephone marketing, mailing lists, print media, response television, publicity, fulfillment, and bounce-backs.

Section three focuses on the preparation and implementation of a direct response program—material that is of general interest to all direct marketers. The topics covered include research, budgeting and math, agencies and staffing, scheduling and critical dates, postal information, legal information, art/layout/design, copy, print production, lettershop and computer applications, and testing/reading results. The appendices include lists of helpful books, information sources, suppliers, seminars, and a glossary of terms.

1

THE BASICS OF DIRECT MARKETING

As a prospective direct marketer, you should understand certain facts about the direct marketing business. First, while the words "direct marketing" may suggest the Sears catalog of fifty years ago, the industry has grown very rapidly, and future growth seems assured. In fact, the Direct Marketing Association predicts that by the year 2000, one dollar out of every four will be spent on direct marketing sales.

Further, according to the Direct Marketing Association, industry sales have doubled in only seven years to over $138 billion. This growth has been fueled by both expanding technology and improved marketing savvy. New marketers are using computer technology to target selected market segments now accessible for the first time. Increased numbers of consumer, retail, business, and industrial marketers are searching to maximize profits and efficiency via direct response. For example, the cost of a personal sales call now exceeds $150. Business-to-business marketers have taken the lead in implementing catalog divisions to handle small orders and inquiry programs.

The use of telephone marketing has increased tremendously with expenditures exceeding $12 billion per year; and the future media of cable TV, home computers, and videotext remain untapped but powerful catalysts for future growth.

While the potential of this distribution channel seems almost unlimited, it is important for each business to consider several factors before attempting to become a direct response marketer.

3

DIRECT MARKETING FLOW CHART

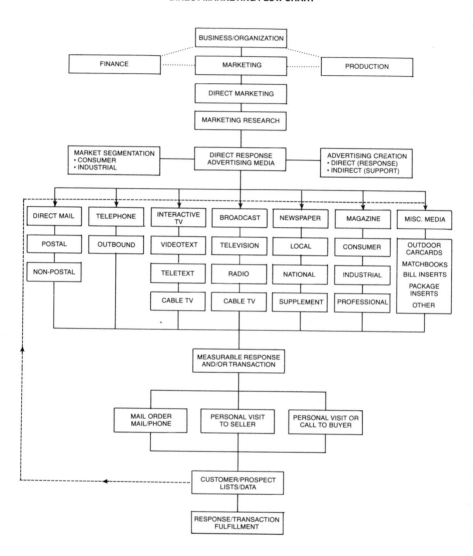

Source: Direct Marketing, Garden City, New York. Reprinted by Permission.

4

SHOULD YOU BECOME A DIRECT MARKETER?

This is one of the most important questions for management to address. And whether you are a bank marketer, retailer, industrial marketer, or kitchen table entrepreneur, the considerations are the same:

1. Is your product or service distinctive and can it be differentiated from alternatives?
2. Can your prospective customer be reached economically through rented lists and media advertisements?
3. Do you have access to existing marketing talent (either in-house or agency) to execute your marketing campaign?
4. Does the price of your product provide the necessary profit margin? Does the price reflect positively on perceived value and competitive pricing?
5. Will the use of direct marketing cause problems with existing distribution channels?
6. Do you have the financial resources to market this new product?

Imagine that you are introducing a new camera that produces instant pictures of superb quality at one-third the price of the competition. The targeted novice camera family of four, parents aged 30–45, should be most receptive to a camera that costs $39.95 and produces instant pictures for only fifteen cents each. Your concern here is with your existing distribution channel, and whether the use of direct response marketing will alienate your existing dealers. While most studies indicate that direct marketing increases the retail market share of a product, many dealers must be educated to the benefits of coordinating retail and direct response channels.

Conflicting distribution channel problems are among the most common that marketers experience. These conflicts can be resolved in several ways. First, you have the option of selling a new product under a new trademark or trade name. Second, you can give the dealer an allocation of product to redeem "walk-in" sales resulting from a direct marketing campaign, or, third, you can syndicate the product to a company with a customer base that is likely to have an affinity for it. For example, World Book Publishing might be an interesting syndication prospect for your new camera.

Few realize the financial commitment involved in launching a new

**TOTAL ESTIMATED
DIRECT RESPONSE ADVERTISING EXPENDITURES**

	1981	(in millions $) 1982	1983
Coupons[1]	94.6	127.1	148.1
Direct Mail (postage, paper & production)[2]	10,566.7	11,359.4	12,692.2
Magazines (mail order merchandise only)[3]	150.0	167.0	188.7
Business Magazines (industrial products only)[3]	59.0	66.0	73.9
Newspapers[4]	73.0	70.6	80.5
Newspaper Preprints[4]	2,228.5	2,500.0	2,850.0
Telephone[5]	11,467.0	12,935.6	13,608.3
Television[3]	295.0	339.0	386.5
Radio[3]	29.0	33.0	37.0
Grand Total	$25,022.8	$27,597.7	$30,065.2

1. Source: Nielson Clearing House
2. Source: Direct Marketing Association, Inc.
3. Source: HAI Industry Statistics/DMA projected growth percentage (1983 only)
4. Source: Newspaper Advertising Bureau/DMA projected growth percentage (1983 only)
5. Source: ATT Communications, DMA estimate for 1983 only; based in part on information from AT&T

Note: Creative costs not included in any of the above figures.

Reprinted by Permission of Direct Marketing Association

product. Yet it is absolutely essential that you, your management, and your banker understand the financial commitment you need to initiate marketing via direct response. Your product development, initial promotion, and some inventory costs almost always occur before the first order comes in the mail. Financial planning is essential.

ARE YOUR OPERATIONS READY?

Let us assume that you believe your product ideas fit the criteria mentioned above and that you are ready to implement a marketing plan. Before you make your move, you must consider several operational issues:

1. Is your computer system capable of processing orders for your new product?
2. Do you have a customer service department?
3. Do you have a warehouse or fulfillment service to ship orders?
4. Are your financial people ready to help manage the flow of funds?

5. Do you have the vendor sources needed to deliver promotional materials? You will also need to select an advertising agency, a printer, and a mailing service.

While the direct response field is growing rapidly, whether or not your organization chooses this channel of distribution hinges on an assessment of marketing, financial, and operational issues.

2

CORPORATE STRATEGY: A DIRECT RESPONSE PERSPECTIVE

Part of the growth in the direct response business during the past decade has occurred because entrepreneurs and corporations alike have recognized that direct response marketing can play a key role in an overall corporate strategy.

For Sears, Roebuck and Company, the retailing giant, catalog business does more than generate profits. Through detailed sales analysis, catalog sales patterns are instrumental in determining likely areas for new retail-store locations. Other companies utilize direct response primarily to generate leads, build traffic, or support media and personal sales campaigns. Regardless of your size, you must consider alternative strategic positions before committing your company and its resources.

THE STRATEGY OF EVOLVEMENT

Many entrepreneurs run their businesses on the premise of "taking the plunge." "I'm an optimist; it will work." This approach sometimes succeeds, as in the case of Roger Horchow, who decided there was a need for a mail-order business to service the affluent, discerning customer who enjoyed unique, expensive products. Mr. Horchow resigned his position at Neiman-Marcus and began what has become one of the premiere direct response companies in the United States. The same is true of Lillian Vernon, Joe Sugarman, and countless others who started with an idea and few resources. Each business evolved into a vital, growing concern.

Did these entrepreneurs establish a formal corporate strategy? Assess the market potential? Consider competitive forces? Perhaps not, or at least not the way you should today. There is nothing wrong with this approach to starting or nurturing a mail-order business provided you recognize its limitations. First, many people overlook competitive forces in plotting their course of action. For example, one new venture, Sportswares, was in business for about three years and lost millions. It failed because there simply was no market for another mail-order catalog servicing the sports apparel customer aged 35 to 55. Companies such as Hills Court, Sports Pages, and thousands of other retailers were already servicing this segment. The entrepreneur who started this venture underestimated both his competitive strength and market potential. He "took the plunge" and relied on his optimism to make it work. You may succeed using this strategy, as no doubt someone will tomorrow and next year; but the odds are against it.

AN ACQUISITION STRATEGY

One way to get into direct response quickly is to acquire a going concern. If you have the resources, this is an obvious option. However, you are still confronted with a number of questions: What kind of business do you acquire? Do you buy an apparel catalog, a business forms company, or a workbench company? How do you assess their relative market values? Which business has reached its potential and which has only begun? How does the prospective acquisition complement your assets? Do you take a chance with a loser and try to turn it around? A case in point occurred when a medium-sized, mid-western direct marketer acquired Hammacher-Schlemmer, aiming to make the company viable both at retail and catalog sales. After a very challenging beginning, company management achieved the turn around, and the business is now profitable. However, turn arounds are risky and should be undertaken only when you are investing in a solid marketing concept.

In short, an acquisition strategy does not eliminate the need for thoughtful planning. Planning is just as critical with an acquisition as with a start-up company.

A DEVELOPMENTAL STRATEGY

Whether you are a sole proprietorship or a large corporation, a well-conceived, properly thought-out corporate strategy will improve your likelihood of success in the direct response field. Your strategy should reflect your plan of attack and address the following issues:

1. *You must focus on the customer and the product or service you plan to offer.* Is your concept truly unique? Will you have to buy your market share? How will your differentiate your product or service?

2. *What is the market potential for your product or service?* Is it so new and unusual that no dollars are currently being spent on it? Is the market growing, stagnant, or receding? Can you achieve your financial objectives with a relatively small share of the market?

3. *Who are your prospective competitors?* Are they growing and profitable, or stagnant and marginal? What is their financial strength? What happens to you if they respond aggressively to your entry? What are their relative market shares? Can you buy a going concern?

4. *How will your new direct response business complement your existing assets?* Will it enhance your existing business or be a drain on profits and management? If you are an entrepreneur, your primary assets are your time and money. Can you manage this new venture by yourself? Do you need a partner?

5. *What do you want direct response marketing to do for your enterprise?* Is it simply an investment for which you expect a certain rate of return? Will it be used as a vital part of a larger overall strategy? What are your long-term objectives?

6. *Can you develop a niche?* Carving out your own niche is classic business theory, but is especially important for the direct response market. Will your perceived market share be large enough for successful profitability but small enough to avoid attracting too much competition?

Whether you are considering a start-up or an acquisition, we recommend that you address each of these points in written form. As your plans develop, you can read, rewrite, and rethink your assumptions. Have your banker, lawyer, and accountant review your plan as well. Each will make points that you will have forgotten or overlooked, and your strategy will develop as your knowledge of the relevant factors improves.

Does this approach guarantee success? The answer, of course, is no. But it does improve the likelihood of success. And success is not restricted to proceeding with your original concept. You may find, after assessing competitive factors, the market potential, and your product or service concept, that your idea was not feasible, or that to succeed you must modify your original concept. Using the guidelines we suggest, you can assess market opportunities *before* making major financial commitments.

A WORD ABOUT MARKETING INTUITIONS

Many marketers clearly have a great ''feel'' for the marketplace. Often a business person may have a product concept that is superb, or he or she may have savvy about a market segment that provides a competitive edge. These are factors that must be considered in formulating a corporate strategy. But savvy and great product concepts are not always enough, and your strategic plan must weigh the relative importance of the variables. Because the direct marketing business is becoming more and more competitive, you should do as much contingency planning as possible to assure success.

HOW TO USE YOUR STRATEGIC PLAN

Let us assume that you have developed a strategy and are confident that the risk–reward relationship is such that you wish to proceed. From your strategic plan, you must develop a business plan. Your business plan may be as simple as resolving to work an extra twenty hours a week to accomplish your established objectives, but you must be sure that you are in a position to execute it. You must plan your financial commitment, hire or retrain the appropriate personnel, review your accounting and operating procedures, and analyze the tax ramifications of your new plan. If you have a computer you must make the necessary programming modifications to service your new venture.

Next, you must formulate your marketing plan, which will depend heavily on the assumptions made in your strategic plan. Your marketing plan sets a time frame for prototyping your product or service, assesses market conditions, indicates planned promotion duties and media and list tests, identifies your target market, and incorporates financial assumptions about results. As you approach your business and marketing objectives, be sure to review your activities against your strategic plan. It's easy to get off course, so make sure that you're doing what you planned to do.

3

A WORD TO RETAILERS ABOUT THE DIRECT RESPONSE FIELD

The following chapters contain special information for those marketers who deal with consumer, retail, or business-to-business prospects. While consumer and business marketers are often quick to see the potential of direct marketing, some retailers resist direct marketing, and have to be convinced of its profit opportunities.

Retailers may opt to focus their direct marketing efforts on building traffic for in-store events, or they may develop separate programs that offer special merchandise for sale by mail or phone only. Often, the retailer's direct response efforts combine these two objectives. But for every retailer who has discovered the profit potential of direct marketing, there are several who have not begun to explore this exciting and lucrative field. Here are some of the reasons why retailers may resist direct marketing, followed by short rebuttals from the experience of successful direct marketing users.

WHY RETAILERS RESIST DIRECT MARKETING

Other promotional activities are more easily attained. Every retailer hears from his or her local newspaper advertising representative on a very regular basis. Most newspapers are glad to "hold the hand" of the retailer, offering layouts, typesetting, and even copy services in some cases. Local television stations may also offer these services, so all the retailer needs to do is select the products to promote and hand over the money.

But direct response programs take planning and effort—exploration of a new way of marketing. And they may seem expensive to the retailer who has never tried them before.

REBUTTAL: The newspaper or TV reps' livelihood depends on their media, and their opinions are therefore likely to be biased. Using the step-by-step techniques in this book, the "how-to" of getting started in direct marketing will become clear to the retailer, who will learn how the necessary planning and effort can result in exciting incremental sales opportunities.

A bad experience turns off the retailer. Some retailers try their own hands at direct marketing, without the services of a professional consultant. They do the best they can, but often break some of the cardinal rules of direct marketing without even knowing it. When their efforts fail, they shake their heads and say that direct marketing is not for them.

REBUTTAL: Retailers who would never attempt to do their own accounting, window dressing, or interior decorating persist in considering themselves advertising and promotion experts. The advice in this book for finding and working with direct marketing consultants should prove helpful in getting the assistance needed for a conservative initial test of direct marketing.

The retailer fears that direct marketing sales will cannibalize his or her retail sales. Many retailers don't bother to produce their own catalogs or mailings, assuming that the sales generated by mail will take away from potential store sales.

REBUTTAL: This "old saw" has yet to be put to rest, even though both Sears, Roebuck & Company and Montgomery Ward openly admit that the introduction of their new catalogs each season has a potent effect on their retail, in-store sales. The efforts of such major retailers as Neiman-Marcus and Marshall Field & Company add evidence that "cannibalization" is not likely to occur.

The retailer considers direct marketing a natural enemy of retailing. The retailer of "preppy" clothing who sees the proliferation of catalogs selling similar lines may feel that such catalog efforts are damaging to his or her livelihood, and resist adding to the perceived "problem."

REBUTTAL: Those in the field generally consider retailers' main competitors to be other retailers, and direct marketers' competitors to be other direct marketers.

Direct marketing is considered junk mail. Some retailers fear their prestige in the marketplace will be hurt if they start producing "junk mail."
REBUTTAL: The creamy, thick paper and lush photography of many retail catalogs (notably those of Gucci and Tiffany) easily raise their status above that of junk mail. What's more, this pejorative term is most often used by consumers who receive mailings in which they're not interested anyway—mailings that were poorly targeted in the first place. The retailer's news and special offerings are not likely to be considered "junk" by loyal customers.

It takes time to produce a good direct marketing effort. Because of the weeks and months required for producing a color catalog, the retailer may feel his efforts are better spent in day-by-day newspaper advertising that can be put together with just a few days' notice.
REBUTTAL: True, direct marketing efforts don't have as immediate an effect as newspaper or even television can. But the medium's assets, such as fine color reproduction, targeting to an exact customer profile, lengthy copy space, and so on make this drawback a minor inconvenience.

A retailer can simply use "canned" direct response material or syndicators—why do one's own? Many retailers are aware of their "clout" with manufacturers who provide them with statement stuffers or even full mailings for special promotions. And some retailers who have larger lists have occasionally let syndicators prepare material for mailing to their retailer's customers.
REBUTTAL: Although these cooperative and syndication opportunities may be lucrative, they are not often well targeted to the retailer's particular market and customer. The opportunity to appeal specifically to one's own market cannot be underestimated.

Now that these common objections have been "put to rest," let us examine some of the benefits of retail direct marketing—still one of the most underutilized direct response opportunities in the marketing world.

REASONS WHY DIRECT MARKETING IS SO VALUABLE FOR RETAILERS

The customer list is a natural. Most every retailer keeps a list of customers' and visitors' names and addresses. Someone's name on that list is your assurance that he or she is interested enough in your products either to buy them or wish to be kept informed about them. Direct marketers without retail outlets would envy the retailer having such a readily available group of "qualified prospects."

Once the retailer understands the power of such a list, he or she may opt to key the list for multiple buyers, "big spenders," fur buyers, purchasers of children's wear, and other special-interest groups. The list can be broken down for very specific offers to highly targeted audiences.

Direct mail allows for a personal slant. Many retailers take advantage of the "personal touch" in direct mail to give early announcement of sales and special events to preferred customers. They may develop in-store events or mail and phone buying opportunities for preferred customers only. Direct mail allows for an "exclusive invitation" approach that is impossible with the mass media of newspaper and television.

The retailer's name already carries an image. Direct marketers without a retail affiliation must spend time and money establishing an image with prospective buyers. The customer may resist sending in an order because he or she has no experience with the firm. By contrast, local retailers carry their local images with them into direct response operations (assuming that they tailor their presentations to reinforce existing images), and the retailer with a reputation for good service and merchandise right away has an edge over an unknown firm.

Direct mail helps avoid constraints inherent in other media. Color reproduction in newspapers is notoriously bad, except in sections that are printed separately as free-standing "stuffers" or parts of Sunday magazines. Television is very limited in terms of copy length, among other constraints, and radio allows for no visuals at all. But in direct mail, the retailer can target the market so specifically that it may pay to send out fabric swatches, offer free samples, print a prospectus costing several dollars a copy, or include several pages of explanatory information enlivened by well-reproduced color photos.

The combination of retail and direct response is a potent one. Back in 1925, Sears, Roebuck and Company—then only a catalog house—opened its first retail store, and Montgomery Ward followed suit in 1926. Even then, retailers understood the potential for retail and direct marketing operations that fed into each other. The 1984 *Fact Book on Direct Response Marketing* from the Direct Marketing Association reports Sears research showing that families receiving a Sears catalog are twice as likely to shop at a Sears store as nonrecipients. Even more significant, these catalog recipients spend twice as much at Sears as non–catalog recipients.

Today, many firms with retail operations use their direct marketing "arms" not only as traffic builders, but also to exploit their opportunities in other product lines and beyond their local traffic areas. Moreover, these firms' retail stores serve as welcome backups to liquidate occasional direct marketing "overbuys" which might otherwise represent a severe loss for the direct marketer.

Credit cards and installment-credit proliferation. Diners Club introduced the first travel and entertainment card in 1950, followed by American Express in 1958 and Carte Blanche in 1959. The first Bankamericard was issued in 1958, leading to today's ever-present Visa and MasterCards. Now that consumers have widely accepted credit cards and installment buying, retailers may offer "high ticket" items via direct response, even to customers who do not hold store charge accounts. All the retailer need do is offer the charge option of American Express, Visa, MasterCard, or some other widely held credit card.

With store charge accounts accepted by customers as a virtual necessity, retailers can launch successful "blanket" mailings to new areas where stores are to be opened, soliciting new charge customers even before the Grand Opening.

Monthly charge statements also become fertile fields for the direct marketer. For the same postage needed to send out the bill, syndicated or co-op offers or the retailer's own direct response pieces can ride along in the envelope.

Vendors are often willing to help pay direct response costs. Today's retailers are smart if they keep their eyes and ears open for opportun-

YOUR OFFER
FROM
ESTÉE LAUDER

18

ities to use a vendor's money for direct response promotion. Here the manufacturer provides a lush direct mail piece imprinted with the store's name and address, and offers a time-dated buying opportunity to the store's customers. The many "free with purchase" cosmetics offers sent out by department stores are but one example of this type of "co-op" arrangement. The customer may then order by mail or stop in at the store to take advantage of the "free with purchase" opportunity.

The oil companies have traditionally been the biggest user of syndicated (see glossary) direct mail pieces. But the energy crisis, the proliferation of statement stuffers of all types, and the rising costs of mailing have combined to bring about a lessening of syndicator activity in recent years. Some larger retailers may still benefit by allowing syndicated merchandise to be offered to their customers through statement stuffers, individual mailings, catalogs, and so on.

Direct response can expand local horizons. Say that you're a retailer of a local specialty: macadamia nuts in Hawaii, for instance, or Navajo rugs and crafts in the southwest. Or suppose you're a firm like

Today's retailers may stimulate store traffic and invite phone and mail sales using "free-with-purchase" cosmetic offers such as this from Estée Lauder.

Gump's in San Francisco or Neiman-Marcus in Dallas, know
reputation beyond your local area, and a place that tourists wa
see when they visit your town. In these cases, and really in any
in which your store offers something that is not readily availab
customers beyond your local area, you may expand your custo
base by offering your products by direct mail and direct response i
dia.

Before you get started, though, keep two things in mind: First, y
must be sure that your products are unique enough to interest customers beyond your local area. Second, you must make sure that your
mark-up will let you sell profitably by mail; the usual 50 percent
mark-up of a retail store that buys merchandise from a middleman
and then resells it may not be sufficient for direct mail efforts where
a minimum three-time mark-up is the rule of thumb.

Direct mail offers you the opportunity to use your buying power. As
a retailer you already have established relationships with vendors in
your field, and will therefore command their attention with your direct response plans. In the sportswear field, for instance, you may be
able to have one of your vendors make custom-designed clothing for
your direct response line—versions that are exclusive to you and
available only by mail. Or, if you wish to play off your success in a
certain department and put together a "deeper" line of that department's merchandise for a direct response catalog or special mailing,
your vendors may be happy to cooperate on the basis of your retail
record.

Your salespeople can benefit from direct mail. The salesperson who
keeps in touch with customers by personal mail or telephone is much
more likely to win customer loyalty than the one who simply waits
for customers to walk through the door. Postcards, standard mailings
with handwritten personal notes, personal invitations to in-store
events, and other means of communication can help your salespeople
build a loyal clientele.

Direct mail can help even out your seasonal business patterns. The
retail store that was bustling with walk-in trade on December 15 can
be a pretty empty place on January 15 unless the retailer has given
the customer reasons to be there after the holidays, such as sales, special events, seminars, continuity offers, and so on. Direct response

techniques can help mitigate slumps by making customers and prospective customers aware of what is going on at a store during traditional "slow periods."

Mail-in or phone-in ordering are also quite appealing to the customer who has to battle a foot of snow to take advantage of a January white sale in person. Thus, direct mail or phone sales can boost the influx of business even when weather or other seasonal factors cut down on walk-in trade.

Pre-test product ideas and pitches. Direct response selling can provide inexpensive "market research" for a retailer, and yield some orders in the process. Try out that new line of merchandise on a limited number of customers by mail, and then evaluate the results before deciding whether to allocate in-store space to the merchandise. Or do a direct mail test using two different themes for a new fall promotion of the same merchandise. The one that "pulls" best then can become the theme for all of your promotions.

Direct mail is good for other types of retailers too. Any business that is selling to individuals rather than other businesses is considered a retailer for the purposes of this section. So if you market a service or other intangible such as car repair, insurance as a local agent, lawn spraying, or dry cleaning, or operate a restaurant, the suggestions here may help you.

A SEPARATE DIRECT RESPONSE DIVISION

Once upon a time, the only merchandise a retailer would offer by direct response promotion was merchandise that could also be found on his or her store shelves. But retailers like Neiman-Marcus changed that by using their expertise as buyers to set up separate, direct response divisions.

"N-M By Post" is a regular catalog that features items available only by mail from Neiman-Marcus. And the regular Neiman-Marcus books carry a disclaimer which says that merchandise contained in the catalog may or may not be carried in Neiman-Marcus stores.

Such non-store offers allow an established retailer to sell merchandise that is more suited to direct response promotion than to instore selling. For instance, some of the charming, small gift items offered in "N-M By Post" would be lost on a large retail counter,

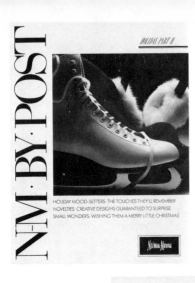

N·M·BY·POST

HOLIDAY MOOD-SETTERS: THE TOUCHES THEY'LL REMEMBER
NOVELTIES: CREATIVE DESIGNS GUARANTEED TO SURPRISE
SMALL WONDERS: WISHING THEM A MERRY LITTLE CHRISTMAS

Neiman Marcus

"N-M By Post" is the separate, direct mail arm of Neiman-Marcus, with its own yearly array of catalogs.

S ilvery snowflakes, sleigh bells, and Santas. These are a few of our favorite things.

8A. Interspersed on a sturdy red string, 1 inch square wooden blocks decorated with Victorian-inspired Santa Claus scenes and large, carved alphabet characters. The garland, measuring 8' long, 15.00 (2.50). From the Trim-A-Tree Shop.

8B. Balls of frosted and bright-tinted glass, festively painted with stripes, dots, sprigs, topped with golden hoops for hanging. 10½" circumference. A set of 6, in the assorted colors shown. 20.00 (2.75). Available through Mail Order only.

8C. Here comes Santa Claus—in a musical hot air balloon! The elaborately detailed taffeta balloon transports a wicker basket carrying Santa, his elf, and a host of toys and gifts. Wind the key on the bottom to hear "Here Comes Santa Claus." Handcrafted and signed by the artist. Hangs from a clear, almost invisible string. 28 inches tall; 12 inch diameter. Colors as shown. 350.00 (7.10). From the Trim-A-Tree Shop.

whereas with proper photography and copy they can become "stars" on the catalog pages.

The retailer might also consider organizing separate direct response divisions for catalogs or mailings that offer merchandise in more depth than would be appropriate for most retail stores. Examples of this would be an Orvis or Norm Thompson mailing offering hunting boots in many different varieties, or an Abercrombie & Fitch flyer offering an entire wardrobe of safari attire.

9A. Typical of an old-fashioned English half-timbered shop—"Ye Olde Curiosity Shoppe", a painstakingly detailed music box lidded with a hinged, thatched roof. Handmade in England of wood and natural materials when possible, the Shoppe plays "God Rest Ye Merry Gentlemen" via top quality Swiss musical movement. 6½" wide x 5" deep x 6½" tall. Painted in the colors shown 50.00 (4.00). From the Trim-A-Tree Shop.

Order toll free Monday through Saturday. Dial 1800-NEIMANS (1-800-634-6267) 8:00 a.m. to 8:00 p.m. Central time.

9B. The mellow jingle of our silver-plated sleigh bell key ring helps you locate your keys in a moment—and keeps you in the holiday spirit at the same time. A Neiman-Marcus exclusive. 1½" diameter. 10.00 (2.40). From Small Leather Goods.

9C,D. Handmade of felt in England, a duo of N-M exclusive Christmas mice, both 4" tall. **9C.** Mouse disguised as Santa to cheer you with a joyful "Ho, Ho, Ho!" 10.00 (2.40). **9D.** As a miserly mouse, Scrooge looks lovable—even carrying his "Bah Humbug!" sign. 10.00 (2.40). Available through Mail Order only.

9E. A pipe-smoking woodsman designed to appear to actually blow smoke from his mouth. Separate the pieces, place lighted incense on the tray inside—the smoke and aroma waft through his mouth. Handmade in Germany of multi-tinted wood, the feathery-haired man carries firewood on his back and a woven basket of mushrooms and sprigs as pictured. Approximately 10½" tall. 32.50 (3.20). Through Mail Order only.

9

4

THE DIRECT RESPONSE BUYER

The key concept for marketing today is "marketing orientation": tailoring products and services to the wants and needs of customers. This tailoring goes beyond the product itself to the other facets of the marketing mix: promotion, pricing, and place (distribution). Thus it is crucial for the direct marketer to understand his or her customer: what the customer wants in a product, and what makes the customer willing to buy a particular product (or be influenced to buy it) via direct response.

This chapter, divided into consumer, retail, and business-to-business sections, covers basic information about today's direct response buyer.

THE CONSUMER DIRECT RESPONSE BUYER

The typical "mail-order buyer" used to be a rural person without much access to retail stores. The original mail-order catalogs from Montgomery Ward and Sears, Roebuck & Company made it possible for the farm community and small-town shoppers to obtain a wide variety of goods without a journey to the "big city."

With today's changing lifestyles, the growth of the suburbs, and the proliferation of mass merchandisers even in rural and semi-rural areas, the complexion of the direct response buyer has changed considerably. To understand his new direct response buyer, let's examine some of the business and cultural reasons why individuals today tend to buy via direct response.

Changing lifestyles. The "classic American family," with Dad employed outside the home and Mom staying at home with two or more children, now accounts for less than one-fourth of American family units. There are more single-parent families and dual-career families than ever before. In fact, women now account for about half of the total work force.

With these changes has come an important alteration in family buying patterns. No longer can a stay-at-home Mom be counted upon to do the family shopping during regular business hours. The stay-at-home Mom often had more time than money, and thus found it appropriate to comb the retail stores for bargains. By contrast, today's working woman often discovers that she has more money than time, and prefers to complete her buying transactions as quickly and painlessly as possible. Direct response offers ways to do this: catalog shopping at home at any hour of the day or night, toll-free 24-hour phone lines for ordering, home delivery, liberal guarantees, free-trial privileges, and much more.

The energy crisis and congestion. Even though gasoline prices have stabilized for the time being, Americans will never again view automobile travel as recreation. Trips, even to the local shopping area, are much more carefully planned than they were in the thirty-cent-per-gallon era. Conservation of energy is just as much a part of the 1980s as conservation of time. And so consumers find direct response buying appealing; it lets them order everything from food to clothing to insurance from their own homes. And the only investment they have to make is a postage stamp or toll-free telephone call.

Congestion at giant, 100-store shopping malls is enough to send many consumers home to their catalogs and direct mail offers. Walking a half-mile from an outlying parking lot and hiking from store to store lacks appeal for all but the "recreational shopper." If the desired merchandise can be ordered by mail or phone, many consumers will opt for the direct response route.

The metamorphosis of direct response sales tools. Today's direct response buyer receives stacks of lush catalogs and mailings with enticing copy and striking art. Most direct response TV commercials have long since surpassed the ''what-a-deal'' pitches of earlier days, and telephone scripting has risen to a high art. Computer personalization fascinates many consumers—as long as we get their names and addresses correct. And who can resist ''action devices''? People love to use stickers or rub off the gold to see if they've won the grand prize.

What's more, as target marketing improves (thanks to advanced computer methods), consumers with special interests are lured to buy via direct response promotions because specialty marketers offer them the best possible selection of collector's plates or ski equipment or organic farming supplies.

WHAT TYPE OF CONSUMER BUYS VIA DIRECT RESPONSE?

A November, 1978 Ogilvy & Mather study highlighted the proliferation of direct response buying. Through a telephone survey to 1,500 adults all over the United States, Ogilvy & Mather uncovered the following information, as reported in the *1984 Fact Book on Direct Response Marketing:*[*]

1. Four out of five adults had purchased something by means of direct response at some time. Two out of three had done so in the previous year.
2. A third of those who had bought by direct response during that year had spent $100 or more. Twenty-three percent of adults had accounted for 83 percent of the direct response sales volume.
3. Families with incomes over $25,000 are much more likely to buy via direct response than those with incomes under this.
4. The age data for direct response customers varies by product type, as does the geographic data. That a certain ''direct response age'' or location cannot be assumed helps explain why it is so essential for direct marketers to zero in on a specific target market.

Reprinted by permission of Direct Marketing Association.

WHAT DOES THE CONSUMER GAIN WHEN BUYING BY MAIL?

Several studies have been done to determine why consumers specifically enjoy buying by direct response. Here are some of the ''plus factors'' they have identified:

- Save time
- Save gas
- Avoid congested stores
- Find out more about item than you can from retail clerks
- Entertainment value of browsing in catalogs
- Convenience (shop at odd hours, home delivery)
- Availability of specialties/exclusives
- Save money
- Confidentiality
- Good guarantees
- Wide selection of merchandise
- Credit availability
- Ease of ordering
- Liberal return policy
- Free trial
- Warm personal contact with owner via chatty advertising copy
- Helpful customer-service department

WHAT MAKES PEOPLE HESITATE TO BUY BY DIRECT RESPONSE?

The Ogilvy & Mather study uncovered an important fact for direct marketers: The number-one reason why people hesitate to buy by mail is that *they don't feel they can trust the company.*

Therefore, the direct marketer must build trust among customers and prospective customers. Check the list of benefits above for some trust builders, such as guarantees, a liberal return policy, free trial, and so on. Others would include a good company image, testimonials, and good overall industry ethics.

THE RETAIL DIRECT RESPONSE BUYER

Most of the information given above for consumer direct response buyers also applies to the retail market. But there are a few additional factors that affect the *retail* direct response buyer specifically as follows.

The decline in personal service. This is one of the most oft-quoted reasons for the increased receptivity to direct response. Rightly or wrongly, people believe that they got better service from their retailers in the "good old days." They remember the time of career salespeople who knew their merchandise well and would provide individual service. They lament the gum-popping salesclerk, paid a minimum wage and no commission, who now reigns over the retail counters of America, reluctantly breaking away from a personal conversation long enough to ring up merchandise selected entirely by the customer.

A good part of this perception of the "decline in personal service" has to do with the changing retail climate. The K-Marts and other self-service, supermarket-like mass merchants have taken their place in the big business category, with even traditional retailers like Penney's and Sears now offering check-out islands and more self-service departments.

Whatever the reason for the change, the customer who dislikes standing in lines, asking questions that the retail clerk can't answer, or spending a precious Saturday afternoon on a wild goose chase for a dress that no one in town can supply, is ripe for at-home buying from well-illustrated, well-written, direct response solicitation. And if it comes from a favorite department store with a fine reputation for quality and service, the customer is all the more likely to buy.

Changing shopping patterns. Even though many shopping centers and malls are open late at least two evenings a week and on weekends, single working parents and members of two-career families have a difficult time fitting retail shopping into their busy schedules.

They also resent standing in line, and have come to realize that time is a precious commodity, not to be squandered on a store-to-store hunt for an item that may not be there. Direct marketing "pitches" with 24-hour toll-free numbers and convenient home delivery have a special appeal to such busy consumers. Some customers even create their own direct response mechanism by calling the store to have staples such as underwear and socks delivered, without even being sent a flyer or catalog offering these items.

The persuasive power of direct mail. Some retail customers shop for the pure joy of it: they show up regularly to see what new merchandise has arrived or what special events are scheduled. But when shopping time is at a minimum, the retailer can reach by mail those customers who don't have the time or inclination for browsing, enticing them to come to the store or take advantage of special opportunities.

The customer wants guidance. Your direct marketing efforts can help customers decide where to shop for unfamiliar items, or build "top of the mind awareness" with customers who may need your service in the future. And if yours is a specialty business, targeted direct mail can reach your potential customers without the undue waste of advertising in newspapers, on television, or in other media.

Direct mail makes you the expert. Economic realities and changing selling methods mean that in many fields, the career salesperson *is* a "dying breed." Thus, even though your store may carry the latest electronic equipment, fashions, home furnishings, or whatever your customer is seeking, the customer may not see you as an expert because your salespeople are not sufficiently informed about these items. However, the retailer can establish this expertise through the mail, by explaining features and benefits of his or her mechandise so that the customer is "pre-sold." Then the customer may purchase the item directly by mail, or the retailer's pre-selling job may serve as the impetus to visit the store and buy the item off the shelf without much discussion or help.

THE BUSINESS OR INDUSTRIAL DIRECT MAIL BUYER

Although many of the business purchaser's personal buying habits and characteristics "carry over" to his or her professional buying activities, there are some very specific differences that direct marketers should keep in mind. Here are some points about the business or industrial buyer:

1. *He or she is spending someone else's money.* As a private consumer, the buyer is fairly free to purchase items on whim or

impulse, without making even a mental list of reasons to justify the expenditure. He or she may buy a brand of cigarettes because of their macho, urbane, or feminist image. Clothing is chosen because of the perceived image it puts forth. A car need not be a practical purchase: it may express some unexplored facet of the owner's personality. But when this same buyer makes a purchase for the company—even a purchase as simple as typing paper or replacement parts—he or she must have a rationale for the purchase based on price, service, quality, or other factors. Thus, the business buyer is generally less given to impulse buying and more impressed with facts and figures, which must be presented in an interesting and usable way.

2. *The business buyer may be a "mechanical type" or a "purchasing type."* Lumping all business buyers together can be a big mistake. The engineer, mechanic, or other business person who will actually use the product is likely to be more concerned with its quality, ease of use, and such personal concerns as enjoyment and status. The purchasing agent is generally interested in getting acceptable quality and service at the lowest possible price. The direct marketer must target his or her pitch according to which of these "types" will be making the buying decision.

3. *The business buyer may not be the "ultimate user."* The business or industrial buyer is concerned with both the use of the product and what will happen when the product contributes to a sale at the next step along the distribution chain. Thus, if you are selling a product to someone who is not its final consumer, make sure you address the buyer's concerns about how the product will contribute to his sales.

4. *The buyer likes to hear from you by mail or phone.* Even though they enjoy buying by direct mail, many consumers complain about the volume of direct response pitches that are directed to them. That's because buying products is a personal or leisure activity for them, not their livelihood. But to at least some extent, the mail and phone contacts a purchasing agent receives are a vital part of the job. Your solicitations can help the agent keep on top of innovations in the field, alert him or her to price breaks, and so on. Studies show that business buyers prefer mail contact above all other forms of contact.

Even though the business/industrial buyer is more businesslike and fact oriented than the private consumer, the direct marketer must remember that this buyer is a human being and not a computer. You'll need to get the business buyer's attention by ''selling the sizzle—not the steak.'' Weave facts into an enticing feature/benefit package, because even more than the consumer buyer, the business/industrial buyer gets scores of pieces of mail every day, and only the most intriguing will gain his or her attention.

5

THE OFFER

The offer is the basis of all direct marketing: the "marketing mix" of product, price, and payment terms, premiums and add-ons, and conditions of sale that faces your prospective customer. Many experienced direct marketers say that in working up any direct marketing proposition, they begin by preparing the order form or ordering information for their product. In this way the points of the offer are succinctly stated, and may be rearranged as needed in other parts of the selling literature or script.

Fine-tuning the offer may well result in dramatic changes in the results of a direct marketing campaign. Without changing anything but the price of an item, for instance, testing, to ascertain the point where total revenue is greatest, may dramatically increase the profitability of a mailing. And pushing or deemphasizing parts of the offer—boxing the guarantee and stating it on each piece of literature rather than burying it in the letter, for instance—may have similar impressive results.

In determining the marketing mix that becomes your offer, remember that beyond your own "givens" for minimum price, terms of sale, and so on, you must be concerned with how your target market perceives this particular offer. In one way or another you must make your offer enticing enough to move the customer into action, exciting enough to make him or her call a toll-free number, mail in an order form with a check, clip a coupon and mark the "yes" box, or perform any one of many other actions that result in a sale or a lead for you.

The easiest way to deter the customer from such action is to make your offer too complex to be readily understood. Other problems are the overlong order form, the lengthy conditions-of-sale statement, and the lack of a business-reply envelope or card (or at least a preaddressed envelope). As Bob Stone, founder of the Stone and Adler Agency, says in *Successful Direct Marketing Methods,* your objective in formulating the offer is to overcome inertia on the part of the prospect. Make it enticing and easy to respond, and your offer becomes much more likely to succeed.

But what will "success" mean for you as a marketer? Are you looking to gain leads or to make immediate sales? If you are going after leads, should they be well-qualified, or is a statement of interest in no-obligation, free information enough of a commitment from your prospect at this stage? Are you more concerned with selling an item now or with "setting up" the customer for a continuity program? Consider both the short- and long-term effects of your offer now, or some ill-considered provisions (such as a 365-day guarantee, or promising a continuity of fifty items on an unproven product line, and so on) may come back to haunt you later.

For more specifics about how to build your offer piece by piece, we will examine the various aspects of your selling proposition and suggest ways to structure each aspect for maximum interest value, short-term sales gains, and long-term customer loyalty.

THE PRODUCT

The products most likely to succeed in direct mail are those that can be demonstrated or dramatized, by means of illustration or descriptive feature-benefit copy, to have exclusivity or convenience value. Personalization is often a "natural" for direct response offers, as are items that may be offered in many different, unusual colors or assortments. To overcome resistance to your product, you must convince your prospect that you have the best item or service of this type, and that buying it directly from you is his or her best available option. Here are some techniques that may help you structure an enticing offering of your product.

Demonstration. Television—where you can show your prospect how that vegetable slicer works or how this piece of artwork will enhance your home—is the medium most often associated with demonstra-

This brochure for the Xerox 610 Memorywriter illustrates the use of *demonstration* in direct mail literature. The copy and photos explain how the machine erases, underscores, centers, indents, and performs other operations.

tion. But in a brochure you can create a similar effect by doing a cross-section of your product, using call-outs to pinpoint its best features, illustrating it from all angles, and so on. Ambassador does this beautifully with its brochures for purses with many compartments, a pen holder, credit card flaps, a checkbook cover, a key case, notepad, and other features all in one piece. If your current product does not lend itself to demonstration, consider designing something in your product line that makes an appealing and active selling story.

Assortment. One of your tasks as a marketer is to help your prospect decide how much of your product he or she needs and how often.

Sell seven bikini briefs in a set, one for each day of the week. Or offer a "family pack" of a food item, or an "executive assortment" of gourmet treats. You can do this with intangibles as well: don't simply offer "life insurance," but provide guidance about how much a person of a certain age and income might want to obtain.

Timely delivery. The fruit, candy, gourmet meat, and book- and record-of-the-month clubs illustrate timely delivery beautifully. Offer your product in such a way that a long-term commitment (more volume for you) also becomes a benefit for the customer. In the service realm, a car wash might send customers an offer for a weekly or monthly once-over at a special rate. Or an insurance firm might offer a monthly premium for continued travel-accident coverage.

Market segmentation. Take a cue from traditional marketers who offer a cigarette brand and fragrance for every personality type and self-image. If you sell clothing, segment your products to fit a clearly defined, reachable group: the sports-minded, sophisticated, career woman, and so on. Record clubs have segments for those who enjoy rock, country, classical, rhythm and blues, and other music classifications. Your choice of mailing lists or ad media will help you reach the prospects who feel most at home with your clearly defined product concept.

Product differentiation. How does your product differ from those your prospect can buy at his or her hometown store or service center? If it doesn't differ enough to excite and interest your prospect, find ways to differentiate it enough so that ordering from you is attractive. Many catalogs offer exclusive items for this reason: items that are unusually status oriented, or especially well designed and which are not available in stores. Examples would be your own brand of golf balls, a cotton shirt that features your company logo, or a popular luggage item that is widely available in vinyl or canvas but which only you offer in leather.

Offer all-in-one kits or outfits. One problem with today's serve-yourself retail stores is that the customer must use his or her own imagination in creating outfits, decorating the home, putting together a stereo set-up, and so on. As a direct marketer, you have the opportunity to do this for the customer, illustrating your choices and carefully explaining why a particular kit, outfit, or decor will look well, work well, save money and time, or whatever. Firms like The

He created some
of the world's
most passionate
music.

Yet he died
whispering the
name of a woman
he had never met.

Lose yourself
in the passion of
TCHAIKOVSKY
as your Introduction
to the Great Men
of Music series.

FREE BOOK! (with purchase of
THE GOLDEN ENCYCLOPEDIA
OF MUSIC

Great Men
of Music

TIME
LIFE
RECORDS

Great Men of Music

FREE BOOK!

This print ad and response card from Time-Life Records represents an example of *market segmentation* based on an offer. The classical music of Tchaikovsky is offered in upscale publications while rock music might be offered in magazines with a younger subscriber base.

36

Sharper Image, which offers everything the customer would need for a home exercise studio, have used this concept beautifully in recent years. American Express and others have selected all the equipment necessary for a deluxe home stereo outfit, and explained its benefits in brochures with many illustrations and lengthy copy.

Let the customer choose his or her own unit of sale. Magazine publishers who let customers choose as many issues of a publication as they want, at x cents per copy, provide the most familiar use of this teaching. The selection process becomes its own mini-action device as the customer chooses his own "comfort level" of months' commitment and dollars spent. A similar choice occurs in insurance when the prospect can select the face amount of his or her coverage.

Let the customer design his or her own product. Some clothiers show outfits made up in various materials and colors and then offer many other color and fabric options. Since custom tailoring is seldom available in today's retail stores, this one-of-a-kind appeal may be very successful. High-ticket direct marketers of furniture and home accessories also offer this option.

The trade up. In its simplest form, this type of merchandising hearkens back to the days where catalogs actually marked their products "Good," "Better," and "Best." Many direct marketers still offer a range of quality/price ratios in any given product type: toasters, work boots, washing machines, and so on. Direct marketing is ideal for such "comparison shopping" because the copy can be written to point out the attributes of the basic model, and then explain how the more expensive items improve upon it.

Club as product. In collectibles, books, records, and other fields, a club is sold as a product in and of itself, with membership benefits that may well include the opportunity to buy related products. If your product can be sold in continuity—if it is something that people collect or want to update regularly—the club concept may work for you. The appeal of a club may be up-front savings (for example, get six books free and buy six more over the course of a year) or exclusivity (only club members will be offered certain products). Or the club may be a forum for the sharing of helpful information as well as for buying opportunities. Or it may be a "share the risks and rewards" venture such as an auto club or Christmas club.

A brochure from United Airlines' "Mileage Plus" Club touts the many benefits of membership. Often a *club plan* may stimulate a wide range of selling opportunities for direct marketers.

Once a club is established and respected in the minds of its members, the mere offering of a product by that club carries the weight of an endorsement. Travel clubs offer everything from luggage to insurance and credit-card protection services. Collectibles clubs go beyond plates and figurines to offer trips to famous porcelain manufacturers in Europe. Related or even unrelated products of interest to your club members receive an automatic "boost" and tie-in to the original product—the club itself.

Product plus accessories. Think of this as the impulse purchase of the direct response field, the equivalent of picking up a candy bar or magazine in the supermarket check-out line while you buy your butter, eggs, and milk. If you can offer an inexpensive, related item to your customer at the time he or she makes the decision to buy a more expensive product, it may well be pure gravy for you. For example, offer a separate-but-matching key case at a special price when purchased along with a purse. Or sell batteries along with an item that requires them; convenient for the customer, and an easily-made, add-on sale.

THE PRICE

Several factors should influence your selection of a price for your product. The first is the prevailing price structure in your field, if your product has competitors. Understanding this will help you avoid unwittingly pricing yourself out of the market.

Second, you should find out how customers perceive your type of merchandise—what their "comfort points" are where price is concerned. Some testing may show you that although your target market is perfectly happy to pay $25 for a pocket-sized, AM/FM radio, it considers $29.95 too high for the same product. People have mental price guidelines that influence their buying decisions; they will say, "I'd like a microwave oven, but I can't see paying more than $200 for one." To zero in on the most comfortable price for your product, do price testing on your test mailing.

Third, you will want to work toward a price that meets your objectives for your direct mail program. If you wish to build your list, selling at a high-volume price will be ideal—assuming the price is high enough to cover your costs, or that you have made the commitment to invest some particular amount for the acquisition of each prospect's name. If you wish to make the biggest possible profit, the highest-volume price may not be best for you. You'll want to determine the level of sales at which your total revenue and profits are best, and this may mean less volume at a somewhat higher price. To see how you are doing at any level of price and sales, use this simple formula:

Dollars received − (Advertising cost + Cost of Merchandise) = Contribution to overhead/profit

Divide your total advertising cost by the number of items ordered to determine advertising cost per unit. Your merchandise cost may vary by volume, so check to make sure you use a cost-of-merchandise figure that squares with your likely total-order quantity, and not just with what you might need for your much smaller price test.

Here is an example:

Total cost of space ads: $4,200.00
Orders received: 250
Individual advertising cost ($4,200 divided by 250): $16.80
Cost of merchandise: $12.00 each
Dollars received: $35.95 each
Dollars received ($35.95) − Ad cost ($16.80) and Merchandise cost ($12.00) = $7.15 Contribution to overhead/profit

Once you determine your best base price for a given product, consider adding one or more of the following pricing strategies to your marketing mix:

Refund for trial. Many firms require prospective customers to pay a small amount to indicate their interest in receiving a catalog or other literature. Often this amount, anywhere from 50 cents for a small booklet to $10 or more for a slick catalog, is refundable with the first purchase. Some firms go this one better and offer double the initial payment as a refund for a customer's first order.

Seasonal discount. If you sell outdoor furniture or summer sports equipment, try offering a discount for pre- or post-season sales. Some companies reuse their fall, Christmas-oriented catalog as a sale catalog in January by attaching a sticker that says ''15 percent off all merchandise,'' or by using a wraparound that lists new prices for items shown inside. For a real splash, you can offer a discount for your product at the height of the season, when people are most likely to want to use it. In this case, emphasize prompt delivery if you have the item in stock, or your customer may fear that the swimsuit season will be over before she receives her new maillot by mail.

Introductory offer. Take a cue from the packaged-goods firms and make a one-time special offer for first-time users of a continued-use product (such as vitamins). Magazines often make introductory offers for new subscribers while making renewing subscribers pay a higher rate. You may want to include a coupon that offers this special discount; a better ploy than initially offering the item at a lower price and raising its retail cost thereafter.

Sale price. Unless you're selling your goods on the basis of snob appeal or limited availability, a discounted price may stir up extra interest. Your sale might be an introductory offer to prospective customers (Spiegel has done this) or a customers-only opportunity. You may wish to do a special sale flyer, catalog, or mailing, use a wraparound on your existing literature, or send a new letter and order card along with a brochure that does not state the price of the merchandise.

Quantity price. This may mean offering two pairs of the same pants for $2 less than two pairs purchased separately. Or you could offer a special on office supplies when bought by the case instead of individually. On the other hand, perhaps your quantity offer will be one that accumulates over time, so that the customer gets a special deal for all of the items purchased if he or she agrees to a certain minimum total purchase each year.

Loss leaders. "Loss leader" is the retail term for an item of universal interest that is priced at or below cost to encourage customers to enter the store. The technique is widely used in grocery and drug-store promotions. In direct marketing, such an item is commonly called an "order starter"—because it is a deal so good that it convinces the buyer to fill out the order form or make the toll-free phone call. And once he or she has made the decision to buy, the customer often decides to make add-on purchases with much less deliberation.

Discounts for order level. When deciding how much volume you need to make a catalog or multiple-item mailing profitable, the average order size is just as important as the number of people who respond. You may wish to encourage a larger order size with a discount structure that provides such an incentive, such as 10 percent off any order totalling $50 or more, 15 percent off orders totalling $100, or whatever works for your proposition.

Comparative price. The Sears catalog best exemplifies this technique. When Sears offers sale merchandise, the firm makes a comparison of previous pricing on equivalent merchandise. The copy will read, "Our lowest price for boys' white cotton underwear since 1978," or "Our lowest price ever for a carousel-style microwave oven." If you use such comparisons, however, make sure you have your facts straight; customers are likely to trip you up if you're wrong.

PAYMENT TERMS

Your terms of sale should combine risk-reducing strategies to ease your customer's mind and the protection you need to be paid in an acceptable manner. Remember that in most cases it is wise to offer your customer more than one way to pay for merchandise—check, credit card, revolving charge, and so on. In this way you're providing a payment plan that suits the customer's needs. Below are some of the payment options you may consider.

Reservation buying. The easier you can make it for your customer to order, the more likely he or she is to do so. That is why the reservation option is likely to help increase your total orders. Here all the customer need do is return a card in the mail or call a toll-free number and say "yes." There is no need for fumbling to write a check or to write down a charge card number. This process provides security for the seller in that he or she can send the reservation customer a bill for all or part of the item before it is shipped. Some reservation customers will neglect to respond when billed, but your net sales may well justify this payment option for you. Many collectibles marketers use the reservation option with the explanation that the final touches are being put on the product, or that the item will be crafted to the customer's order.

Free trial. Remember that the direct response customer does not have the opportunity personally to examine your merchandise before making the buying decision. Thus your offer of a no-obligation free trial may take the place of the usual retail store "try on" or "try out" for the customer. Make sure you play up the free trial in all parts of your presentation; many marketers get used to offering a free trial and don't "push" it enough. Remember that your offer is new to the customer and that he or she is looking for reassurance.

Be very clear about the time period involved in the trial. Ten, 15, or 30 days are the most usual periods. You may opt to send the bill along with the product or to send it separately once the stated time period is up, along with a letter saying that since you have not heard from the customer, you know that he or she is enjoying the product, and that it's time to pay for it. Before granting a free trial to a customer, you should make a credit check, especially on a relatively high-ticket item.

As you might logically expect, a free-trial offer will net you more returned goods than an offer with less liberal terms. But firms that offer free trials report that the returns are more than compensated for by the additional orders and payments received. If this is not the case with you, make sure that your advertising is not overselling your product, and that the customer isn't disappointed in what he or she is receiving.

Money-back guarantee. With this offer the customer pays all or part of the cost of the product before it is shipped. He or she then has the

Southern Living® Gallery offers collectors a thirty-day *free trial* on its "Southern Forest Families" plate, and a free stein which the collector may keep even if he or she returns the plate.

FREE! Return this special certificate with your reservation card, and you will have the opportunity to own this beautiful stein as our *free* gift to you.

4¾ inches tall 12-ounce capacity fine first-quality porcelain special commemorative backstamp

This fine collector stein is yours free just for agreeing to examine "Eastern Cottontail Rabbit" in your own home.

This handsome collector stein, as useful as it is decorative, displays details of Dorothea and Sy Barlowe's original young wildlife art from the series. A $35 to $40 value yours whether or not you keep the plate.

Display it with pride, or give it as a precious and timeless gift to someone you love. This lovely stein compares with others selling for $35 to $40 or even more—yet it's yours free, when you agree to examine "Eastern Cottontail Rabbit."

Even if you return "Eastern Cottontail Rabbit," the collector stein is yours to keep forever—with the compliments of *Southern Living Gallery.*

Dorothea and Sy Barlowe, the noted American illustrators, created the splendid rendering of young wildlife expressly to complement both the first plate of the SOUTHERN FOREST FAMILIES series and this precious stein.

The stein is fired with first-quality, pure porcelain, banded with 24-karat gold. A special backstamp commemorates the issuance of this stein *only* to preferred collectors invited to participate in the SOUTHERN FOREST FAMILIES collection by *Southern Living Gallery.*

This is a Private and Limited Invitation
Please respond by March 15th

Southern Forest Families

with this
PREFERRED RESERVATION CARD
Send no money now

YES. Please enroll me in the SOUTHERN FOREST FAMILIES collector plate series and send me "Eastern Cottontail Rabbit"—the important first-edition plate—for a *risk-free* 30-day examination.

I understand that you will assign me the lowest registration number available and that the same number will appear on every plate I decide to collect in the series. My special member price of $39.95 (plus postage, handling and insurance) applies to every plate I collect and is guaranteed, regardless of any price increases incurred in Europe or the United States.

I need send no money now. I will be invoiced when "Eastern Cottontail Rabbit" is ready to be shipped. If I decide to keep "Eastern Cottontail Rabbit" after my 30-day risk-free examination, you will send me additional plates in the series at the same low price with the identical registration number at the rate of about one every other month. Each plate will be sent to me for a 30-day examination and I may return any I do not wish to keep. I may cancel my membership anytime I choose simply by notifying you. The stein will be mine to keep even if I return "Eastern Cottontail Rabbit."

Please correct any errors in your name and address
Southern Living Gallery
P.O. Box 1847, Birmingham, Alabama 35282

We reserve the right to reject or cancel subscriptions at any time.   FF082 option of returning it within 10, 15, or 30 days, or whatever period of time you set, for a full refund or credit. Once again, make sure you play up your guarantee to the fullest; display it in a box with a "value border" and mention it in your letter, brochure, order card, or other material. Also, make sure to state whether you expect the customer to insure the merchandise upon returning it and whether you will refund the shipping cost.

The money-back guarantee provides more security for the seller than does a free trial, but may well result in fewer net orders since it requires more of a commitment "up front" on the part of the customer. You may wish to test a free trial versus a money-back guarantee offer and see which produces better bottom-line results for your proposition.

Cash up front. A check or money order provides maximum security for the seller (especially if he or she does not ship until the check clears). Some customers prefer to pay for their purchases up front, avoiding a later bill and the cost of another stamp.

As an incentive for customers who pay up front, you might forgive them the postage and handling charges for their payment. Or you might simply offer cash payment as one option among various partial-payment or split-payment options. Of course, the cash payment (and the various charge options) may be combined with a money-back guarantee to lessen customer hesitation.

Split payment. To encourage customers to make big-ticket purchases, many direct marketers split the payments without finance charges. This allows customers to make an up front payment of less than the full price of the merchandise, and to then continue to pay month by month. Firms with their own credit-card systems, such as American Express or the oil companies, can offer the option of adding one-half, one-twelfth, or some other portion of the total price to the charge card statement each month. Customers who pay cash might receive a monthly bill or a coupon book with slips to return with each month's payment.

Charge-card option. With so many consumers using American Express, Diners Club, and bank cards regularly, a charge-card option is very likely to justify its extra cost. You pay a small percentage of your receipts to the charge-card company to cover its costs for processing your orders. In turn, the credit card company pays you for each pur-

Preferred Reservation for *Great Animals of the American Wilderness* Collection.

Please enter my subscription for the *Great Animals of the American Wilderness* Sculpture Collection exclusively from The Hamilton Collection. The collection includes eight original sculptures by renowned wildlife artist Herman Deaton, presented as a limited edition of hand-painted sculpture in cold-cast bronze. Each figurine will bear the artist's name and will be accompanied by a numbered Certificate of Authenticity. Each of the succeeding seven sculptures will be shipped at two-month intervals. The original issue price for each is $75.00, payable in two equal installments, with the first installment due prior to shipment.

I prefer to pay the initial installment for my first sculpture as follows:

☐ With this order. I enclose my initial payment of $37.50.*
☐ By credit card. Charge my initial payment of $37.50* to my credit card as follows:
   ☐ MasterCard ☐ Visa ☐ American Express ☐ Diners Club
Full Account Number _____ Expiration Date _____
☐ No payment now. I will be billed $37.50* prior to shipment.
*Florida residents add $1.88 sales tax.
Illinois residents add $2.63 sales tax.
Please allow 6–8 weeks for delivery

Guaranteed only if mailed by:

August 17, 1984

Signature _____ Telephone No. (___) _____
Charge orders must be signed to be valid. All applications are subject to acceptance by The Hamilton Collection. 37945 FLF1

Mountain Lion

First issue in the
GREAT ANIMALS OF THE
AMERICAN WILDERNESS
*Sculpture Collection
by Herman Deaton*

Worldwide edition limit: 7500
Individual Limit:
One set per collector

100% Buy-Back Guarantee
The Hamilton Collection guarantees that you may return any figurine you receive, undamaged, for 100% of everything you have paid for it within 30 days of receipt.

This order form exhibits the *split payment* option and also offers the buyer an opportunity to reserve the items with no payment now.

chase, and your customers pay it. Qualified holders of major credit cards already have passed at least a cursory credit check, and are therefore attractive prospects as customers for you. Note that you will generally pay a larger percentage to American Express and Diners Club than to the bank-card firms. The percentage you pay depends on the volume and continuity of your business with the credit-card firm. Contact the local bank that runs a MasterCard or Visa service for more information about charge-card billing, or contact American Express or Diners Club directly.

"House" charge. Like many retail stores, you may wish to offer a charge-account of your own. To decide whether this is warranted, balance the administrative work and debt collection procedures involved against the potential interest income and goodwill factor. A check of most major catalog and direct marketing firms shows that unless they are in the credit card business themselves (such as some retailers, oil companies, American Express, and so on), they are unlikely to offer their own charge option. Instead, they probably accept a variety of credit cards as well as cash up front.

Cash on Delivery. Cash on delivery (COD) is much less used today than in the past, when most households had a homemaker around to meet the deliveryman. It may be arranged through the United Parcel Service or U.S. Postal Service for a fee, but conventional wisdom today is that it is not worth the extra cost, the refusal rate, and the "nuisance" orders that it may encourage from children and jokesters.

PREMIUMS AND ADD-ONS

Most everyone likes a free gift, especially one that is personally appealing or related to some product they're considering buying. When you offer a premium, make sure you and your prospect both are absolutely clear about what qualifies them for the premium: whether it's merely inquiring about the product, trying it, buying and paying for it, buying some of the items in a continuity program, or whatever. The degree of commitment needed for qualification will substantially affect both your response rate and your bottom line.

For instance, if you are selling a stereo system by direct response, you might offer a record or tape as a premium. You must then decide whether the record will go along with the merchandise, or be shipped later, once the free-trial period is over and payment has been received. And if the customer sends back the stereo, spell out in ad-

A *premium slip* like this one highlights the item being offered for free as well as the terms under which the customer will receive it.

vance—so as to avoid problems later—whether he or she gets to keep the record as your gift or has to send it back to you as well.

If you are selling a set of records, books, collector plates, or making any other continuity proposition, you may wish to offer a display device as a premium. Decide whether the premium will be included in the first shipment or later in the series. If you provide it right away, you will have to factor it into the cost of doing business with each and every customer. If you offer it later, you not only provide an incentive to stay in the continuity program but also cut down the overall cost for your premiums, since you needn't send the premium to those who drop out along the way. A good rule of thumb is to use past sales records to determine the average number of books, records, or whatever you sell to your continuity customers, and to ship the display device or other premium right before this average is reached. This will encourage the average customer to purchase more merchandise, with the incentive of filling up his attractive new display device or otherwise fully using his premium.

Sometimes the premium you offer is itself continuous or offered at regular intervals. For instance, all current customers of your firm may receive a newsletter as a premium. Or you may send a Christmas thank-you gift to all customers whose yearly expenditures with you remain at a certain level. If your continuous or regular premium is attractive enough, it will encourage customers to keep up their level of expenditure with your firm.

Remember that the cost of your premium cannot be tied to an arbitrary percentage of sales or rule of thumb. When testing one premium against another, look at the bottom line for the best net result. A $5 premium of great appeal may net you more money than a $2 premium that provides little incentive.

In addition to a simple premium-with-purchase offer, you might test offering gifts at certain order levels to encourge a larger average order size on a catalog or multiple-item offer. If last year's average order size was $40 and you're hoping to up that to $50 this year, why not offer a universally appealing free gift for each order of $50 or more?

Another way to use premiums to your advantage is the "member-get-a-member" pitch. Book and record clubs do this quite well, offering members a certain amount of free merchandise or credit for each new person they can sign up and convince to commit to a certain level of purchasing. Watch out for this tactic in regulated industries such as insurance, however; here such enticements may be considered unethical or illegal.

Or, instead of a separate, free gift, consider "add-on" offers to the items you sell. You might, for instance, offer a free gift box or gift wrapping to everyone or only to customers whose orders reach a certain level. Or you might offer a bill-to/send-to arrangement at no extra charge to facilitate gift giving.

SWEEPSTAKES

Sweepstakes can create an excitement that enlivens a routine offer or convinces "fence sitters" to try your product or service. Human nature assures that even though buyers and non-buyers stand an equal chance of winning a sweepstakes, your prospect believes he or she has a better opportunity by buying something.

Large and well-known sweepstakes, such as that put on by Publisher's Clearing House, can provide you with a wealth of ideas and inspiration, especially in the areas of package design, TV support, and prize selection.

Consult a firm with expertise in contest management early in your consideration of a sweepstakes or contest; the rules, regulations, and laws in this area of endeavor are many, and beyond the scope of the average direct marketer's knowledge. Ventura Associates and D. L. Blair are two of the best-known firms in this field. For fledging direct marketers or those with small budgets, the costly and complex sweepstakes option is not recommended.

Sweepstakes—such as this example of the famous Publishers Clearing House offer—add interest to a proposition because they promise a number of prizes, and because the recipient may win with or without a purchase.

CONDITIONS OF SALE

Urgency

Convincing the customer to buy—and to buy right away—requires an urgency appeal. Every sales presentation needs a call to action, but this is especially vital in direct marketing, since there is no face-to-face contact with a salesperson. The customer does not necessarily have to say "yes" or "no," as is necessary when facing a salesperson; he or she can say "maybe" and put your sales piece aside. But if you offer the prospective customer an enticement to act now, an immediate sale is much more likely to result. For example:

Time limit. Tell your customer that your offer is valid only until "x" date. Give a reason for this—that the items cannot be made after that time, seasonal needs require a cut-off date, or some other.

Subscription period. When combined with a reduced-price pitch, a limited subscription period often is used in periodical promotion. But a "subscription block" (a time or quantity limit) may also apply to collectibles, special financial accounts, or other investment-related appeals.

Charter member. Tell the customer that he or she will be a charter member of an organization or charter subscriber to your product if he or she responds by a certain date, and that he or she otherwise risks being just a "regular" member or subscriber, with a resulting loss of status, and perhaps of present or future special privileges.

Limited edition. This strategy is widely used in the art and collectibles fields, and in some cases for books and other decor or status items. The edition of a product is limited to a certain number of items, or "firing period" (number of days plates will be fired), time period, or span of time. After that time no more are to be made, and the unlucky prospect will have to purchase the item on the "secondary market."

Frequency and Terms

"Fine tuning" your offer may mean testing different ways to structure a continuity pitch or long-term proposition such as a book or record club. Here are some ways in which marketers have combined

customer convenience with guaranteed additional sales for themselves. Although these methods may seem more adaptable to books,
records, and collectibles than to any other product, brainstorm a bit:
perhaps a "load up" or "ship 'til forbid" concept (see page 51) could
also work for your product.

Negative option. This is a carefully worded offer by which the customer agrees to take shipment of products as they are made available
at intervals unless he or she specifically indicates otherwise. The
marketer then sends out the product at a monthly or some other regular interval. The customer must return to the marketer, by a given
date, a card indicating that he or she does not want the chosen product, or prefers to receive another optional product or products. Otherwise, the chosen product of the month is shipped to the customer
along with an invoice. This method may prove very lucrative to the
marketer, but the initial agreement for such a system must be worded
carefully so as to avoid legal problems and misunderstandings. For
pointers on how to word negative-option offers, you can check the
promotions done by some of the larger book and record clubs.

To entice customers to agree to a negative option, many marketers
offer a certain number of products free or at a very low "up-front"
cost. The customer may then be asked to commit to buy a like number
of products over a period of time, usually one or two years.

Positive option. This is another way to structure a regular product
offering, but it differs from the negative option in that the customer
does not receive merchandise unless he or she specifically orders it.
Periodic newsletters or product offerings are sent to the customer,
who then returns an enclosed card with his or her selections. If the
customer does not wish to purchase in any given month, the card need
not be returned. In general it will be easier to get a customer to commit to a positive-option than to a negative-option plan, but fewer
guaranteed, regular sales will result. However, the amount of merchandise returned should be less with this plan; in a negative-option
plan the customer may refuse merchandise on arrival if he or she simply forgot to return the card in time asking that it not be shipped.

Load-up. In continuity or open-ended programs, shipping costs can
become prohibitive. Sending one book or record at a time is much

more costly than "loading up" a boxful and asking the customer to remit his or her full payment on a month-by-month basis. Some marketers make the load-up a regular feature of their offer, while others make it an option. The marketer must balance the bad-debt potential of shipping merchandise in bulk before it is paid for against the high shipping costs of month-by-month delivery. Once the load-up is sent, the marketer may invite the customer to finish out his or her obligation by paying the entire net due, and may even offer a premium or discount for doing so. Alternatively, the marketer may send the customer either a coupon booklet to encourage regular monthly payments, or send individual statements, which are much less costly than monthly product shipments.

Ship-'til-forbid. This option works well with fairly homogeneous products or products that are consumable, such as foods or pantyhose. The customer agrees to receive and pay for a regular shipment at intervals, unless and until he or she notifies the marketer to cancel. Many customers see this as a welcome service for regularly used items, while marketers gain some predictability in sales.

Membership fee. When a club program is appropriate, a membership fee separates the curious from those who are genuinely interested. Ideally, the customer should be able to see how the membership fee translates into specific benefits worth at least as much as he or she has paid. For example, a travel club might offer trip planning, discounts on lodging and car rentals, and members-only travel/accident insurance. A collectibles club might offer a members-only limited edition at regular intervals, or market updates, a newsletter, or travel opportunities. Or a membership fee may entitle a member to ongoing discounts or other privileges. Most membership fees are either one-time or annual. Another option is the "lifetime membership" which comprises perhaps five to ten times the annual membership fee, paid at one time.

Continuity. Whereas negative- and positive-option and ship-'til-forbid plans may continue indefinitely, a continuity plan includes a specific number of related items. The terms include a regular interval of shipment, method of payment, and determination of whether or not the customer is obligated to purchase every item or may pick and choose among them.

TYPES OF GUARANTEES

Beyond the ''guarantee of satisfaction'' are a wide range of promises or guarantees that a marketer might offer to ''sweeten'' the agreement with a customer. The following are examples of these.

Guarantee of acceptance. This is typical in insurance. The older person or person with a history of medical problems may be wary of his or her acceptability to an insurance company, and some prospects are put off by the idea of a medical examination for eligibility. The guarantee of acceptance states that (usually within certain age ranges) the prospect cannot be turned down for health or other reasons. Moreover, buying insurance by mail is appealing because of its simplicity, which adds to the prospect's ease and confidence in responding.

Guarantee of quality. This may come from the manufacturer, from the marketer, or from a third-party source like Underwriter's Laboratories or *Good Housekeeping* magazine. Such a statement helps reinforce the decision of a buyer who has not had the opportunity to examine the merchandise in person before responding.

Guarantee of repair or replacement. This guarantees is usually valid only for a specified period, but it cuts down buyer resistance caused by lack of service from the direct marketer. The customer who feels he or she can get an item repaired or replaced through you does not have to worry about finding a proper service facility.

LEAD GENERATION

In many cases, an offer is not a pitch to sell a product, but to send a brochure, catalog, or more information to a prospective customer. Such lead-generating activities are most useful for high-ticket or complex products. An advantage of lead generation is the list of inquiry names it produces, since those that do not respond to the current offer may well be excellent prospects for a later offer of a similar type.

Leads may be followed up by another direct marketing effort such as a mailing package or telephone call, by a personal sales effort, or by a combination of these. Below are some of the offers marketers make to solicit leads for these ''two-step'' programs.

Free information/free facts. This sounds much less threatening and obligating than a salesman's call.

Free book/booklet/catalog. A worthwhile piece of literature at no cost often weaves in the sales message subtly, as opposed to selling in a pushy manner. A lead-generating booklet for insurance, for instance, might offer information about Social Security and retirement planning.

Free analysis, estimate, demonstration, sample. These are all promotional ways of gaining leads that can be followed up with a sales call or telephone contact. Again, this sounds much more enticing than a sales call.

With all of these offers, make sure to stress that there is no obligation to the prospect.

If you respond to your leads with a direct mail kit, make sure the recipient realizes that the material is coming in response to his or her request. You can usually use an ordinary direct mailing piece for this purpose, with two important modifications: an outer envelope with wording such as ''Here is the Information You Requested,'' and a letter acknowledging the prospect as someone who requested this literature.

LOOSE LEADS/TIGHT LEADS

You can exercise some control over how many leads you receive from a promotion and their quality. If you are sending out an inexpensive mailing package for leads, you may not have to tighten your list to address only the ''sure prospects.'' But if you are searching for a small number of highly qualified prospects for your limited personal sales staff to follow up, tightening your lead list will be important.

A ''loose'' lead is someone who has indicated interest in your proposal but has not taken a great deal of trouble to respond, and may or may not be a qualified prospect. Here are ways to ''loosen'' your lead-generating activities:

- Make it easy to respond. Provide a stamped envelope or one with a Business Reply Card; use bind-in cards in magazine ads; provide a toll-free number; provide a prelabeled card that the prospect can just drop in the mail.

- Offer a premium for a response. The less the premium has to do with the product you're selling, and the more it is worth to the prospect, the looser the lead.
- Emphasize the "no obligation" aspect. Promise that no sales-person will call.
- Talk "sizzle" in your copy. Tell the customer all the benefits of your product or service and very little of the how's and why's.

A "tight" lead is a person who has indicated a strong interest in your product or service, either by means of a payment, some effort on his or her own part, or by accepting some obligation. Here are some ways to "tighten" your lead-generating activities:

- Tell the customer the price and payment terms. This is a natural "tightener" for high-ticket products.
- State that a salesperson will call to do an "energy audit," give a free demonstration, or do something else.
- Tell the prospect exactly what will happen when he or she responds—whether they will be invited to buy, try the product, or whatever.
- Charge money for the information or service rather than making it free. This may be softened by applying the charge to any purchase made later.
- Require that the prospect stamp his or her reply, or write a letter and address an envelope, rather than simply using a Business Reply Card.
- Talk about how the product works and why it does what it does, besides "sizzling" about its benefits. Zero in on your particular product rather than talking generally about the attributes of this type of item or service.

RETAIL OFFERS

This section will provide retailers with some ideas for direct market-ing offers that will help build traffic, combining in-store traffic with additional mail or phone sales, developing a separate direct response division, and providing support for the retail operation.

Traffic Builders

When you open a new store or outlet. If a new store is in an area that may be convenient to some or all of your existing customers, let them know about it and its location. Doing this may be as simple as a special message in one month's charge statements, such as: "Visit us at our new Highland Park Store, opening June 8 at 123 Park Avenue." Or you might send existing customers a special offer to get them to visit the new store: a coupon, announcement of a sweepstakes that must be entered on the store's premises, fashion show, celebrity appearance, or other special event.

When you wish to obtain charge customers for a new store. You can rent lists of residents of your new trading area by zip code, and "blanket" the area with charge-card solicitations. Make sure you take only the most likely zip codes; don't mail to poor sections if yours is an expensive specialty shop, for example. To sweeten the deal you might offer a free gift with the first use of the new charge card, sending the customer a coupon to redeem on his or her first visit to the store. Steketee's, a Michigan department store, did such a mailing when the firm opened a new store in Muskegon Mall. The results were impressive: 7 percent of the area residents who were solicited opened Steketee's charge accounts.

When a customer has not used his or her charge lately. Keep track of your customers' frequency of purchases. If they haven't charged an item in the last six months, year, or whatever interval you choose, make them a special offer. You might offer a free premium with any charge purchase or simply ask them to stop into the store for a free gift and to acknowledge that they want to keep their charge account open.

To encourage newcomers to trade with you. Most communities have Newcomers or Welcome Wagon groups that can supply you with lists of new arrivals in the community. A direct mail offer to these people, giving them some incentive to stop into your store and open a charge account, can establish a loyal clientele of people looking for stores and services to rely on.

To establish a continuity program. Burger King, McDonald's, and other fast-food outlets use continuity programs that other retailers can emulate. They have special inserts stuffed into the local Sunday

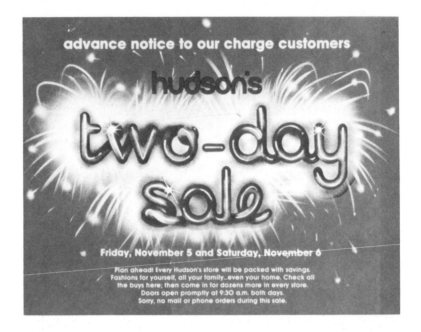

advance notice to our charge customers

hudson's

two-day
sale

Friday, November 5 and Saturday, November 6

Plan ahead! Every Hudson's store will be packed with savings.
Fashions for yourself, all your family...even your home. Check all
the buys here; then come in for dozens more in every store.
Doors open promptly at 9:30 a.m. both days.
Sorry, no mail or phone orders during this sale.

Retailers may use direct mail to offer their preferred customers an *advance notification of sales*. This advance notice to charge customers tells about customer courtesy days at Hudson's Two-Day Sale.

newspapers containing dated coupons for obtaining free or discounted products. This encourages customers to visit the restaurant at least once a week during the continuity program. Dry cleaners might try a mailing to local residents or a newspaper insert with discount coupons or two-for-one offers on suits one week, blouses the next, and coats the next.

To "get the jump" on a seasonal event. In the fall, customers start thinking about winterizing their cars or getting the carpet cleaned before Thanksgiving. These and other seasonal concerns offer fertile fields for the direct marketer, who can get a message into the hands of the consumer along with a "sweetener" to spur action. For instance, a local service station might send out discount coupons for a full winterizing program to past customers, and an "occupant" mailing to the nearest neighboring zip code areas as well.

To offer a personal-courtesy touch. The smart retailer knows who his or her most valued customers are, and can use direct mail to reward them with a gift, gain them a private audience with a special visitor, or give them some other thank-you. Last year's fur coat buyers, for instance, might be offered a free cleaning of the coat the following spring just for stopping into the fur department to see the end-of-season values. A book store might arrange for top customers to attend a private cocktail reception with an impressive author-visitor, announced only to selected people via direct mail. A salesperson with a customer who likes a certain maker's custom suits might drop that customer a line and enclose sample swatches of fabric when a new shipment of fabric arrives at the store.

To bring customers in for a sale. Perhaps some of your best customers are people who wouldn't see your sale advertised in a local paper or hear it announced on radio or TV. You can mail them a notification of the sale, its dates, and some of the things to be offered, and can sweeten the offer by arranging as "Customer Courtesy Days" a period of several days before the general sale starts. This will give your customers the best selection of merchandise and avoid their having to fight the crowds when the general sale begins.

Combined Store and Mail/Phone Offers

Retailers are most likely to maximize their total sales during a sale or special event, by sending their customers a sale announcement with the option for them to order by mail or phone rather than having to come in person. Customers who can't shop during the sale hours, or who dislike the crowds that sales may turn out, may find such a mail or phone-in order appealing. Moreover, by mailing your sale or special event catalog or flyer to prospective customers in surrounding zip code areas, you may entice new customers to visit your store or call or mail in orders, which in turn may make them into regular customers for you.

Support for the Retail Operation

Direct mail to keep people informed. Direct mail can help a retailer keep customers aware of new locations, store policies, changes in business hours, and other important facts. What's more, when such an informational mailing is made, stuffers offering merchandise or services can be sent along with them. For example, a Grand Rapids, Michigan, tree-service firm mails its customers a list of recommended services, keyed to each customer's own yard, in the spring and summer. Along with each service list come solicitations for products of interest to homeowners, such as fireplace inserts, lawn spraying offers, and so on.

To collect overdue accounts. Before resorting to the expense of a collection agency, many retailers try a series of collection letters to nonpaying customers, seeking the response of a prompt payment. The early letters in such a series might take the tone of ''have your overlooked something?'' If such a gentle approach doesn't work, the retailer might try a terse, simulated telegram format and finally a letter stating bluntly that the account will be turned over to a collection agency if payment is not received within 10 days. Books offering standard formats for business letters give suggestions on such collection letters, or you can ask your direct marketing consultant or agency to create a ''collection series.''

BUSINESS-TO-BUSINESS OFFERS

In most cases, the general advice about direct response offers applies to business-to-business situations. However, it is important to remember the business buyer's motives as contrasted with those of the individual consumer. As a professional buyer, he or she is spending a company's money, rather than his or her personal money. The buyer's concern is to ''look good'' to the boss and the company, and the points to stress in an offer to business buyers therefore differ from those in consumer marketing. Benefits should be discussed in terms of the good of the company rather than of the individual. The crucial benefits are those that make the buyer's life easy: good service, one-stop shopping, automatic re-buys, and so on.

Reasons for business-to-business offers. Many business mailings center on news and information. Since the business buyer makes a profession of purchasing, it is in his or her best interests to keep up on new products and new applications for existing ones.

Thus, the introduction of a new product is a good reason for a business-to-business offer. A timely offer is also appealing, as with a special price on a seasonal item or a stock-up sale in which the buyer can gain a substantial discount for his or her firm.

Lead generation and personal sales. When generating leads for a business-to-business sales staff, it is essential to determine how many leads each salesperson can handle within a given period. A mass mailing may produce hundreds of qualified leads, but if there are only two salespeople to follow them up, precious good will may be lost in the interim. A much better approach would be mailing in waves, so as to provide a manageable flow of leads on a continuing basis. If too many leads arrive at once, a telephone follow-up or even a letter can acknowledge the receipt of each lead and promise full attention as promptly as possible. Such a follow-up can also help qualify prospects and "sniff out" those who are ready to buy, tagging them as "must-see" individuals.

Premiums. The business premium differs from the consumer premium in that it may or may not go directly to the purchaser. For some products, a good premium might be support literature, product brochures, or continuing news about the product and how to use it. In other cases, a premium may be offered through a two-step process, such as with a mailing suggesting that the prospect stop into the marketer's booth at a trade show, and get a free gift. A personal gift meant for a purchasing agent may be quite effective but must be handled discreetly so that it does not appear to be a bribe. It is best simply to describe the premium, and not state in the promotional copy whom it is meant for or what will be done with it.

6

DIRECT MAIL FORMATS

Direct marketers—and especially direct mailers—have more freedom than those who advertise in most other media. Those who advertise in the print media, for example, are constrained by page sizes and paper types, as well the positions available in a magazine or newspaper. Television and radio advertisers must work within prescribed time slots. But except for postal codes and budget factors, the direct mailer is free to size his or her promotional pieces, select the papers and reproduction techniques to be used, decide how many inserts will be included in each mailing, and generally provide the tone and "personality" of each mailing package.

The main purpose of every direct mail package is *to bring about action*. Marketers should keep this goal firmly in mind in creating each and every direct mail piece, from the selling letter to the business-reply envelope.

The format for a mailing flows from the objectives it must meet, and becomes a visible and active statement of the marketing strategy. Both format and strategy are based on the target prospect, the budget for the mailing and for the overall campaign, competitive factors, company image, and so on.

The basic direct mail format includes a letter, brochure or flyer, reply form, and Business Reply Envelope, all contained in an outer envelope. But while many mailers find this basic format highly effective, others modify it, add to it, and test various other inserts. This chapter will discuss the basic direct mail formats and ways to enhance them, together with other techniques that may induce more of a response to a direct mail campaign.

THE LETTER

No direct mail solicitation is complete without a selling letter. The letter is a "personal sales" device that takes the place of one-on-one contact with a salesperson; it usually comes from the president of the firm making the direct mail offer, although it may come from another official of the marketing firm. Sometimes, when the pitch is from a family-owned company and the objective is to make the customer feel that he or she is buying from a small, cottage industry, the letter comes from the spouse of the owner, who talks about the great products his or her spouse has worked so hard to provide. At other times the pitch is just the opposite: snob appeal. In this case the letter might come from an advisor to the firm whose credentials qualify him or her to make authoritative comments on the merchandise being offered.

The selling letter refers to the product features and benefits as shown in the accompanying brochure, and explains to the prospect why this product or service will benefit him or her personally. The word "you" is used frequently in most good direct response letters: the focus is on the prospect—his or her wants, needs, triumphs, home, family, interests, and comfort. How does this product fit into your prospect's life, and why is it that he or she should not go another day without it? The letter should explain these things and create mental pictures for the prospect in which he or she imagines using and enjoying the product or service.

Direct mail letters feature short sentences, short paragraphs, lots of indentation, use of second or even third colors, and many other attention-getting techniques. As a new direct marketer you may be skeptical about the effectiveness of these methods. But they will make more people read your mailing, and your response will usually be higher than if you use a plain letter that more closely resembles business correspondence.

The writing of a direct mail letter is an art—one that is best left to skilled, experienced direct marketing copywriters. But to critique the work of your writer, you should recognize and understand typical direct mail letter techniques and characteristics. Some of these are as follows:

Direct mail letters are long. To tell the story of your product, your writer probably will recommend a letter that is at least two pages long, and possibly four pages. Rather than request a two-page letter, tell your writer that you want a letter that is long enough to do the job. This may be a page and a half, four pages, or more. The keys are readability and salesmanship, not brevity.

Direct mail letters are personal. Don't expect your direct mail letter to read like a business letter to a client; it is more likely to be a chatty narrative broken up by lists of reasons for buying your product and indentations for important points.

Direct mail letters often have headlines. You may summarize your offer or make your most important point in a heading before your salutation. Unless your letter is to be auto-typed or computerized, you may eliminate the salutation altogether and flow right from the heading into the body of the letter.

Direct mail letters often have subheads. Subheads help organize the letter and allow the prospect to pick up your main points even if he or she is skimming.

Direct mail letters feature promotional ploys. These may include underlining important points, different typefaces for subheads or lead-ins, a heading in a box at the top of the page, and handwritten messages at strategic places.

Here are some additional pointers and ideas to incorporate into your direct mail letters:

- *Your letterhead is important.* The letterhead you select should reflect the image of your product and firm: economical or expensive, modern or traditional, liberal or conservative, sporty or elegant. Some firms add a list of advisors or board members to the letterhead to reflect the historical, religious, or authoritative nature of the company and its products. Most direct mail letters are printed on 8½-by-11-inch stationery, using both sides. Monarch-sized stationery looks more personal, and might be used for an additional letter with a special, one-to-one appeal.
- *Try using paper other than letterhead for a special effect.* For instance, a simulated memo in the form of a last-minute note from the president or other company official might be used. Or you might print a letter on "plain brown wrapping paper" and talk about how your product will be shipped in this same paper

for the sake of confidentiality. Yellow notebook paper might indicate that the letter is very casual and comes from a down-to-earth, blue-collar individual who ripped a sheet of paper from his or her child's notebook. Printing a letter on the back of a sheet of holiday wrapping paper might emphasize the gift-giving possibilities of the product, or highlight the point that you will gift-wrap and send the product for the customer.

The United States Historical Society *letterhead* helps establish the organization as an expert in the field of Antique Arms by listing the distinguished members of its Antique Arms Committee. The eagle logo reinforces the company's image.

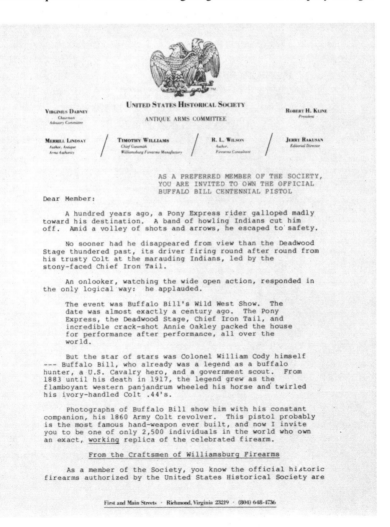

UNITED STATES HISTORICAL SOCIETY

ANTIQUE ARMS COMMITTEE

VIRGINIUS DABNEY
Chairman
Advisory Committee

ROBERT H. KLINE
President

MERRILL LINDSAY
Author, Antique
Arms Authority

TIMOTHY WILLIAMS
Chief Gunsmith
Williamsburg Firearms Manufactory

R. L. WILSON
Author,
Firearms Consultant

JERRY RAKUSAN
Editorial Director

                    AS A PREFERRED MEMBER OF THE SOCIETY,
                    YOU ARE INVITED TO OWN THE OFFICIAL
                    BUFFALO BILL CENTENNIAL PISTOL
Dear Member:

     A hundred years ago, a Pony Express rider galloped madly
toward his destination. A band of howling Indians cut him
off. Amid a volley of shots and arrows, he escaped to safety.

     No sooner had he disappeared from view than the Deadwood
Stage thundered past, its driver firing round after round from
his trusty Colt at the marauding Indians, led by the
stony-faced Chief Iron Tail.

     An onlooker, watching the wide open action, responded in
the only logical way: he applauded.

     The event was Buffalo Bill's Wild West Show. The
     date was almost exactly a century ago. The Pony
     Express, the Deadwood Stage, Chief Iron Tail, and
     incredible crack-shot Annie Oakley packed the house
     for performance after performance, all over the
     world.

     But the star of stars was Colonel William Cody himself
--- Buffalo Bill, who already was a legend as a buffalo
hunter, a U.S. Cavalry hero, and a government scout. From
1883 until his death in 1917, the legend grew as the
flamboyant western panjandrum wheeled his horse and twirled
his ivory-handled Colt .44's.

     Photographs of Buffalo Bill show him with his constant
companion, his 1860 Army Colt revolver. This pistol probably
is the most famous hand-weapon ever built, and now I invite
you to be one of only 2,500 individuals in the world who own
an exact, <u>working</u> replica of the celebrated firearm.

          <u>From the Craftsmen of Williamsburg Firearms</u>

     As a member of the Society, you know the official historic
firearms authorized by the United States Historical Society are

First and Main Streets · Richmond, Virginia 23219 · (804) 648-4736

- *The P.S. is important.* A great percentage of direct mail letters have a P.S. at the end. Conventional wisdom is that most readers look at the signature of a letter first, to see who it is from. In doing so, they may also glance at the P.S., which is therefore a good place to make an important point or enhance the urgency of the offer. The P.S. may also emphasize a money-back guarantee, state the prime product benefit, or refer the prospect to another piece in the mailing package.

- *Computer letters are a mixed blessing.* The consumer who receives a letter with computer fill-ins that are all correct and well integrated may be pleased by this personal touch and encouraged to respond. However, if any part of the computer message is incorrect or mishandled, the computerization may do more harm than good. There is no guarantee that a computer letter will generate more of a response than a simple "Dear Friend" letter would, so test to see how it will work for your offer. Computer letters may feature fill-ins on a preprinted form, or they may be typed completely by the computer to eliminate telltale differences in the type darkness or positioning of filled-in sections. Writing computer letters for fill-in is something of an art; usually the fill-in of the customer's name, address, or other personal information must be put at the end of a paragraph to avoid problems with differing line lengths or numbers of characters. Many printing-sales representatives can acquaint you with the latest computer and laser printing techniques, and offer quotes on test and roll-out quantities.

- *Change your letters to suit the prospect.* Printing different letter versions is one of the least expensive ways of tailoring your offer to different interest groups. For example, you may use the same brochure for both previous buyers of the product and new prospects, and acknowledge the status of the recipient in the letter. If you rent a list of people who are all Auto Club members, you might acknowledge this in a special letter and use a different letter for a group of people who are all Corvette owners.

- *Endorsement letters supplement selling letters.* If you are able to obtain an endorsement for your product by a respected or authoritative group, or the executives of a club or organization whose members will then be more likely to want to buy, one of the best ways to utilize this endorsement is in a separate letter. This letter should probably be signed by the president of the endorsing organization. In it he or she will mention some of the product's features and benefits from the organization's point of view, and recommend the product to your prospects.

• *Publisher's letters answer buyer objections.* In personal sales, one of the most important aspects of closing the deal is overcoming the prospect's objections. In direct mail, many marketers use a "publisher's letter" or "Why not?" letter to do the same thing.

This *endorsement letter* from the Royal National Rose Society lends credibility to a collection of plates inspired by roses which the Society selected as prize winners.

 The Royal National Rose Society

PATRON:
HER MAJESTY QUEEN ELIZABETH, THE QUEEN MOTHER

CHISWELL GREEN LANE
ST. ALBANS
HERTFORDSHIRE AL2 3NR
Telephone:
ST. ALBANS (0727) 50461

To all lovers of Roses:

In the gentle world of rose gardening, real excitement is rare indeed. But I can still remember the thrill at the Society when the "Irish Gold" variety received the Gold Medal.

And this morning I experienced that magic once again when I was presented with a beautiful bone china collector plate from the Boehm Studios. I'm not an expert on fine porcelain, but it's little short of a miracle how faithfully Boehm has captured the very spirit of "Irish Gold." You can almost smell the blooms!

I'm delighted that we are associated with this artistic venture. It has been several years since we first envisioned sponsoring a fine collectible that would honor our most prized variety of roses. Now that dream has come to life through the artistry of Boehm.

I hope you will consider acquiring this fine limited-edition plate. If you derive half as much joy from it as I have, your investment will be more than worthwhile.

Cordially,

Jack Shotter
President

AFP
AMERICAN
FAMILY
PUBLISHERS

"The Winner Who Threw Away
One Million Dollars!"

Dear Friend,

Soon, on behalf of American Family Publishers, I will be awarding the first MILLION DOLLAR PRIZE in history in a by-mail sweepstakes!

I may be awarding it to you, personally — but only if you return your entry. If you don't, you could be throwing away ONE MILLION DOLLARS! Because...

"Someone Just Like You Actually Threw Away A Fortune!"

I've just learned how it all happened. Recently, someone just like you received the winning Grand Prize Number, and "he went and threw away all that money!"

He failed to return the winning number and his prize was awarded to someone else.

I would be sorry to see that happen to you — especially since you

Over Please...

FCS 13V

---

may have already won this historic prize of ONE MILLION DOLLARS!

Remember, the winning number has already been selected and sealed away — it may be one of your numbers!

It could be your name announced as the first MILLION DOLLAR WINNER on national television on the TONIGHT SHOW on March 25!

But this is your LAST CHANCE to return your Personal Prize Claim Numbers and claim this fabulous prize. Do it today! And good luck to you!

Cordially,

Ed McMahon
For American Family
Publishers

PS. Don't be "The Winner who threw away ONE MILLION DOLLARS!" Return all your Personal Prize Claim Numbers today!

© 1983 AFP

Such a supplementary letter is customarily folded or contained in a separate envelope. On the outside it might say something like ''Please do not open this note unless you have already decided not to respond to this offer.'' Few readers can resist opening such a note, especially when they have been told not to. The note brings up common objections to the product and refutes them. For example:

OBJECTION	REFUTATION
Perhaps you think that responding obligates you to buy more items.	All future purchases are optional.
Perhaps you're afraid you won't wish to keep the item when you get it.	The item carries a money-back guarantee and you may return it for a full refund with no questions asked.

- *Telegrams, mailgrams, and fake telegram formats.* One way to enhance the urgency of your message is to replace the usual business-type letter with a real Western Union telegram, a Mailgram (overnight service), or a letter in telegram format from one of a number of services. The Western Union services are somewhat costly, but may be justified, especially for follow-ups; test to see how they compare with a regular mailing. Unfortunately, Western Union does not allow additional inserts; however, there are several telegram format services that send computer-printed pieces resembling telegrams via first-class mail. These services will often allow the insertion of a simple brochure and business reply envelope. Or you might design your own telegram-like mail piece and have a computer service print your message. Make sure your design is sufficiently different from those of Western Union or other services to avoid copyright infringement.

Some *publisher's letters* answer objections directly, while this letter from American Family Publishers answers them indirectly. In addition, the letter from Ed McMahon exhorts the reader not to miss a chance to win $1,000,000.

THE BROCHURE

Brochures also are called circulars, flyers, folders, or booklets. Their functions are to illustrate the product, demonstrate its use and benefits, and give interesting background information about it. Just as a good direct mail letter contains all the main sales points for a product or service, so does a good direct mail brochure.

Some direct marketing experts say that the brochure should contain all points of the offer on a single surface, so that the prospect can "take it all in" at one time without flipping pages or switching from a letter to the brochure. Many successful direct mail brochures, however, have been done in booklet form with various points of the offer explored on various pages. Whatever your format, make sure that the brochure copy ends with a closing statement designed to make your

Here is an actual Western Union *telegram* format used in direct mail efforts. Some mailers use "pseudo telegrams" instead.

prospective customer act; don't leave him or her hanging with a mere recitation of facts.

When their budgets permits, many direct mailers are tempted to create brochures that are pleasing to their own egos—colorful, expensive, splashy, and impressive. For high-ticket, status items this may be the right alternative. But the best way to select a brochure format is to consider the target market and characteristics of the product. A three-for-$29.95 polyester slack offer does not require an eight-page color brochure on 100-pound coated stock. By the same token, a $999.95 stereo system may not be adequately sold in a black-and-white flyer on offset paper. Gather the brochures your competitors use or those in similar fields for ideas on paper sizes and stocks, the use of color, and supplementary illustrations.

Make sure your brochure fits with the other items in your package. An expensive, slick brochure should be complemented by a tasteful letterhead and a well-designed order form on good-quality stock. By contrast, a two-color flyer on offset stock looks fine with an inexpensive letter and order form.

Few direct mail brochures are done in black-and-white, although some firms use this one-color approach for a ''homey'' or ''small company'' look. Most brochures feature at least two colors, and the majority are done in four colors. This is because more colorful brochures generally pull larger responses than those without this added interest factor.

In most cases the brochure provides you and your art director with the greatest opportunity for creativity where size and folds are concerned. One ''standard'' brochure is the 8½-by-11-inch sheet folded twice into a ''C-fold'' flyer. Many brochures look like booklets and may be stitched or stapled to keep their pages together. If you want your prospect to keep and carry your brochure, consider making it of pocket size. If you want to make a big splash, design a ''broadside'' which opens up to a flat size of 17 by 22 inches or more. Save brochures with designs you like and discuss them with your art director to see how they might be adaptable to your own products and offers. But before committing to an odd size or fold, check with a trusted printer or two. This will help you avoid paper waste and extra bindery charges. Also remember that any brochure you design for machine insertion into an envelope must have a closed edge for the inserting machine to ''grab.'' This will save you costly and time-consuming hand-insertion charges.

THE REPLY CARD

It is essential that your reply device breeze the customer through his or her buying decision and reinforce the wisdom of it. If the reply card is confusing, complex, or intimidating, your sale may be nipped in the bud.

The reply card should summarize all elements of your offer, and should be able to function as a free-standing sales piece. Some customers save only the reply card and put it aside for a later decision; they should be able to use the card to refresh their memories and return an order with confidence.

The reply card should also help reinforce the urgency of the buying decision, and should comfort the buyer with a restatement of the guarantee or other risk-reducing aspects of the offer. It is also a good idea to picture the product on the reply card.

The reply card can be called an "order form," but many direct marketers opt for a term that focuses more on "sizzle" and less on the nuts and bolts of ordering and paying money. You might refer to the card as a "Reservation Form," "Invitation," "RSVP Card," "Free Information Ticket," or "Membership Application" if these terms apply.

A reply card labeled or ink-jet printed with the prospect's name and address makes it easier for him or her to order. Design the reply card so that the label shows through a window in the outer envelope, and it will serve as the means of addressing the piece as well. If you must ask the customer to fill in his or her name and address on the reply form, make sure there is ample space for them and that the paper stock is easy to write on: some coated stocks do not take well to pens or pencils of any kind. Also make sure you request specifically the customer's name, address, city, state, and zip code, or many of your respondents will provide you with inadequate information for delivery. And use a light-colored stock, so that any color pen or pencil will show up. Believe it or not, some misguided art directors have actually created reversed-out reply forms that would require sales prospects to use pens with white ink!

When your prospect is returning only an inquiry or reservation, and no payment is required, you may opt for a postage-prepaid Business Reply Card that the prospect can simply drop in the mail. But if you are asking for any confidential information on the card—a credit card number or the customer's age, for example—or if the nature of your

This *action device* asks the customer to move the golf ball from left to right and "tee it up" to emphasize 50 percent savings.

product is at all confidential, a Business Reply Envelope may ease your prospect's mind and make him or her more likely to respond.

You may also add to your customer's confidence by providing a tear-off stub on one end of your reply form, which he or she can save for future reference. This stub should have your firm's address on it, and allow room for the customer to record what he or she ordered, the date it was ordered, by what means it was ordered, and when delivery is expected. A statement on this stub of any applicable guarantees is also a good idea, and the stub provides another, more practical benefit: you may design your card so that removing the stub makes it just the right size for one of the standard Business Reply Envelope sizes. (If the card were sized this small in the first place, it might well float around too much in the outer envelope, so that the address label would not show through the window.)

To stimulate action with a reply card, many marketers use involvement devices of various kinds. These include:

- A page of stamps representing various products available for purchase or premium options. The prospect affixes to the reply form the stamps for the products or premiums he or she wants.
- A picture of the product or premium offered, either tipped onto the letter or another piece or on one side of the order form. The prospect affixes the product or premium picture to

the order form he or she returns to indicate acceptance of the offer.

- Yes/No stamps. To stimulate action, some marketers ask the prospects to respond whether their answer is yes or no. Sometimes the prospect is entered into a contest or receives a free gift for doing so. In this case the prospect chooses the appropriate stamp and affixes it to the reply device.
- A temporary membership card, which the prospect can remove from the order form, keep, and return the order form with his or her membership dues. The marketer then sends a permanent membership card with other club or organization information.
- A regular postage stamp affixed to the reply card. The prospect is asked to use this stamp in responding. This is much more dramatic than a Business Reply Envelope, albeit more expensive since with the latter you pay only for those envelopes that come back to you.
- A label to transfer from one piece of the direct mail kit to the order form. Pressure-sensitive labels may be used to address the letter or outer envelope, and can then be removed by the prospect and affixed to the order form.

One *Newsweek* renewal effort used an *actual stamp* to encourage response.

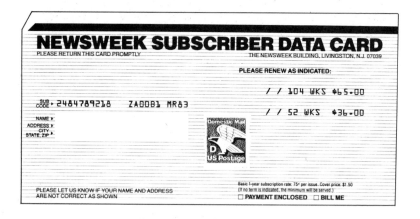

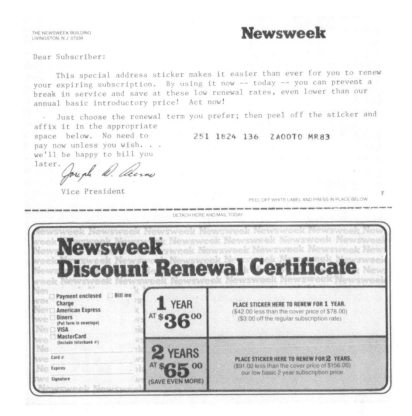

THE NEWSWEEK BUILDING
LIVINGSTON, N.J. 07039

Newsweek

Dear Subscriber:

This special address sticker makes it easier than ever for you to renew your expiring subscription. By using it now -- today -- you can prevent a break in service and save at these low renewal rates, even lower than our annual basic introductory price! Act now!

Just choose the renewal term you prefer; then peel off the sticker and affix it in the appropriate space below. No need to pay now unless you wish. . . we'll be happy to bill you later.

251 1824 136   ZA00TO MR83

Vice President

PEEL OFF WHITE LABEL AND PRESS IN PLACE BELOW   F

DETACH HERE AND MAIL TODAY

Newsweek
Discount Renewal Certificate

☐ Payment enclosed   ☐ Bill me
Charge
☐ American Express
☐ Diners
(Put form in envelope)
☐ VISA
☐ MasterCard
(Include interbank #)

Card #
Expires
Signature

1 YEAR
AT $**36**00

PLACE STICKER HERE TO RENEW FOR 1 YEAR.
($42.00 less than the cover price of $78.00)
($3.00 off the regular subscription rate)

2 YEARS
AT $**65**00
(SAVE EVEN MORE)

PLACE STICKER HERE TO RENEW FOR 2 YEARS.
($91.00 less than the cover price of $156.00)
our low basic 2 year subscription price

Another renewal pitch from *Newsweek* asked the customer to *move the address label* from the letter section to the renewal certificate form.

THE BUSINESS REPLY ENVELOPE

Time and again tests show that the cost of providing a Business Reply Envelope for your prospect is justified in that it encourages a greater level of response. The customer finds it much easier to return his or her order in a postage-paid, self-addressed envelope than to search around for a plain envelope and stamp.

To use a Business Reply Envelope you need a permit from your local post office. To get this you will fill out a form, pay a yearly fee, and receive a reply number to use on your envelopes. You will pay the current first-class rate plus a small surcharge for all orders that are returned to you. Provide the post office with money in advance which it may draw against as mail arrives; this will help avoid delays in your receiving your mail.

Business Reply Envelopes must be designed and sized in accordance with post-office rules. The specifications for Business Reply Envelopes and Cards are available at your post office. In most cases your art director will be familiar with these rules, assuming that direct mail is a specialty for him or her.

There are standard sizes for Business Reply Envelopes, the most common being the 6³/₄ and #9 sizes. You may use other sizes within post-office guidelines, but they may be more costly if they must be custom ordered from your envelope house. Make sure that the Business Reply Envelope you select fits easily into your outer mailing envelope, and that the reply form fits easily into the reply envelope, preferably without folding.

THE OUTER ENVELOPE

The outer envelope makes the initial impression on your prospect, and must therefore be selected and decorated with care. The paper stock, typeface, and even the type of postage used on an outer envelope help the prospect decide if he or she will consider a mailing piece appealing enough to open, or simply a candidate for the "round file."

Some direct marketers advocate perfectly plain outer envelopes bearing only the return address of the sender. They say that a plain envelope arouses curiosity in the recipient, and that an overly promotional outer envelope turns people off. A plain outer envelope is a cost saver, since it can be used for many different mailings. And plain envelopes can have their own "personalities," with the look of an invitation or of personal stationery. The personal look may be taken a step further when the return address, or "corner card," is that of an endorsing organization or person rather than of the marketer. Sometimes there is no corner card at all, but simply a totally "blind" mailing. This is most effective with stationery that is quite elegant and a mailing that appears to be an official invitation or announcement.

Other direct marketers suggest the use of decorated envelopes and envelope "teasers." A "teaser" is a statement on the outer envelope which helps lure the prospect inside with the promise of a special offer, free gift, important or intriguing information, or something else. Sometimes a teaser makes a statement and then trails off like this . . . , enticing the reader to pick up the rest of the message inside the envelope. Other marketers begin their letters on the outside of the envelope and stop in mid-sentence, inviting the reader to continue the story inside.

Teasers do not have to be written, however. A motif that typifies the product might decorate the envelope, such as a horse's head for a horse-related product. This would entice people interested in horses to look inside. Windows in the outer envelope can show through to a picture of the product, the premium, or a sweepstakes prize.

Some marketers decorate their envelopes all over with pictures of the product and its uses, or with "sizzle" about benefits of the product or prizes to be won. Others encourage a prompt response by showing the final date of ordering through a small window in the envelope.

All of these techniques and many more will provide testing opportunities for your direct mail program. But your basic outer envelope should be a #10, a 6 by 9, or 9 by 12 with a window for the label on the order form to show through. Many other sizes are acceptable to the post office: European sizes, monarch sizes, and so on. Check with your postmaster for details. And also check with your envelope house to make sure that you're not designing a very expensive custom envelope whose cost may not be justified.

As for the method of affixing postage, the easiest way is to print your Bulk Rate Mail Permit on the envelopes, but this is a dead giveaway of a direct mail piece, and may dilute the effectiveness of an invitation- or personal-letter-look mailing. Alternatives include metering with a Pitney Bowes machine, which gives a look more like a regular business mailing and can be done using the Bulk Rate amount; and Bulk Rate stamps, which are more costly to affix but provide more of a personal-letter look. Check with your lettershop for more information about the pros and cons of these methods, and the costs for their use.

OTHER INSERTS AND FORMATS

Testimonial flyers. If you have or can obtain flattering and believable testimonials from satisfied users of your product, a flyer containing these testimonials may make a good addition to your kit. Optionally, you may work some testimonials into your letter copy or put them on a panel of your brochure.

Premium slips. The customer who barely skims your mailing may not realize you are offering a premium unless you devote a special piece to it. The premium slip should discuss the features and benefits of the premium, its dollar value if impressive, and what the prospect must do to obtain the premium.

Buckslip reminders. These small flyers are most often used to simulate "last minute news." A buckslip might be inserted to tell the prospect that a certain item being offered is now sold out, thus stimulating urgency for buying other items offered. Such a piece might highlight your toll-free 800 number if you have one. Or the buckslip

An *article* from Southern Living® Gallery tells the history of collector plates with subtle plugs for this firm's products.

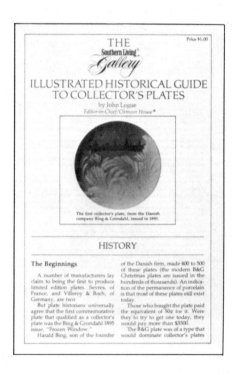

Damart included this *sample swatch* to prove how warm, light, and soft its thermolactyl material is.

might explain a recent improvement in the product or the offer. It should cover the offer thoroughly enough to make sense to a reader who has not read your promotion kit.

Article or ad reprints. These pieces add credibility to your offer by including statements from "independent" articles or ads. In many cases such articles are written specifically for the direct mail kit and never appear in any publication, but only look as if they had. Where ads are concerned, the marketer might obtain reprints of an ad run in a particular publication and overprint a message such as, "In case you missed our ad in XYZ magazine . . . ."

Questions and answers. A question-and-answer piece gives you the opportunity to restate your offer and the attributes of the product in a new and simple-to-understand form. For example, one question might be: "What do I need to do to obtain the XYZ product on a thirty-day free trial?" The answer would explain the procedure.

Samples of the product. If the product is inexpensive and easy enough to send, you might include a sample of it in your mailing. Products that may be sampled in this way would include newsletters, stationery, fabric, and so on. Swatches of fabric may be enclosed in clothing offers as well.

Gimmicks. To induce a response, some marketers send their prospects actual checks for small amounts of money, which the customer may endorse and cash for responding to or even for simply receiving the mailing. Or the marketer may send a penny or other coin or coins to create interest value, with a line such as ''A penny for your thoughts.'' Advertising specialities firms can provide a wide range of gimmick items that may be enclosed or tipped onto your promotional pieces. Examples of these might be a little package of two aspirin tablets for a product that ''takes the headache out of spring cleaning,'' or a packet of instant coffee with a letter that says, ''have a cup of coffee on us and sit down and read about XYZ product.''

Follow-ups. In a series of mailings, varying your formats may inspire fresh interest from your prospects. You might, for example, send an actual photocopy of your original letter, with a handwritten note saying ''in case you missed this special offer the first time around . . . .'' Using different outer envelope sizes will encourage prospects to read mailings sent later in a series, as will printing a two-color brochure in a different color combination.

Self-mailers. While the standard direct mailing includes various separate pieces enclosed in an envelope, self-contained mailers come in a number of attractive formats. A self-mailer may be as simple as a mimeographed sheet with an ordering device separated from a letter by a dotted line, or it may be a complex format with ingenious folds, perforations, and combinations of paper stocks to provide a brochure, letter, order form, and preformed Business Reply Envelope all in one. In general, mailers find that they get a better response to envelope mailings than to self-mailers. But people are more likely to pass a self-mailer along to a friend or associate than they are an envelope mailing. So if your offering appeals to a ''cult'' audience or special interest group, the self-mailer may work beautifully for you. And because some self-mailers cost less than envelope mailings, the cost per order with the self-mailer may be less, even if you get fewer total orders. Usually the self-mailer concept is worth a test. Work with an experienced printer to find a cost-efficient format, and try it against your standard envelope mailing.

RETAIL DIRECT RESPONSE FORMATS

Many of the formats discussed above will also be applicable to some retail direct response efforts. But there are certain formats that are especially helpful for retailers to consider.

The catalog mailing. Chapter 7 of this book contains the basic "how-to" information for consumer, retail, and business-to-business catalogs. Suffice it to say here that retailers today use catalogs in all shapes and sizes, both to supplement and advertise in-store efforts and as separate sources of profit. Chapter 7 provides more information on how to get started with your own retail catalog.

Single-item mailings. Retailers who have a very special item with broad appeal to the customer base may use the standard one-item offer with a letter, brochure, reply card, and Business Reply Envelope, or such an offer may be made using a self-mailer.

Brooks Brothers has done single- and multiple-item mailings to sell such merchandise as classic men's shirts with the store's well-known logo embroidered on them. Firms such as Neiman-Marcus have also done single- and multiple-item mailings, perhaps to groups on their customer list identified as clothing buyers. A colorful self-mailer for silk dresses might even include swatches of the various colors available, contained in a small plastic bag which is tipped or stapled onto the mailing piece.

Mutli-flyer mailings. Rather than print a catalog that will be outdated after one season, some retailers choose to do a modular mailing piece with flyers of the same size for each piece of merchandise. All of the flyers may then be housed in a small "portfolio" with a flap to keep them together. For the next mailing, the retailer again includes the flyers for merchandise that sold well and is still available, replacing those for outdated, sold-out, or slow-selling merchandise with new flyers.

Letters only. A simple letter in an envelope, especially if it is or appears to be hand-typed, can be a very effective way for a retailer to communicate by mail with a customer. Such a letter might serve as a personal invitation to an upcoming event, a "thank-you" for opening a new charge account, notification of a new store policy, a collection letter, or part of a customer-service reply. You might try designing your letterhead so that the usual company name and ad-

A *portfolio* may hold scores of different product offerings all presented in one mailing. This American Express® mailing is one example.

dress information appear on the bottom, leaving the top free for promotional language and headings.

Computer letters. Some oil companies have used computer letters in an interesting way to thank their customers and generate increased loyalty and traffic. Using computerized records, they send the letters to charge customers, thanking them for their x dollars in charge business last year, with the exact amount filled in by computer. Other retailers might use such a computer fill-in to thank charge customers and offer them a special gift, or to announce the arrival of some type of specific merchandise that might interest the customer, just to name two possibilities.

Handwritten letters or cards. Salesclerks who have been encouraged to keep good customer records will know just who to drop a line to when that new shipment of needlepoint kits and yarn or XYZ-brand dress shoes arrives at the store. Personnel at service stations might want to write to customers when it is time for another oil change or brake check, and carpet cleaners would want to write to their customers to let them know that a year has passed since the last cleaning job. Be sure your salesclerks are supplied with stationery or cards with your store name, and that they're encouraged to use them to correspond with customers.

Self-mailers. To gain immediate attention, try using a self-mailer. This piece may be as simple as a sheet of offset-printed paper folded and stapled, or as elaborate as a beautifully printed four-color piece, with a letter printed on a different paper stock as an insertion. Self-mailers may also serve double-duty as free-standing stuffers in your local newspaper, package inserts, and so on.

Fake telegrams. Because of their appearance of urgency, mailings with a telegram look can help a retailer announce a sale or other special, time-limited event quite effectively. Get yourself a real Western Union telegram for inspiration, but don't follow it literally enough to risk infringement. Try a "Sale Gram" or a "Back-to-School Gram"—whatever name fits your offer best.

The invitation/ticket approach. Retailers can build walk-in traffic beautifully with invitations to special events or sales, or with tickets to fashion shows, appearances by celebrities, "Breakfasts with Santa," and so on. One way to do this is to make the invitation look like a formal, personal one by using a squarish outer envelope, fine paper stock, and an R.S.V.P. card. Or you can use an envelope "teaser" that says "Your Are Invited" and leads the prospects inside to find out what they are invited to.

The coupon book. To build traffic for an ongoing product, item, or special event, consider offering a book of coupons, or individual coupons for specific items of merchandise or services. You might also send several free-with-purchase or x-amount-off coupons for your next sale to your current customers. Or offer a coupon book with dated "deals" to encourage repeat customer visits over time.

BUSINESS-TO-BUSINESS FORMATS

Once again, the previous sections of this chapter will offer many ideas for the business-to-business direct marketer. In business mailings, however, the list of prospects is often relatively short and the cost of the item being sold relatively high. Thus the marketer can spend more time and money pursuing each individual customer by mail, even to the extent of sending a specially written letter to each prospect.

A campaign by *Cuisine* magazine illustrates this point. *Cuisine* wanted to reach a relatively small circle of media buyers and prospective media buyers who might wish to advertise in the magazine. The theme of its campaign was: "If You're Not in *Cuisine,* You're Not in the Kitchen"—meaning that *Cuisine* readers were highly in-

Retailers have an excellent opportunity to provide personal mail reinforcement for sales. This letter came with a box of expensive chocolates, in thanks for a luggage purchase in excess of $1,000.

I.magnin 1525 LAKE COOK ROAD . NORTHBROOK, ILLINOIS 60062

December 6, 1982

Ms. Susan Kraus Jones

Dear Ms. Kraus Jones:

Ms. Marilyn Levin, of our Luggage Department, was pleased to serve you recently. We trust you are enjoying your purchases.

It was a pleasure to have you visit our store, and we hope you will visit us again soon.

As an expression of our appreciation, Please accept this box of chocolates.

Sincerely,

R. A. Gifford
General Manager

Encl.

SAN FRANCISCO . PALO ALTO . OAKLAND . WALNUT CREEK . SAN MATEO . SANTA CLARA . VALLCO FASHION PARK . CARMEL
PORTLAND . SEATTLE . LOS ANGELES . BEVERLY HILLS . PASADENA . SOUTH COAST PLAZA . SANTA ANA . DEL AMO
SHERMAN OAKS . LA JOLLA . SANTA BARBARA . PALM SPRINGS . PHOENIX . CHICAGO . OAKBROOK . NORTHBROOK . WHITE FLINT

fluenced by the magazine's ads when they chose items for their kitchens. The first of a series of mailings in this campaign was actually a shipment: a box containing a handsome crock filled with wrapped candies. Printed on the crock was the theme message, while the crock itself was a handsome piece that could be used and displayed in the prospect's home. Each crock was accompanied by a selling letter.

About a month later, each prospect received another selling letter along with another type of candy to fill the crock, which presumably had already been emptied by the hungry media buyer. Throughout the series, each letter was accompanied by a different food item—in an amount just sufficient to fit in the crock.

The cost of this campaign certainly was high—probably much more than most marketers would be able to spend on a regular consumer prospect. But because of the small target audience and high stakes involved, the expenditure in this case could be justified on the basis of its impact.

As mentioned in Chapter 5, on "The Offer," business-to-business buyers are concerned with value and with justifying their expenditures to their superiors. Thus most direct-response formats for business sales are more serious and factual than are consumer appeals. Forget the puns involving scantily clad young ladies and other "cute" ploys; they come under the category of "borrowed attention"; in other words, they get attention for their sensationalism—not for the product. Here are some of the factual and persuasive formats you might consider:

The file folder. Many of the items that you mail to business prospects are expensive: price lists and catalogs, for instance. It is important that the customer perceive these items as something to be saved and filed. To that end, try designing a piece that comes in an actual file folder—tab and all—in just the right size for a standard file drawer. Just as stamps to affix to a reply form are action devices for the consumer, this file-folder format inspires many business prospects to action—in this case putting your kit in a handy file drawer for continued reference.

The loose-leaf notebook. If your price lists and catalog sheets change frequently, why not provide important customers and prospects with a good-quality loose-leaf notebook, decorated with your company logo, in which to keep the updates. Then you can do periodic mailings including new material and explaining what items and price lists should be eliminated.

The newsletter. Many company newsletters have become respected in their fields as fact-and-opinion letters that industry leaders want to receive. A newsletter of this type can mix well-researched articles with subtle "plugs" for the sponsoring company, becoming an ongoing public relations tool that may eventually produce sales or at least give the company that sends it an edge obtaining the right to bid.

How-to booklets. Just like a newsletter, booklets or even books from your firm may become highly sought information pieces, even as they provide a subtle message about the expertise of your firm.

Testimonials. Statements by representatives of respected firms that have purchased and used your products successfully can provide a very powerful business-to-business selling tool. In choosing them, try to include as many specifics as possible about dollars and time saved, effectiveness, service, and so on.

Other formats and reasons to mail. A special report on a topic of interest may create an excellent opportunity for a mailing to your customers and prospects, since it can show your understanding of the question at hand. Marketing surveys provide a similar opportunity, as do seminars you are planning, announcements of new offices and services, and so on.

7

CATALOGS

The reasons for the growth in general direct marketing set forth in Chapter 5 apply directly to the consumer catalog business. What's more, retailers have embraced the catalog concept as a way both to stimulate in-store traffic and to sell to the customer unwilling or unable to purchase items in person. And the retailer with a unique concept or a reputation for quality and service can use a catalog to expand his or her horizons beyond the local clientele.

Business-to-business marketers have used catalogs for years as leave-behind pieces for personal sales representatives. Today, however, more and more businesses, including such giants as IBM and Control Data, have come to understand that a catalog can also work on its own, selling office supplies, replacement parts, and much more—often without a single personal sales call. And this flexibility becomes increasingly important as the cost of that sales call edges toward $200.

THE GLAMOUR . . . AND THE REALITY

The growth of catalog marketing comes as no surprise to any American consumer who is a mail-order buyer. In the months before Christmas of each year, the frequent mail-order buyer may receive an average of ten to fifteen catalogs *per day,* offering goods as diverse as chocolates and leather chairs, televisions and custom t-shirts, evening wear and fishing gear.

Unfortunately for their originators, many of these catalogs make only a one-time appearance in the marketplace. Caught up in the glamour of slick, well-photographed presentations and exotic goods, these entrepreneurs figure "if Roger Horchow could do it . . . so can I." And so they introduce yet another gifts-and-accessories catalog, forgetting that when Horchow started in 1971 his book was one of a kind. Or our ill-fated catalog marketer may then find himself under-financed and unable to build a mailing list fast enough to cover his costs and keep growing. Or his products may attract many would-be buyers, but lack of follow-through and poor customer service create ill will and result in poor word-of-mouth reputation for his firm.

This is not to say that successful catalog marketing is a myth. On the contrary, this field has new and exciting success stories each year, such as the recent "Sharper Image" book of electronic items and jewelry, or the new crop of catalogs tuned to the business traveler— "Innovations" and "Dimensions in Travel" to name just two.

But starting a catalog is serious business, and a great deal of up-front planning, financing, and operational work must be done to maximize the chances for success. This chapter will outline the "how-to's" for catalog marketers and provide some helpful benchmarks for novices in the field.

CONSUMER CATALOG MARKETING

Ways to Get Started with Catalogs

There are two contrasting ways for a catalog business to get started, and either may be vastly successful if handled properly. The first way is "from the ground up"; the second involves a "pay-out plan" in which a going business or investor funds the catalog until it can pay back the investment and stand on its own.

Building from the ground up. Few individual entrepreneurs have the capital necessary to plunge into the catalog business right from the beginning. However, they can work into a stable catalog operation stage by stage. First, such a company might find one good and appealing product to sell via space advertising, affordable solo mailings, or both. Once this product is launched, either similar products or different products with demonstrated appeal to the buyers of the original item may be offered to the list of these buyers by means of package inserts, invoice stuffers, newsletters, and other communications.

In this cautious, step-by-step way, the company learns which products are most appealing to the customer base. As the firm builds up a "stable" of products that sell well and appeal to its customer profile, the framework for a small, initial catalog is formed. This first catalog might contain all the firm's proven "winners" plus additional test items—logical extensions of the product mix that has already proven successful. With time the catalog would grow as more proven products and merchandise categories emerged from such testing.

For example, let's assume that a marketer has developed a special jalapeno pepper jelly that he can sell profitably via small space ads. Using bounce-backs, the marketer might begin selling other preserves and jams to maximize the dollar value of the names he or she has acquired while at the same time doing some inexpensive product-versus-product testing.

Eventually, the package inserts and stuffers the marketer creates might become foldouts or mini-catalogs, growing with time to include related gourmet food items such as nuts, candy, and so on, until the marketer has enough proven products to provide the "anchor" for an initial catalog offering to established customers and rented-list prospects.

The pay-out plan. In recent years a number of large American firms have entered the catalog marketing field, often with no expense spared. Companies like Corning, Pfaltzgraff, and Zale's Jewelers are among the manufacturers and retailers who have added catalogs to their marketing mix.

Take Pfaltzgraff, for example. This Pennsylvania firm manufactures dinnerware which it sells at retail, mostly via department stores. But in the late 1970s the company recognized another viable channel of distribution: direct marketing to consumers by means of a catalog. The consumer would then have the opportunity to purchase a wide range of accessory items that most retailers were unwilling to keep in stock, and Pfaltzgraff could take advantage of handsome margins by direct selling—without middlemen.

The result of this strategy is "Country Notebook," a catalog that blends Pfaltzgraff's country-look stoneware lines with decor items, giftware, and collectibles having a country theme.

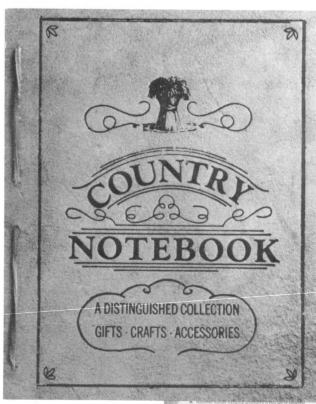

COUNTRY NOTEBOOK

A DISTINGUISHED COLLECTION
GIFTS · CRAFTS · ACCESSORIES

...t home in today's American country kitchens and
...ood... appropriate for any room where family and
...authentic Yorktowne look of the past will be applauded.

...great green salads and other foods can be "well
...ed" with Yorktowne's three-compartment server
...ed holder has tinware base; comes with three
...ing spoons.
...Relish Server   07-043H...$16.25

...mugs with their own decorated wood rack. Convenient
for coffee or tea.
4 pc. Mug Set/Rack   07-292K...$27.25

C. Complete the look you want with this very functional
addition to your set. Utensils not included.
Utensil Crock   07-300A...$11.00

D. Oil and vinegar have a home in their own little
Yorktowne jugs. You may even eat more healthy salads,
just to use them!
Cruet Set   07-440K...$11.00

E. Lazy Susan with three compartments and dip holder in
center. Perfect for parties.
Lazy Susan , 07-130W...$28.75

G. TV snacks are special when served on the Yorktowne
"chip and dipper." Just right for company, too. 12" diameter
Chip 'n Dip (12")   07-180K...$12.00

H. Your table can be charmingly complete right down to
these attractive Yorktowne napkin rings. Set of four.
Napkin Ring Set   07-013A...$6.75

Although Pfaltzgraff has run space advertising to acquire the names of new prospective customers, the firm did not take time to build step-by-step from the ground up; rather, it invested in a full-scale catalog from the very beginning, and projected a pay-out plan whereby the catalog operation would gain funding from the parent company during its start-up period.

Planning the Successful Catalog Venture

To determine whether your catalog concept has a good chance of succeeding, consider the guidelines set forth below on the target market, positioning, merchandising, and operations.

Pfaltzgraff's "Country Notebook" catalog projects an image in keeping with today's popular country look in tabletop and home decor.

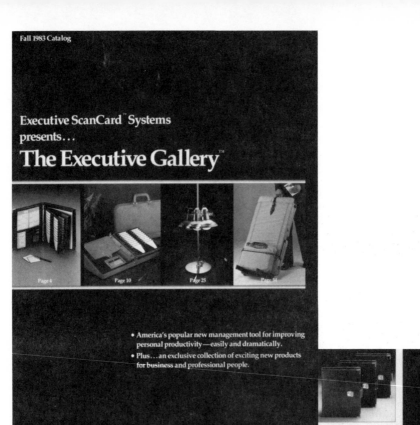

Fall 1983 Catalog

Executive ScanCard™ Systems
presents…

The Executive Gallery™

Page 4 Page 10 Page 25 Page 31

- America's popular new management tool for improving personal productivity—easily and dramatically.
- Plus…an exclusive collection of exciting new products for business and professional people.

The Chairman of the Board

It's like a traveling office.

This deluxe model of the Executive ScanCard System fills every requisite for executive organization, in and out of the office. The Chairman initially offers three ScanCard panels which handle up to 120 projects. Additional panels can be added to expand to 200 projects. In addition, it has an appointments calendar, phone index, built-in multi-function calculator, business and credit card compartments and concealed pocket files for important or private papers. 300 color coded cards are included, and the cover is personalized with the user's name or initials. Edges are handsomely stitched for appearance and durability, and all hardware has an attractive goldtone finish. In leather-like vinyl (black, brown or tan) Item CB31 $99.95 (54). In genuine cowhide leather (black, brown or burgundy) Item CB50 $149.95 (54).

Credit card orders, phone
800-848-2618
In Ohio call 800-282-2630

Satisfaction Guaranteed
If, for any reason, you are not satisfied with any item purchased, you may return it within 30 days for a complete and courteous refund. You take no risk.

The target market. To succeed in catalog marketing, you must define your target market as specifically as possible. Many catalog marketers make the mistake of approaching too broad an interest group, and succeed only in making a mediocre impression on a broad range of consumers.

Be sure that you also focus on a target market that is reachable. There may be millions of Americans dying for the opportunity to buy left-handed back scratchers, but if there is no publication or direct mail list by which they may be reached, your efforts may well be doomed.

And make sure you understand the difference between a sharply defined target market and a special-interest group that is too small to make for profitable operations.

Here are several examples of recent catalogs that have carved out

"Executive Gallery" serves a wide range of needs for today's executive at work, at home, and during leisure.

acceptably large yet distinct target markets. Use these as food for thought in your own planning process.

Target Market	Catalog	Merchandise Profile
Executives	The Executive Gallery	Luggage, attachés, self-improvement cassettes, travel helpers
Chocolate lovers	The Chocolate Catalogue™	Gourmet candies, chocolate novelties
Decor-oriented persons	The Stevens Catalogue™ Bed and Bath Fashions	Fine-quality coordinated towels, sheets, accessories, and so forth
Organization-minded	Hold Everything! A Catalog of Containers from Williams-Sonoma	Containers for gifts and kitchen, office, and closet items
Teddy-bear lovers	The Bear Necessities®	Teddy-bear-related toys, apparel, decor items, and gifts
Innovations	The Shelburne Company	The latest (mostly electronic) items for travel, personal care, home, and entertainment

Your appeal to the market. Your challenge is to offer the consumer a range of related products that he or she does not perceive to be readily available from any other source. You may achieve this on the basis of any number of attributes, such as:

- *Better selection.* Most consumers know that they can buy cotton turtlenecks at the local shopping center. But if you offer reasonably priced cotton turtlenecks in twenty-five different colors and twenty different sizes, your catalog may be perceived as having a ''better selection.''

- *Finer quality*. Here once again, the perception factor is at work. The consumer who buys a jacket off the rack in a mid-priced department store is unlikely to hear about its construction and wearability from the salesclerk. But if you can explain these attributes in copy, you may well win the customer's admiration as a source with "finer quality."
- *Uniqueness*. To create uniqueness, take a readily available product and add a special twist to it, or create a worthwhile item that your customer can buy only by mail. For instance, you might win the exclusive right to import macadamia nut cake from a special source in Hawaii. Or you might offer a portable, personal-sized color television when all other sources have it only in black-and-white.
- *More affordable price*. Once again, perception is at work here. It may be that a local retailer is more affordable than you are, but if the consumer perceives your product as a value, you may win the sale anyway. One crude but classic example of this is the discount catalog practice of showing the list price for every item in a mailer as well as the discounter's price. Or you might explain how volume buying power lets you price your items lower than others, or offer quantity discounts, discounts for members of a "club" you devise, or similar enticements to show consumers how affordable your merchandise is.
- *Appealing presentation*. For many consumers, catalog shopping is more fun than shopping in stores. If they can select their Christmas gifts while gazing at your rich, four-color catalog and reading your comforting copy, why shouldn't it be? But appeal need not be based on high-cost production techniques alone. Some catalogs win loyal followings with a down-home attitude as well.

Catalog positioning. Each year, hundreds of catalogs are published that successfully sell women's clothing, and scores that market sporting goods. Even though they may seem to offer similar items on the surface, their positioning is different enough so that each can carve out its own particular interest group and customer base. They may do this by means of the merchandise they sell, the format of their presentation, their price range, spokesman or spokeswoman, and many other factors.

🐻 THE BEAR NECESSITIES 🐻

MERRY CHRISTMAS AND A HAPPY NEW BEAR

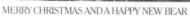

SNUFFLE OFF TO BUFFALO

Snuffles™ by Gund. One of the cutest bears this side of the Black Forest. He has an ultra soft coat made exclusively for Gund, and a unique weighted stuffing that makes him a joy to play with. (He's a 13" bear and comes in three handsome colors.)

#2050	Tan Snuffles	$21.00 ($2.50)
#2051	Brown Snuffles	$21.00 ($2.50)
#2052	White Snuffles	$21.00 ($2.50)

THE WELL READ BEAR

This famous storybook character comes complete with two of his own storybooks. Your child will spend hours reading with his new friend.

#8063   Corduroy (with 2 books, 14" $25.50 ($2.50)

DECORATE A BEAR ROOM

You'll be up, up and away with our beautiful porcelain balloon and bear wind chimes. Hand crafted by Jam Ceramics, their pleasing tintinnabulation will leave you tingling.

#7033	Bear with Balloons	$18.00 ($2.50)
#7032	Bears in the Air	$15.50 ($2.50)

94

20

In the womens' fashion group, for instance, contrast the following firms and their orientations:

- *Victoria's Secret:* Designer lingerie; fine nightwear and undergarments.
- *The Talbots:* Classic, medium-priced clothing with a preppy, New England look.
- *Lawson & Marcia Hill:* All shoes, in all sizes from 4 to 11 and AA to D widths.
- *Garnet Hill:* Natural-fiber garments; clothing of 100 percent wool, cotton, and silk.
- *Lew Magram:* Formerly calling itself "shirtmaker to the stars," this firm now offers "fashions to the stars" for women, selling high-fashion looks at a mid-price range.

"The Bear Necessities®" serves today's fast-growing market of teddy bear afficionados.

The
Natural
Fibers
Catalog

garnet hill

Fall
Winter
1982/83

A. Oak Knoll Sweater
These handsome sweaters are made of a heavyweight yarn. The extra length and zipper front make them almost a car coat. There are two handy side-seam pockets and a front zipper and nice turtleneck. Offered in Burgundy or Navy.
#57W1   Sizes: S, M, L $55.00

B. Men's Cotton Turtleneck
This turtleneck rides just a little lower than most turtlenecks. Its flat knit is made of soft spun cotton that has been pre-shrunk for easy care. The ribbed collar and cuffs give it a handsome finish. It is sporty enough to be used for skiing, and dressy enough to be worn under a blazer. Colors: Camel, Silver, Navy.
#1259   Sizes: S, M, L, XL $24.90

C. Women's Cotton Bouclé Turtleneck
Is made of 100% cotton bouclé yarn. It is tightly knit, and the irregularity of the nubby yarn gives an almost dressy look. The natural color makes a very versatile sweater. Machine washable. Color: Natural.
#12W6   Sizes: S, M, L $28.50

D. Homespun Sweater
This sweater is like a jacket because it has the natural undyed bulky yarn in it. It is nicely finished with side pockets, front zipper, and high crew neck. Color: Gray Tweed.
#17X1   Men's Sizes: S, M, L, XL $60.00
#17W2   Women's Sizes: S, M, L $60.00

- *Lilly Pulitzer:* If The Talbots catalog is for the New England preppy, Lilly Pulitzer is for the Sun Belt preppy. Bright prints and resort looks in classic styles.
- *FBS:* Very trendy, New York looks for younger women; mostly junior sizes.
- *Aunt Abigail's Attic:* This firm's motto is "Country clothes for particular women"; the catalog carries the same styles year after year, including smocks, middy dresses, prairie dresses, and calico prints.
- *Saint Laurie Ltd.:* This firm calls itself a "manufacturer of classic business suits," with women's styles as carefully tailored as men's.
- *Royal Silk:* Mostly blouses, all silk, and affordable.
- *Britches:* High-quality classic looks, but with a touch more sophistication (and more cost) than The Talbots.
- *Esprit:* Inexpensive, faddish clothes for junior sizes. Bright colors, targeted at the young and fashion-conscious. More casual than FBS.

One of a very wide range of apparel catalogs serving special needs is "Garnet Hill," The Natural Fibers Catalog.

Tennis Lady

FALL/WINTER 1983

T

THE MUST-HAVES!
DESIGNER ORIGINALS
LOADED WITH FASHION
WIT AND SPORTY SPIRIT

26A

28B

26D

26A Adrienne Vittadini Sport. Big on bulky knits and European chic. Gives you the comfort and confidence it takes to make you feel like a winner, even if the most active thing you do is jog around the block for the paper. In soft, natural, fleece-back cotton with giant rib-knit cowl and cuffings. S(4-6), M(8-10), L(12-14) sizes 118.00.

28B Ralph Lauren's spirit starts with a flag shirt in birdseye cotton. S-M-L sizes 26.00. 2 cable knit vest in na navy/multi stripes. S 72.00. **28D** Famed, shorts with adjustab waist, in fine, all cot twill. 4-14 sizes 59.0

28

98

And in the sporting goods areas, look at the difference among these firms, which are loosely grouped under the ''sporty'' category:

- *Banana Republic:* Safari gear that is as much for the stay-at-home ''hunter'' as for the real African traveler.
- *Duncraft for the Birds:* Everything for the bird watcher and his feathered friends, including feeders, how-to books, seed, bird houses, and bird-oriented decor items.
- *Delta Arms:* Everything for the hunter, from guns to camouflage clothing to whimsical plaques for his office or den.
- *Sportpages:* Offering sporty attire, this firm is moving further and further away from the sporting-goods category with each issue, but its catalog still contains warm-up suits, exercise supplies, and related items.

There is a catalog for most every type of sports buff, including ''Tennis Lady'' for women tennis players.

h Lauren, the American
gner who believes more in
— than fashion. And
s it with this season's
ick that flash primary
s loud and clear, take on
r, better-than-ever new
na. Fabrics — light
ns or heavy-duty
ns. Looks — even better
rrow than today

Ralph Lauren's heavy-duty
fleece-back sweatsuit coffons
S(4-6), M(8-10), L(12-14) sizes.
Black/white hooded jacket
over yellow polo shirt and
black drawstring pants.
29A Jacket 84.00. **29B** Pants
64.00. **29C** Shirt 26.00.
29D Yellow cardigan 89.00.
29E Royal blue pants with
patch knees (for praying you
win.) 65.00.

☎ CALL
TOLL FREE
From anywhere in the
continental U.S.
Central time
1-800-527-7923
In Texas - call collect
214-263-9631
MONDAYS - FRIDAYS
8:30 a.m. - 5:00 p.m.

29

- *Tennis Lady:* Tennis-related attire and equipment for women and their families.
- *Sporting Dog Specialties:* Everything you need to pamper your talented hound dog and make it easier to live with.
- *Damart® Thermolactyl:* Thermal underwear and nightwear of every size and description.

These examples show how important it is to "fine-tune" your catalog's subject matter and your merchandising, going far beyond some general category such as women's clothing, sporting goods, giftware, or decor. Determine your positioning on the basis of an identifiable need in the marketplace and your ability to fill that need, and communicate the strengths of your product to the target market.

Selecting and evaluating catalog merchandise. Catalog merchandising is a semi-science. The "science" part involves careful research into your own past results, the activities of competitors, and the available merchandise (new and repeat) from vendors in your field. The "semi" qualifier applies because no matter how well-chosen your merchandise is, the response of consumers is not completely predictable. It is to be hoped that before too long you will develop a reliable "sixth sense" to help you in making merchandising decisions; a "feel" for the market based on past experience, talking with consumers, and the relative attributes of the products you're marketing.

Here are some ideas to help you in merchandising your catalog:

Consider needed mark-up. Unless you can sell a product for at least twice—preferably three times—its cost to you, the profit margin is not likely to be sufficient.

Check the competition. In order to become an active buyer in your product category, send for a copy of every catalog you can find in this category and "decoy" buy from a number of them. Note what types of products are merchandised with one another, and their price ranges, as well as items that seem to appear in every catalog. Consider how much space is allocated to certain types of items. Read the copy and note which product attributes it stresses. Cut out those layouts you feel are most effective and save them to discuss with your layout artists. Try filling in your competitors' order forms and note which are confusing and which easy to use. Note your competitors' policies about shipping and handling; is there a shipping charge for each item, or is this figure computed on the basis of the size of the order? Or is the shipping charge figured into the price of the merchandise? Do your competitors sell merchandise on the front cover of their catalogs? On the back cover? Characterize each catalog in terms of its target marketing and positioning. Where is there an "open" category for you to explore?

Attend trade shows. You or your buyers should be "regulars" at all major trade shows—here and eventually abroad—that feature your line of merchandise. Approach vendors whose merchandise fits your profile and explain your catalog concept. Work with them to determine which of their products would enhance your catalog. Negotiate to obtain the best profit margins you can. Find out how much advertising allowance your vendors will offer toward your catalog costs, and what you need to do to take advantage of these funds.

Consider exclusives. Some vendors will work with you to create exclusive merchandise just for your catalog. In the clothing line, this might be something as simple as a trim color on a standard skirt or blouse, or a warm-up suit with your company logo. Remember, however, that you must balance the exclusivity factor against the chances of getting "stuck" with excess inventory; you'll have to buy very carefully on an exclusive item, especially a fashion item, since your vendor won't be able to sell it anywhere else if you overbuy.

Look for order starters and impulse "add-on" items. Whimsical items in your interest area may encourage the customer to begin filling in an order form and to then move on to the bigger-ticket merchandise in your catalog. In sporting goods, for instance, a set of three monogrammed golf balls for less than $10 may lead a customer to your order form, and while he's ordering he may go ahead and also order a new golf bag or set of club covers. So don't steer completely away from low-end merchandise that may have a special appeal to your target market. And the same goes for especially appealing merchandise at sale prices.

Order carefully and spread your ship dates. One of the trickiest areas of catalog management is buying your merchandise in the proper quantities. If you underbuy you risk losing good orders—and good will—as your customers wait for you to re-order. If you overbuy you tie up good money in an "aging" inventory that may have to be sold at or below cost, if it can be sold at all.

Here is one proposal you can make to your vendors that will minimize this problem. When you select an item, figure your "worst-case," "probable-case," and "best-case" sales for that item. Ask your vendor to reserve the "best case" quantity of items for you, and to ship in three segments as follows. At about the time your catalog is to be mailed, accept delivery of the "worst-case" amount of goods. Then—once your orders come in and you can project the total amount you'll sell—decide whether or not to accept a second shipment that will bring your stock up to your "probable-case" level. Finally, if things go really well and you can project sales at the "best-case" level, take a third shipment at the proper interval to fill your later catalog orders. If at any point your projections indicate that your sales will be in the "worst-case" category, you can then cancel your later shipments in accordance with your predicted sales figures.

The table shown here demonstrates how this system might work for a catalog marketer selling crystal vases at holiday time:

Catalog mail date	September 10
Worst case sales projection	100 vases
Probable case	150 vases
Best case	200 vases
Ask vendor to allocate	200 vases
With ship dates as follows	100 on September 1
	50 on October 10
	50 on November 1
Order projection as of 10/10 (Authorize October 10 shipment)	156 vases total to be sold
Order projection as of 11/1 (Cancel November 1 shipment)	143 vases total to be sold

How to allocate space by product. Once you have some idea of the product selection for your catalog, you will need to allocate space to each of the items you'll be promoting. Although you may be tempted to give the most "photogenic" items the biggest play, the most practical way to assign space is "by the numbers." Use your sales history with the item to determine its relative strength. In most cases you will use total dollar sales rather than unit sales to allocate space.

For a general idea of how many units of a product should sell for it to "carry its weight" in a quarter-page space, determine the total sales level you will need to break even on your catalog, and work back from there. The following is an example of how to do this.

Let's say the total cost of your products, inventory, mailing costs, and minimum contribution to overhead comes to $200,000. Assume that you have a twenty-four-page catalog with an order form that takes up two of those pages, a non-selling cover, and two non-selling, informational half pages included in the book. This leaves twenty pages for merchandise promotion, for an average requirement of $10,000 sales per page. To deserve a quarter-page space, therefore, on average a product would have to gross at least $2,500 in sales, and to merit a half page, it would have to bring you $5,000. Please note, however, that if some of your products carry better profit margins than others, their actual "contribution to overhead," and not just their gross sales, should be considered.

On your first go through, estimate the sales that you expect each product to bring, and allocate its catalog space accordingly. This doesn't mean that you have to limit your designer to quarter-page boxes, but rather that each item and its copy should occupy roughly the amount of space allocated to it when the catalog layout is prepared.

Once you have done your first catalog mailing and received your response figures, evaluate the performance of each product against your expectations. Then, for your next catalog, you can decide if its space allotments are correct. If an item did twice as well as you projected, you might try allocating it more space to see if it can do even better. But test this, because some products can do beautifully in a small space while others only "bloom" on a half- or full-page layout.

For items that did not live up to their expectations, consider whether to cut back their space allotments or drop them entirely. An item may live up to a quarter-page space while not measuring up to the sales volume needed to justify a half page. However, cutting an eighth-page item back to one-sixteenth of a page may not be worth the effort. In this case you may be able to replace the weak product with another item that will perform more respectably.

When you present your page lineup to the layout artist, along with a written listing of your products, it is a good idea to provide a rough layout that shows the basic space allocations for each product. Paste up actual photos of each item where possible. This will help both you and the artist see how the products integrate on the page or spread.

Design and organize your catalog. To help your designer obtain the right "look" and "feel" for your catalog, clip the layouts, type styles, photography concepts, and product presentations that you like from other catalogs and mail pieces. Then work with your designer and your copywriter to determine the positioning of your catalog and the design elements that will emphasize this positioning to your target

Harry and David® projects a "down-home" image in this letter that accompanies its fruit catalog.

market. A modern office-supplies catalog, for instance, might go for a streamlined look in design and for clean, sans-serif typefaces for its headings. By contrast, a firm that wants to project a down-home, cozy image might use serif typefaces and even stick to black-and-white or sepia-and-white rather than using color for its illustrations, simply to keep that "family business" aura.

As your catalog design shapes up, make sure that one of your foremost goals is to make the catalog appealing and easy to use. Spreads should flow together in a pleasing whole, and such essentials as the order form, your return address, and your toll-free number should be easy to find. The copy should expound on the product features and their related benefits. Diagrams, close-up shots, testimonials, and product-in-use ideas will all help "activate" your catalog and make your products seem real and desirable to the prospect.

When evaluating your photography and copy, remember the principle of PPIPU: "perfectly plain if previously understood." Often you will become so close to a product and its presentation that you fail to notice essential missing visual or written elements—things a customer needs to know. To avoid this, have unbiased outsiders look over your photos and copy and ask them if anything seems confusing or would turn them off as a prospective buyer.

Even more important, once you design and typeset your order form, is to have a number of people attempt to fill it out and tell you where the "glitches" are. The order form does not have to be strictly "learn by doing" thing; check your competition and some of the more established direct mail marketers to see how they handle such essentials as postage and handling, bill-to/ship-to arrangements, gift wrapping and enclosure cards, charge and credit options, and so on.

The hot selling spots. As you plan and design your catalog, keep in mind what marketers now understand about the prime selling spaces in your book.

First, although the front cover can be a prime selling space, most catalog marketers today opt to use this first page as a "theme setter." They may show a group of merchandise items that are available for sale inside the catalog, a scene that characterizes the company and its goods, or a seasonal vignette.

The back cover, however, should in most cases be used for selling products with a high sales potential. Be careful that the products you

This "World's Fare" catalog represents the concept of a *theme-setting cover* with its gourmet fare and copper serving pieces.

depict on the back cover also characterize what's inside the catalog. If they are too different from the mainstream of merchandise in your book, prospective buyers may never make it past the front or back covers.

The inside front cover spread and the spread after that are next in the "prime territory" race, along with the center spread and the inside back cover. The spread near the order form also carries a high potential. And don't underestimate the power of the order form itself for selling merchandise, especially the add-on or impulse variety. Talk with your designer or printer about bind-in order-form designs that give you some extra selling space at an affordable cost.

Use the same catalog, but make it look different. Catalog planning and production are expensive, and especially if your merchandise line-up doesn't change dramatically over the course of a year you may wish to create a single catalog and use it for several mailings to the same target market. There are several ways to make sure your prospective customers see the catalog as a fresh mailing each time it's received.

- *Remail at an interval.* You may well find that you reach acceptable levels of response by remailing the same catalog at sufficiently long intervals. Psychologically this may have the same effect as repeating an effective space ad: the consumer who considered buying from you before may finally decide to buy after an additional "impression" or catalog mailing.
- *Use a catalog wrap.* You can take your existing catalog and bind it into a four-page "wrap" that states a new seasonal theme, offers special values, promotes certain merchandise, or otherwise freshens your mailing. This is an inexpensive way to make your catalog look new while adding a promotional flair to it.
- *Change the cover.* The insides of your catalog may remain exactly the same, but if you change the front and back covers you'll gain a new look that encourages the customer to read through your book again. Your new cover look might be seasonal; Downs' Collectors Showcase, a collectibles catalog, does this. In the fall, its catalog first appears with a Halloween or harvest theme; the next remailing might have a general cover; and a third would use a Christmas approach. Another approach to the new cover is to "splash" it with merchandise that did exceptionally well inside the catalog on a first mailing, to encourage an even greater response with the remailing.
- *Change the signatures around.* As in book publishing, larger catalogs are produced in 16-page "signatures." If you wish, you can provide a new internal look for your catalog by changing these sections around. You might keep some 16-page sections exactly the same but change their order, and create a new introductory signature keyed to the time of year, special merchandise, a sale, or something else.
- *Use a separate price list.* If your merchandise remains the

same year after year, but your prices do not, consider creating a very fine catalog without prices and providing a separate price list. High-end merchants like Gucci and Hermes do this, as do some hard-goods marketers. An extra advantage of this for the international marketer is that a single catalog can be printed in many different languages for various locations, with appropriate price lists. The disadvantage of this system is that it makes it more difficult for the customer to order.

Publishers Central Bureau utilizes a *catalog wrap* to tell customers about a sweepstakes offer. The same catalog might be used again with a different wrap or cover.

Producing and directing your catalog. Before that first catalog goes in the mail, you should have systems devised and people ready to handle order processing, customer-service questions, shipping and returns, credit- and charge-card purchases, telephone orders, and all of the operational functions that spell the difference between contented customers and those who may never order from you again. If you are just beginning, you may wish to engage the services of an order-processing and fulfillment house rather than setting up the entire mechanism from scratch.

RETAIL CATALOG MARKETING

Most of the consumer catalog material discussed in the preceding sections is also important to the retail catalog marketer. However, some additional comments are in order.

Traffic building and direct response. Retail marketers should keep their objectives for each catalog firmly in mind. Is the catalog designed to bring the customer into the store, to solicit mail and phone orders only, or a combination of both? Promotional ideas such as coupons, privileged notification, "phone order specials," and so on can be planned to help achieve your goals for the catalog.

Many retailers whose original non-store marketing efforts were aimed strictly at traffic building have learned that they can increase total sales and profits by seeking mail and phone sales more aggressively. This is important for several reasons.

- *Disenchantment with retail shopping.* The customer who has decreasing time for "recreational shopping" may still wish to purchase your goods, and may welcome the option to do so by mail or phone.
- *Expansion of customer base.* By offering a direct response catalog, retailers can entice customers in their area who might never visit their retail store. What's more, mailings outside the retail buying area let the retailer reach a new and vast universe of customers (assuming that the products and image promoted are unique enough to compete in the regional or national marketplace).
- *A separate direct response division.* Neiman-Marcus led the way for this concept with its "N-M by Post" and other mailings promoting merchandise that was often unavailable in the

company's retail stores. Trading on its national reputation for fine taste and good merchandise, Neiman-Marcus has been able to woo mail-order buyers who have never visited its retail stores, and to sell additional and different merchandise to those who also visit its retail stores.

But here is an important word of caution: Don't expect all of your retail, in-store customers to buy by mail. Some folks just aren't mail-order buyers, even though they know your reputation and lines of merchandise. Certainly you should mail your catalog to your list of charge customers, since they are likely to give a better response than the members of any other list you might rent or exchange. Over a period of time, however, you may "weed out" groups that are unresponsive to your mailings and continue mailing your offers only to your retail customers who prove to be mail-order buyers as well. Large retailers may wish to consider a "merge/purge" of their charge customer list against lists of known mail-order buyers in their product category. The names that emerge as both charge customers and known mail-order buyers are then the "prime targets" for direct response offers.

The vendor-sponsored catalog or section. Most retailers are aware of today's many opportunities to sponsor catalog mailings, spreads, or sections with money from vendors. This can be profitable for both sides, but a few words of caution are in order.

Before you agree to a vendor-supported program, find out how much control the vendor expects over the "look" of your catalog. Does he expect to retain certain pages and positions for his merchandise? Or want a certain graphic presentation that clashes with your firm's image? The best vendor-sponsored catalog sections or pages are those that "don't show," with the result that the prospective customer has no idea that the section is any different from any other part of your catalog.

BUSINESS-TO-BUSINESS CATALOG MARKETING

Business-to-business marketers will find the meat of what they must know about catalogs in the consumer section of this chapter. Here are a few additional guidelines.

Catalog as salesperson. As the cost of a personal sales call rises, firms that have relied almost exclusively on person-to-person contact are finding themselves in need of alternative forms of effective marketing. One such alternative is to break your accounts into groups on a volume/profit basis, and to market to each group according to its importance and potential. The marketing mix for such a plan might include a varying combination of personal contact, phone contact, direct mail letters, and catalogs. Thus, a potential customer whose account size does not warrant many personal contacts may be kept active by means of a catalog and other direct mail efforts.

Catalog for aftermarket sales. Another business-to-business catalog use is for aftermarket and/or supply sales. The purchase of an IBM typewriter, for instance, may be transacted via a personal sale. But for selling the typewriter buyer regular supplies of ribbons, correcting fluid, paper, and so on, telephone and catalog contacts are more cost-efficient. And aftermarket items like typewriter pads, additional typeface elements, and others can also be sold effectively by catalog.

Creative Ideas for Business-to-Business Catalogs.
- *Be informative but not boring.* Don't ignore good promotional language and graphics simply because you are selling a business product. Don't bog yourself down in an explanation of the features at the expense of "sizzle" about the benefits of a product. Some industrial catalogs read more like instruction manuals than selling documents. Remember that you can explain the intricacies of how the product works once it's in the customer's hands. What he or she needs in advance is to know how it can help him or her; what it can do personally and for the company.

  Avoid "talking jargon and technicalities to yourself" in the presentation of a technical product. Non-technical buyers may be turned off, fearing that your product is way beyond their technical understanding.
- *Be organized: Use an index.* While only the largest consumer catalogs provide a merchandise index, this component is a must for the business customer. And although you'll be striving for an interesting presentation, keeping similar products together will help your business customer make direct comparisons of costs, features, and benefits.

- *Intersperse how-to's with products.* Show your expertise in your field by providing testimonials and product-in-use information along with the products themselves. This makes your catalog presentation more lively and helps customers visualize how to use your products.
- *Make ordering easy.* Just as consumer marketers test their order forms and instructions on prospective customers, it's a good idea to approach people in your target market to see if your catalog is easy to use. Is there a phone number the customer can call to expedite matters? Is it clear whether the customer needs a purchase order? Must he or she put money down now, or can they be billed later? How long does shipping take? All these specifics are more important than ever in a business situation, especially when the customer is evaluating you against a competitive retail or personal-sales situation.

8

MAILING LISTS: THE VITAL CUSTOMER LINK

How do you reach the consumer most likely to purchase your product or service? This vital question represents a never-ending challenge to direct marketers of all sizes. Experienced marketers most often resolve it by using existing customer lists and renting prospect lists from competitors or other available sources. For smaller or less experienced marketers, who may well be in the formative stages of developing a business, selecting the proper list is often critical not only to the success of the offering but to the marketer's financial survival.

Regardless of size or years of experience, direct marketers agree that *a strong product offering and proven promotional package will fail when mailed to the wrong list.* This axiom is absolutely basic to the direct response business, and is perhaps best understood by examining the types of mailing lists available to direct marketers.

CATEGORIES OF MAILING LISTS

There are any number of ways to categorize mailing lists, but it is perhaps most useful if the direct marketer thinks of the available list options in terms of those prospects most likely to respond to a select mail-order offer.

Customer lists, sometimes referred to as "house lists," yield by far the greatest responses to direct marketing campaigns. Every direct marketer, save for those involved in new ventures, has a customer

113

base of active buyers who have purchased goods or services at least once. These customers have established a relationship—a *customer franchise*—with the direct marketing firm and are comparatively the most responsive for a number of reasons: (1) they need or want the company's goods or services; (2) they are satisfied with the prices and quality of the products or services they've received, and usually have a recurring need; and (3) they know and trust the company and have few doubts about its reliability.

Customer lists are often complemented by inquiry and referral lists. The prospects on these lists usually have not yet purchased a product or service, but have directly expressed interest in doing so or have been referred by an active customer. They are usually more responsive than prospects on lists rented from outside services, but less responsive than those on current buyer lists.

Mail-responsive lists are mail-order buyer lists rented from other direct marketing firms for the purpose of prospecting for new buyers. Because the direct marketer can prequalify prospects, the persons on mail-responsive lists are usually considered next after those on customer lists in the hierarchy of responsiveness. Knowing such factors as a person's product- or service-purchase history and frequency and dollar amount of purchases lets the marketer bring his or her product or service to the attention of the group of prospects most likely to want or need it. For example, a mail-order marketer of a new line of fine French chocolates might want to test such mail order lists as those of Omaha Steaks, the House of Almonds, and the Collin Street Bakery. Each list would provide prospects who have already demonstrated a propensity to purchase food via mail, an affinity for epicurean delights, and the necessary affluence to buy, as indicated by the average order amount of $55 to $60.

There are thousands of mail-responsive lists available to direct marketers through a variety of list owners or brokers. These lists are the lifeblood for both new and seasoned marketers.

Compiled lists are usually created from a data base of information compiled for purposes other than promotion. Such items as membership, automobile-registration, and telephone directory listings, or standard industrial codes may form the basis for this kind of list. Because marketers often lack the ability to prequalify prospects on the basis of compiled lists, such lists belong on the bottom of the hierarchy of list responsiveness.

The compiled list also offers the greatest degree of risk, but it is possible to use it with success. The basic composition of a compiled list may pinpoint specific marketing opportunities. For example, a direct marketer of medical equipment may prospect with the American Medical Association membership list; or a publisher of transportation law and deregulation guides may mail to prospective customers on the basis of a Standard Industrial Code selection for transportation businesses with 100 or more employees. Some of the larger mail-order companies use sophisticated computer-marketing techniques, such as regression analysis, for selecting the most responsive segments of compiled lists, but many small and medium size mailers find that using this technique is prohibitively expensive.

ESTABLISHING A LIST BROKERAGE RELATIONSHIP

The first role of a list broker is as an advisor on which list should be tested and rolled out (see glossary). Periodically, you will receive from your broker recommendations in the form of list data cards, carrying the latest information on prospective lists, including such vital items as the approximate universe, average dollar order, and available segmentation for each list. The broker will study the various list profiles and test results, and recommend new test possibilities. The broker is also usually responsible for placing and expediting all rental orders, and therefore receives a commission from the list owner (usually 10 to 20 percent of list rental sales). In many instances, the list broker becomes an integral part of the marketing team, providing valuable objective advice.

The role described above for the broker is an ideal one. If you are a large mailer (above 10-million rented names per year) you probably have a professional list broker with whom you have established a mutually profitable working relationship. If you are small or a new direct marketer there are a number of realities about the list-brokerage community that you should understand. First, your brokerage business will initially be comparatively small, and there will be a direct relationship between the volume of names you rent and the quality of the brokerage service and information you receive. Like any other business, the brokerage community must allocate its resources in accordance with volume and profit, making a smaller commitment to developing newer enterprises that may, eventually, become valuable accounts.

HORCHOW

DATE: January 8, 1985
726,028 24 months buyers
506,761 12 months buyers
332,733 6 months buyers

AVERAGE ORDER: $65

SELECTIONS AVAILABLE:

Last 12 months @ $5/M
Last 6 months @ $10/M
$30 + @ $7.50/M
$50 + @ $10/M
$75 + @ $20/M
NEW $100 + @ $30/M
Multi buyers @ $10/M
NEW Multi buyers selected by *average* sale @ $20/M
SCF, State, Sex @ $5/M
Zip select (with zip tape only) @ $5/M
NEW Product Select @ $10/M
☐ women's apparel
☐ men's apparel
☐ homewares
☐ jewelry
☐ collectibles
☐ food
☐ food service
☐ children's
☐ desk/office
☐ bed/bath

For merchandise offers $80/M
For subscriptions or fund raisers $55/M

PROFILE:
Affluent mail order buyers who have purchased fine quality merchandise from The Horchow Collection catalogues. Successful past rentals include: gifts, collectibles, women's apparel, publications, men's apparel, electronics, fund raising and financial offers.

ADDRESSING:
Magnetic Tape, 9 track, 1600 BPI
4-up Cheshire labels
Pressure sensitive labels @ $5/M
Any running charges @ $5/M
Keying @ N/C.

CONDITIONS:
Sample mailing piece required. Minimum order is 5,000. Allow 2 weeks for delivery.

LIST MAINTENANCE:
List is cleaned minimum of 6 times yearly.

PLEASE CONTACT:

List Manager (214) 385-2700
HORCHOW MAIL ORDER, INC.
4435 SIMONTON ROAD, DALLAS, TEXAS 75234

3,000,000 LILLIAN VERNON BUYERS

PRIMARY LIST SEGMENTS:

2,400,000 Buyers last 12 mos. (1984) .... $55 per M
1,300,000 Hotline buyers last 6 mos. (Jul-Dec '84) .... $55 + $5 per M
900,000 Hotline buyers last 3 mos. (Oct-Dec '84) ...... $55 + $10 per M
740,000 Catalog requests (1984) .... $35 per M
inquire Change-of-address buyers (twice yearly) ......$50 per M

Jan. 1985

CUSTOMER PROFILE:

source: 98% direct mail sold
sex: 98% female
average age: 43
average order: $35.00
average household income: $36,000

work status: 63% working women
education: above average
product preferences: items from the Lillian Vernon Catalog—see "product selects" below

ADDRESSING:
—4 or 5 up Cheshire
—9 track/1600 BPI
—pressure sensitive labels at $4.50 per M
—magnetic tape—$15 non-refundable fee per tape

KEY CODING:
—$1.00 per M up to ten digits

SELECTS:

multi-buyers .... +$5 per M
dollar amount ordered
—over $10.00 ... +$5 per M
—over $20.00 ... +$10 per M
—over $30.00 ... +$15 per M
—over $40.00 ... +$20 per M
—over $50.00 ... +$25 per M
—over $75.00 ... +$30 per M
geographical
—State .... +$3 per M
—Zip .... +$4 per M
—SCF .... +$3 per M

credit card buyers... +$5 per M
product selects (+$5 per M each) *
—decorative accessories
—bed and bath
—dining and entertainment
—kitchen and pantry
—leisure, hobbies, collectibles
—toys
—stationery
*Inquire about other product selects available in our list rental program.

REQUISITES:
—5000 minimum
—sample mailing piece is required

for further information, please call:
JOY CONTRERAS

LILLIAN VERNON®
510 South Fulton Ave., Mount Vernon, New York 10550   (914) 699-4131

THE SHARPER IMAGE

FEB 20, 1985

428,364 1984 MAIL ORDER BUYERS $90.00/M
325,579 1983 MAIL ORDER BUYERS $80.00/M
196,984 1982 MAIL ORDER BUYERS $65.00/M
** HOTLINE - INQUIRE **   + $10.00/M
SPECIAL RATE FOR FUNDRAISERS $65.00/M

MINIMUM ORDER: 5,000
4/5-UP CHESHIRE
MAG TAPE: 9T 800/1600 BPI

THE PREMIER HIGH-TICKET MERCHANDISE LIST ON THE
MARKET. THIS PRESTIGIOUS GROUP OF MAIL-ORDER BUY-
ERS HAS PURCHASED TOP-QUALITY ELECTRONIC PRODUCTS
AND HEALTH & FITNESS ITEMS FROM A TRULY INNOVATIVE
AND IMAGINATIVE CATALOG, WITH PRICES RANGING FROM
$29.95 TO $4,000 (A TANNING BOOTH). THIS HIGH-IN-
COME, WELL-EDUCATED AUDIENCE WILL RESPOND TO OF-
FERS FOR GIFTS AND MERCHANDISE, CLOTHING, MAGA-
ZINES, BOOKS & RECORDS, COLLECTIBLES, FUNDRAISERS,
FOOD, AND INVESTMENTS.
SOURCE: 90% DIRECT MAIL, 10% SPACE IN UPSCALE
PUBLICATIONS: POPULAR SCIENCE, ESQUIRE,
SMITHSONIAN, SCIENCE '84, TIME, SIGNATURE
AND THE WALL STREET JOURNAL.

A SAMPLE MAILING PIECE IS REQUIRED FOR APPROVAL.

---------- SEX ---------
75% MEN
- AVERAGE UNIT OF SALE -
$150.00
------ SELECTIONS ------
$10.00 CREDIT BUYERS
$ 5.00 STATE
$ 5.00 SCF
$ 5.00 ZIP
$10.00 HOTLINE
$ 1.50 KEYING
$10.00 SEX
$ 8.00 P/S LABELS
$ 5.00 RECENCY
$10.00 $50+ BUYERS
$20.00 $100+ BUYERS
$ 5.00 SPLIT KEYING

UPDATED COUNTS

MAG TAPE NON-RET. $20.00

THE LISTWORKS INC. / MANAGEMENT DIVISION
40 Radio Circle, P.O. Box 459   (914)
Mount Kisco, N.Y. 10549-0459   241-1900

List data cards provide essential marketing information for potential testing.

As a small or new direct marketer, you should be honest with prospective brokers about your planned volume, and sell them on your product or service. Furthermore, it is just common sense to consider choosing a small or medium-sized broker, so as to mitigate your volume deficiencies as much as possible. And while larger companies utilize numerous brokers, you should place all of your business with a single broker, to ensure as much as possible that the broker will spend some research and development time on your business. Finally, and perhaps most importantly, choose an experienced broker and, if possible, one who is knowledgeable about your field of direct response but not working directly with your competition.

It is important to understand that you do not have to use a broker, especially if you have a grasp of the kind of lists that will work for you. Many an entrepreneur has begun by contacting list owners directly after referring to the Standard Rate & Data Service Directory of lists. If you do this, you must, of course, assume the analysis and expediting functions that would ordinarily comprise the package of brokerage services.

TESTING PROSPECTIVE LISTS

Now that you have an understanding of the various classifications of lists, and what to expect and not expect from a list broker, you should focus on the proper utilization of the lists you decide to test.

What Is a Good Response

The novice's most embarrassing and unfortunately naive question is the often asked "What is a good response?" The answer is, "A good response is not a predetermined percentage but a response that achieves the marketing and financial objectives established for the product line." For example, assume that you are marketing two distinct lines of insurance and testing two identical 10,000-prospect segments of a physicians list rented from the American Medical Association. One of your insurance lines is an inexpensive term policy on which your break-even is ten orders per thousand mailed; the other is a more expensive whole-life policy requiring a minimum of four orders per thousand mailed. After mailing, assume that you receive an identical response of eight orders per thousand on both offers. Which of the two is a good response? Obviously the whole-life offer proved to be an economically viable one, while the other offer fell short. Understanding the need to meet a specific goal is essential for accurately assessing the results of a direct mail test.

Perhaps the most controversial point in list testing is how large a test cell the marketer needs in order to achieve accurate results. What is the reliability factor? Must you be 75 percent sure or 96 percent sure? Traditionally, marketers have tested 10 percent of the universe (whole list), but this has become prohibitive as list universes have grown into the millions.

Let's assume that you and your broker have selected a variety of fifteen new lists to be tested during your next direct-mail campaign. How large will your list test be? 5,000, 7,500, 10,000, or 15,000 randomly selected prospects? This range for list tests is often used by a variety of companies, with what seem to be basically good results. Of course, you can apply regression analysis and probability tables (see glossary) to ascertain your reliability factor, but the basic economic reality influencing marketers of every size is that testing is expensive, and therefore can only be done at whatever level the marketer can afford.

Generally, a test cell of 7,500 to 10,000 prospects selected at random from each list should provide you with an adequate, reliable reading on most offers. However, there are several other factors to consider. First, *test deeper, not longer*. If you are tight for test dollars and your choice is between two 5,000-name tests or one 10,000-name test, choose the larger single test; your results will be more reliable and you will avoid the likelihood of an unreadable test. Second, *consider the price elasticity of your offer*. For more expensive items ($100 or more) make your test cells larger (15,000 to 20,000 prospects). For less expensive items (in the $15 to $20 range), you can use test cells of 5,000 to 7,500 names, thereby expanding your total test-list universe. *Don't forget to test your house list!* You can often improve your offerings and profitability by testing your house list first. Because your house list is the more responsive, a test of 1,500 to 2,500 is often all that is needed for reliable feedback on your newest idea. *Make price tests large.* Because you want to make sure you are getting a proper reading, your price-test cells should be a minimum of 25,000 names each. *Always validate your tests.* Following an initial positive test result, validate your results by mailing an interim test segment before committing yourself to a full rollout of a list.

If you follow these general guidelines for establishing list-testing parameters, you will be off to a reasonable start, and you can add more sophisticated methodology as you garner the necessary resources.

WHAT THE "MERGE/PURGE" CAN DO FOR YOU

Initially, when a mailing is small, it is not practical to try to eliminate duplicates among the various lists beings mailed. However, as your volume grows and expands, it becomes most cost-effective to utilize "merge/purge" techniques to eliminate duplicates. For example, when using merge/purge it is not unusual for a mailer to eliminate 12 to 15 percent of the total names rented for a given promotion. At a mailing cost of $300 per thousand, you save yourself up to $4,500 on each 100,000 names rented.

In addition to eliminating duplicates, most merge/purge programs will let you suppress your house list against rented lists, provide listings of multi-buyers, remove pander names (people who have told the Direct Mail Association that they do not wish to receive direct mail offers), and divide your outputs into qualifying and nonqualifying carrier-route segments, enabling you to mail more efficiently.

While the use of a merge/purge program should save money, remember the importance of choosing a good merge/purge service company.

You or your broker will have negotiated "net down" arrangements with each list owner. Your merge/purge instructions to the service bureau should always prioritize the lists, giving the lowest priority to the most expensive lists with the most liberal net-down arrangements. This will improve your cost effectiveness, since you will pay for the most expensive names only as a last resort.

THE CUSTOMER LIST AS A SOURCE OF INCREMENTAL PROFIT

As your customer or "house" list grows, you should consider the incremental benefits of list-rental income. You may rent your own list through your broker, who will advise you on a per-thousand rental charge for your list. You should generally charge what your competitors charge, which is probably also the simplest list-pricing technique. The broker's commission for renting your list is usually 15 to

20 percent of your rental price for it. In addition, the list management firm—a firm that maintains and updates your lists—will normally charge 8 to 10 percent for processing your rental orders. Therefore, you, the list owner, pocket 70 to 75 percent of each list-rental dollar. More to the point, if you rent 75,000 names at $40 per thousand each month, your incremental income after processing and brokerage fees is about $2,100 monthly. Assuming you rent this file once a month, your net list rental income would be $25,000 per year. This is "found money" if you are currently not renting your file—incremental income in the truest sense of the word.

Some marketers are reluctant to rent their lists because they fear competing offers will reduce the response to their own offers. Conversely, many marketers feel that noncompetitive mailings tend to keep the buyer active and more productive for longer periods.

Finally, if you decide to place your house list on the market, or if you are already on the market, you need to examine your broker and list-management arrangements. Whenever possible, you should consolidate the two relationships into one. If possible, choose a small or medium-sized broker/manager. This will maximize your clout and minimize the likelihood of having overdue receivables.

9

DIRECT MARKETING TESTING

Direct market testing is often intimidating and misunderstood by experienced and novice marketers alike. This chapter will pinpoint areas worthy of testing and outline basic test guidelines.

DIRECT MAIL TESTS

Marketers are forever in pursuit of the improved sales results that correspond to improved profits. If you are a new marketer you must decide on the criteria to be used for establishing your control package (the control package is a tested, proven approach to marketing a given offer). If on the other hand you are an experienced marketer you may have an idea of the refinements you wish to make. In either case, you should utilize grid testing. For example, if you have a 6-by-9-inch package with six identical inserts and different test letters, your grid would read as follows:

	Description	Quantity
Control A	Two-page letter	25,000
Test B	Three-page letter	25,000
Test C	Four-page letter	25,000

Reading the results from this test would enable the marketer to make any cost-effective refinements in his or her plan. For example, a four-page letter may outpull a two-page letter, but not by enough to pay for the cost differential between the two. Further, you must consider sample size when evaluating list- or package-test results. As we mentioned in an earlier chapter, the size of the sample will determine the reliability of the results. The following test-size guideline may be helpful:

- For copy and creative tests, 10,000 to 20,000 names per cell (a composite of sample names randomly selected from a list universe) should be sufficient in most cases. List tests usually are reasonably accurate with 5,000 to 10,000 names per cell. Price tests need a minimum of 25,000 names per test cell to provide reasonable results.
- For those who must test on a limited budget, fewer larger tests are better than a number of small tests. In tandem with this, the most important items, such as the package test, should be tested first and the more obscure, such as the letter P.S. test, left for later; this will enhance the return on your dollars.

After you have the most efficient direct-mail package, you can work on refining each component.

A WORD ABOUT PREMIUM TESTING

Whether you're testing in the media or in the mail, you should consider the following points: First, most marketers find that a premium that complements the product proves to be best. If, for example, you are selling books via direct response, a bookcase to hold the selection of books may prove successful. There are, of course, many exceptions to this rule, and you should consider a variety of ideas before

	Description	Quantity
Control A	Collection of six books No premium	20,000
Test B	Collection of six books; free bookcase, value: $12.95	20,000
Test C	Collection of six books; free author's guide, Value: $12.95	20,000

testing your ideas. If you are a new marketer, delay premium testing until you have developed a control package that serves your needs. However, when you do decide to test your premium concepts, you should use the same grid approach given on page 121.

TESTING IN PRINT

Testing in print requires the same discipline as testing by mail. Perhaps the most basic print test is the A-B split. Here a marketer splits an advertisement so that half of the readers in an area see one offer and the other half see a different offer. This lets the marketer test the viability of the product or service over the entire area while at the same time testing a varied approach in offer, price, headline, or copy. Some publications do not offer A-B splits, and you may have to test a split in comparable publications. For example, some marketers use the *Smithsonian* magazine as a bellwether for *National Geographic*.

Another media testing technique is called multi-split-run testing or telescopic testing. With this technique, you can test a control advertisement in several regional editions of a publication. For example with advertisement A as a control, the grid would be as follows:

Control		Tests
Ad A	*vs*	Ad B
Ad A	*vs*	Ad C
Ad A	*vs*	Ad D

This technique lets you test a larger number of alternative offers, enhancing your likelihood of success. Furthermore, you will be able to roll out faster, with presumably better results.

One final note about media testing relates to the kind of buyer you're acquiring. If you have been selling primarily to mail-order buyers, you should modify your purchasing assumptions for the potential buyer who will see your test in the media. Because the media person is more of an impulse buyer, renewals and continuity purchases often are not as strong as with the mail-order buyer.

PRODUCT OR SERVICE TESTING

In some cases you can test product or service viability only by executing a mail or media test. However, before doing this, there are two techniques that can be used to get feedback about whether or not a new offering will be well received. First, a mail survey showing pictures or a description of the new product, or both, can be done with prospective buyers. Usually you will get a strong response, in the range of 15 to 25 percent. This is especially true if you are mailing to existing customers. Further, if you can identify existing customers as well as prospects, you may set up a series of consumer panels to review and comment on your new product ideas. While neither of these techniques is fail-safe, each will provide you with more insight into the viability of a product or service. These techniques can also greatly enhance your product concepts, as well as help you close down offers and save thousands of test dollars.

10

PRINT MEDIA: STRATEGY AND EXECUTION

Use of the print media is one of the most fascinating disciplines within direct response marketing. While many consider print advertising "black magic," with an intimidating mystique, others recognize this medium for what it is: another tool for achieving marketing objectives. Throughout this chapter, we will help the marketer focus first on developing a media strategy, and then on executing this strategy.

DEVELOPING A PRINT-MEDIA STRATEGY

Whether you're an experienced marketer or new venturer, your general planning should be the same. Consider your current or forecasted position in the market, determine how much you can afford to spend on overall promotion, and evaluate what your competitors are doing. Ultimately, after weighing all the variables, you must set down a print strategy with goals and objectives that complement your overall marketing strategy. For example, many marketers choose print media as an extension of direct mail, to be used only after their core lists have been depleted. Others use print media to create entirely new markets for some products that are too pluralistic for direct mail. Still others take a more institutional approach, using print to generate inquiries that will later be converted to sales by either personal sales or direct mail.

While it is difficult to generalize in this area, there are several factors that should be considered when formulating your plans, as follows:

1. *Are there a large number of targeted lists available for your product?* For example, if you're a direct marketer of gourmet foods, there are more core lists available for your use than if you're marketing industrial widgets. And as a marketer of industrial widgets, you would therefore plan on a more dominant use of print media than the gourmet food marketer who has more and better list alternatives.

2. *Consider your product life cycle.* If you have a new product and are unsure of its market potential, print media can be used to affirm and develop the existing market. For example, some years ago, *Runners' World* was launched as a publication designed to service the growing joggers' market. Initially it was very difficult to isolate clusters of lists for use in building circulation, so the magazine's marketing people launched an eclectic media campaign that resulted in establishing it as a viable entity.

3. *Assess the economics of print.* In some cases, especially on lower-priced, impulse items, mail costs may prove prohibitive. Print is often preferable because you will be able to reach so many more people on a media offer.

In summary, when formulating your print-media strategy, you must assess not only your competitive and marketing positions but also the product life cycle, print economics, and core-list variables before determining your course of action.

EXECUTING YOUR MEDIA STRATEGY

Selecting the Right Stuff

Making media decisions is not much different from making list decisions, except that competitive information is often more readily available. Initially, you should list all the publications that your competition uses. Then, within that group, pick the most frequently used publications for the competitive product most similar to yours. These two exercises will allow you to use your competitors' advertising expenditures to your advantage, and increase the likelihood of success with your initial media tests. This method is not foolproof, because your competitors may have different profit objectives. However, it should help focus your activity toward those publications with the greatest affinity for your product or service.

Assuming that you have a new product, or that your competition does not use print media, you should consider further factors. First, you should look for publications with editorial affinity—an editorial content and focus that are similar in subject matter to the product you're offering—and readers with a good propensity to buy via mail order. If you're selling Cuisinart Gourmet Cookware, *Bon Appetit* magazine would be a publication with editorial affinity. Furthermore, *Bon Appetit* also has a good percentage of mail-order advertisements in each publication, and therefore also fulfills the mail-order propensity criterion. Unfortunately, you will not often find this combination in one publication. When making a test choice, always test the publication that has the greatest mail order activity. The odds of the test choice working are clearly in your favor. Editorial affinity alone will usually not produce the results you need if the mail-order profile is absent.

When making your test decisions for print advertising, you should select publications that are benchmarks for their disciplines, just as you do with mailing lists. For example, if you were marketing men's jewelry, you might select a regional edition of *Playboy,* a regional edition of the *Wall Street Journal,* and a regional edition of *Business Week.* If each of these tests works, these are obvious similar publications which you would wish to test as you expand your universe.

You should also consult the directories published by the Standard Rate and Data Service to locate prospective publications in which to place ads. Each directory is classified by type of publication—such as consumer, business or farm—and within each directory, publications are grouped by editorial similarity. In addition, each publication listing provides the media buyer with the complete information needed to make a comparison with other publications. Rate policy, discounts, black-and-white and color rates, closing dates, split-runs, and so on are included. For your reference, the following is a typical magazine reference listing as shown in SRDS.

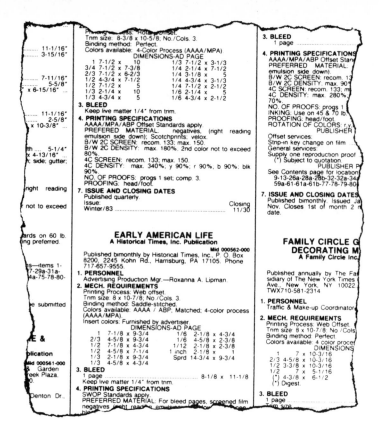

Reprinted by Permission of the Standard Rate and Data Service

Determining the Character of Your Print Media

Now that you have identified the publications you wish to test, you must determine the appearance of your advertisement. How large will it be? Will it be graphics-oriented or copy-oriented? Will it be color or black-and-white? What typeface should you use? Will it be a coupon ad or will you use a bound-in reply card? What image will be projected? Ultimately, a combination of these elements will determine the character of your print-media campaign.

Image projection is often unfortunately overlooked until after an advertisement is published. The image your advertisement projects should be consistent with your marketing strategy, reflecting the image of your company and its products or services, and complementing your long-term goals. For example, the ads for a discount marketer of books, such as the Doubleday Book Club, will have a completely different "look" than those for a marketer of expensive, leather-bound, limited-edition books such as The Franklin Library. The marketing strategy of each business is different and the reader's perception of the print-media campaign clearly reinforces the basic market position of each business.

In determining the size of your advertisement, there are several issues to consider. First and foremost is how much can you afford to spend. If you can afford only a quarter-page advertisement in the publication of your choice, the decision is made for you by simple economics. Of course, you must have the space to advertise your product effectively, or you should not do the advertisement at all. Probably the best rule of thumb is to determine the smallest space unit that will still sell your product. Use this size for your control and test upward in unit increments to see if the larger ads increase the response enough to justify the additional cost. As you may know, larger advertisements do not always perform proportionally better, and you must therefore test to be sure that you're not wasting money. Here again, a review of competitors' advertisements may prove helpful in making your size decisions.

After deciding on your space commitment, you must decide on the balance of your copy and graphics. This decision is often subjective, but should be made after considering some fairly objective points about the product or service being offered. For example, if you are selling a "how-to" product, you would probably want to use graphics or pictures liberally to help the customer understand the use and the derived benefits of the product. There are any number of good examples of this, such as the Rid-A-Bug campaign, which both sells the pest-control benefits of the product and demonstrates its ease of use.

On the other hand, if you're selling an intangible such as life insurance, you will probably want to orient more toward a copy emphasis, because you will need more space to explain each feature and benefit. In short, you must assess your product offering and bias your media presentation in the direction of maximum sales.

You must also decide whether you will use black-and-white or color advertisements. As mentioned previously, a four-color ad should be used only when it truly enhances your product presentation. Unless your product will benefit from this additional expenditure,

This full-color, two-page spread from Easton Press represents an upscale appeal for book buyers.

130

you should use black-and-white. Generally, a four-color advertisement will outpull a black-and-white advertisement, but your cost per order may well be the same or slightly more on the color split. Moreover, the black-and-white advertisement will give you far greater flexibility if you are planning to maximize your advertising dollars via R.O.P. (run of press—position can be anywhere) or remnant buys. Finally, most marketers seem to agree that you should do either four-color or black-and-white—not two-color or three-color ads.

Another book offer, for The Executive Program®, presents a much more businesslike image than that of Easton Press, befitting its prospective customers' perceptions.

Understanding Your Buying Options

You should begin your print-ad campaign by understanding that you can beat a publication's rate card almost every time. And because you are a direct marketer who runs each campaign as a separate entity, buying smart will tremendously increase your chances of being successful in media. First, many publications offer mail-order advertising discounts ranging from 10 to 15 percent. This gives you a nice break, but placement of your ad may well be a problem, since in such cases mail-order companies' ads are often placed together in one section of the magazine or newspaper. There are volume and frequency discounts available, but these are usually most beneficial to the many large advertisers, such as the book and record clubs, who can make a commitment for every issue of a publication, for a year at a time.

The small and medium-sized marketer is probably better off shopping the remnant and R.O.P. deals. Almost all publications sell remnant space. This is space that is either unsold or results from late cancellations. It's not unusual to be able to buy this space from 50 to 70 percent off the rate card figure and it is therefore ideal for testing new products. Most newspaper space is sold R.O.P., which means that your advertisement can appear anywhere throughout the publication. And while you can negotiate more costly positions with some papers, R.O.P. rates, just like remnant rates, put a significantly lower break-even demand on the marketer and provide the best opportunities for him or her to succeed over time.

Despite what most advertising agencies suggest, you can effectively establish an in-house agency if your advertising volume is sufficient. This allows you to save the 15 percent agency commission that most magazines and newspapers grant. The agency usually keeps 15 percent of the billing. But you must have significant advertising activity to make this option viable. Otherwise, you should select a good agency and take that route for as long as it serves your needs.

Print-Media Test Considerations

In the following material testing is discussed in conjunction with buying options because testing decisions and buying options are often interrelated.

With the larger newspapers and magazines, you would obviously not run your ad in a national edition without having tested it first.

Usually your test should comprise either a regional-edition test or a representative-remnant test. It is rare that a remnant buy is clustered enough to permit a proper read, so to assure that you have a controllable test you should buy regional editions. The test will cost you more on a per-thousand basis, but your total dollar commitment should be reasonable against your risk/reward criteria. Otherwise, you should not do the test. Keep in mind that your test cost per response will be higher than your rollout CPR. When you do your test analysis and forecast for subsequent campaigns, be sure to use your rollout cost per thousand in lieu of your test cost. Remember that the advantage of buying regional editions is that it allows you to test responsiveness to your offer without buying advertising in the entire issue of a publication. This technique should be used wherever possible, but especially when testing the publication as a viable medium.

In conjunction with testing for the most responsive media, you must also structure tests that will help you analyze alternative offers, products, and copy approaches. The best way to do this is to use A-B testing, using different advertising approaches for a product in equally divided runs of a publication issue. This allows the marketer to read separate key responses to distinct offers, copy platforms (slants) or products. If for example, you segment a regional edition of *Better Homes and Gardens* into a perfect A-B split, you can test different headlines against each other to determine which is the most effective. Subsequently, you could roll out to the entire national circulation with your most productive ad.

However, it is important to recognize that split testing is a complicated matter, and you should be aware of several problems. First, many publications do not make A-B splits available. This is especially true of vertical (specialized readership), medium-sized publications such as the *Smithsonian* magazine. And unless you have a product that appeals to the masses, enabling you to use *TV Guide* and *Time* magazine, you may have difficulty employing the A-B technique at all.

You Do Not Control Position

One of the realities of being a print advertiser is that you have little control over your position in a magazine or newspaper. Unless you spend some big dollars for the back cover, your position is more often than not determined by someone outside the publication's advertising department. Most marketers agree that the closer you are to the front, the better you will do in magazines and newspapers. While some would say you should test your positions, many marketers have difficulty controlling this variable. Probably the best way to assure favorable placement is to negotiate hard with the advertising salesperson and get your mechanicals in far in advance of publication. If you're late with your advertising materials, you can be assured your position in the book will deteriorate.

Generally also, right-hand pages pull better than left-hand ones and, as mentioned previously, back covers are particularly strong. The inside back cover usually pulls well, as does the first right-hand page. If you select one of these prime pages, make sure your insertion order documents the exact commitments made to you prior to publication.

A Word about Timing

Just like a good golf swing, your print-media success may ultimately depend on timing. You must plan your test so that you have time to react and roll out. This is especially important when you're selling seasonal items such as Mother's Day gifts or Christmas cards.

Seasonal peaks and valleys must also be taken into account when evaluating tests and targeting roll out months. Generally speaking, direct marketers rate the months of the year as follows:

Best Months	Fair Months	Poor Months
January, February, September, October, July	March, August, November	April, May, June, December

This ranking doesn't mean you can't have a successful campaign in April or June. But it does generally pinpoint the consumer's buying behavior, and when you are testing you should include a seasonality factor in your forecasting model. Finally, while you must remember that the competition for consumer attention is most challenging during the peak months for your business, you might want to test in the "off-months" to make sure that they really are weak months.

11

TELEPHONE
DIRECT MARKETING

Telephone marketing is a wide-open field with exciting prospects. But it is expensive and complex, and should be approached with caution by small-budget marketers and those inexperienced in its use.

Telephone marketing is the only kind of marketing that combines the direct response and personal sales techniques: a human being in communication with a prospect. And yet to be cost effective, the message communicated must be carefully scripted and as uniform as humanly possible.

The telephone offers marketers the opportunity to "enforce themselves" on selected prospects, ringing a bell in the prospect's own home and asking him or her to respond at the time the marketer chooses. But this power must be used carefully to avoid invading the privacy of the prospect, approaching him or her at an unseemly hour of the day, or otherwise creating offense.

The phone also provides the ultimate "ease of ordering" device: a prospect simply calls a toll-free number and answers a series of questions to order merchandise or get information. Yet even though some telephone-marketing firms quote impressive statistics on sales improvements through the use of incoming and outgoing phone marketing, many companies, even good-sized direct marketers with healthy budgets to spend, say that their telephone efforts have not resulted in any appreciable increase in sales, profits, or good will.

Entering the telephone-marketing field is a significant and costly step for any direct marketer. And because phone marketing most often becomes an important factor only after a firm is established in mail or space advertising or both, a full discussion of it is beyond the scope of this book. This chapter will provide a brief overview of the opportunities available for telephone direct marketing today. For an excellent, in-depth presentation of the field, consult *Telephone Marketing: How to Build Your Business by Telephone* and *Telemarketing Campaigns That Work!* by Murray Roman (McGraw-Hill). The Direct Marketing Association offers a week-long series of seminars on incoming and outgoing telephone marketing which will be of great help to the marketer entering or exploring this area.

CONSUMER TELEPHONE MARKETING

One of the first questions a new phone marketer needs to answer is whether to use an in-house or outside telephone-marketing service. Many of the pros and cons here are the same as those discussed in the context of selecting a direct response agency or setting up an in-house operation. The in-house group is under firmer control, but is a fixed-overhead item that may be costly in "down" periods. It can be taught to understand your firm's products better, but may not be exposed to as many new ideas and techniques as an outside service. The in-house group may also save you money on a per-call or per-sale basis, assuming that your volume is stable enough to predict. But if your phone efforts are at all seasonal, you may find it wiser to engage an outside service as needed.

The time and manpower commitments necessary to set up an in-house phone operation are substantial. You will need WATS lines, trained personnel (or you will have to train them), facilities for them to work in, a fair and workable compensation package, and other elements. In general, then, new phone marketers may well opt for an outside service, at least until their volume increases and they feel comfortable enough with phone marketing to make wise decisions independently of an expert firm. Most outside telephone-marketing services are located in central states such as Nebraska or Kansas, rather than far-flung states where long-distance calls to the other coast are higher in price. To understand the WATS rates and how you may set up your phone system in the most economical way, contact the business sales department of your phone company.

Outgoing phone marketing. In general, marketers have found that approaching a prospect by phone works best when some form of relationship already exists with that person. The cost of one-on-one telephone sales is so high that random calling seldom pays off—and even renting lists of likely prospects, as you would for a direct mail solicitation, may well result in impossibly high costs per order.

Many firms make their first telephone sales efforts to established customers as a follow-up to a mailing. The pitch might be: "Mrs. Smith, we haven't yet heard from you about our offer of the second collector plate in the Norman Rockwell series. We're calling to alert you that you must act promptly before the limited edition is fully subscribed."

Book sellers might call previous buyers of a Civil War series to tell them about a new series on World War II. Insurance marketers might call present policyholders to solicit leads for a new life insurance plan.

The timing of your phone calls is very important—and of course, take time zones into careful consideration. Calling before 9:00 A.M. on a weekday or before noon on a Saturday or Sunday will handicap your offer, since it will inconvenience many prospects. Calling much later than 8:00 P.M. may bother those who end their day early.

Scripting your telephone solicitation messages is an art best left to experienced telephone-marketing writers. However, if the writer is new to your field of endeavor, have your regular direct mail copywriter check the script to make sure that the most important benefits and action devices are being utilized.

Taped messages may be used very effectively in some outgoing phone campaigns, but only if they are preceded and followed by an actual human voice. Automatic sequential dialers, which offer a computerized message with no human contact, are generally received rather poorly by consumers. Moreover, they are seldom very selective, and selectivity is an important key to telephone-marketing success.

The taped message should come from a celebrity, expert, or authority figure who will be familiar to the prospect. For instance, an insurance company that uses Art Linkletter as its spokesman might call prospects with a special, recorded message from him. Or a collectibles firm whose direct mail letters are signed by its president might offer a taped message from the president to established buyers.

Some marketers have used outgoing telephone offers to test and fine-tune their product, price, and accessories promotions. They can select test groups and use the calls in a sort of "telephone market research" to determine the relative reaction to two test prices, two payment plans, or whatever. This is much quicker and less costly than a mail test, although it should be considered preliminary information and not necessarily conclusive.

Incoming telephone marketing. The toll-free 800 number offers an important customer benefit in ease of ordering. Especially in conjunction with television offers, in which a Business Reply Card or Envelope cannot be provided, such a number allows the customer to order without much effort.

Many catalog marketers now offer toll-free ordering for customers who use credit cards. You will be wise, however, to test the toll-free option against a regular phone number to make sure that its extra cost is justified. Some catalog marketers have found that they get just as many orders, and just as large, without the use of an 800 number.

Whether your incoming 800 number is handled in-house or by an outside firm, make sure that sufficient personnel are available at peak ordering times. This must be carefully coordinated with TV advertising, from which all of the calls are likely to come within a very short period. Catalog marketers must be aware of when their pieces have "dropped" into the mail to make sure a sufficient number of operators is available for the peak ordering period.

TELEPHONE MARKETING FOR RETAILERS

Most retailers with catalogs offer toll-free 800 numbers, or at least a regular telephone number for customers to use in ordering. These firms must decide whether to use an in-house or outside service, and must make sure that a sufficient staff is on duty during their peak ordering periods.

Outgoing phone marketing for retailers may well also be a fertile field. Salespeople may call established customers with news of exciting new merchandise. Many retailers sell and renew service contracts and insurance plans by phone. Even without the benefit of a sophisticated WATS-line system or a professionally written script, many local retailers have been involved in telephone marketing for years. As customers become increasingly direct-response oriented, all retailers will benefit by giving attention to telephone marketing and its growing potential, especially for repeat sales, accessories, and service applications.

TELEPHONE MARKETING FOR BUSINESS-TO-BUSINESS

The telephone serves as a cost-efficient means for qualifying prospective customers for many business marketers selling high-ticket items. With the cost of a personal sales call nearing $200, the more qualified the prospect in terms of ability and readiness to buy, the better. Salespeople or their assistants can use the telephone to pre-qualify customers and determine their immediate and future wants and needs before any travel or time investment is made.

Additionally, many firms have benefitted by categorizing their customers and prospects by the means and frequency with which they are contacted. In the office-supply business, for example, some small customers are sent only a catalog and yearly updates, and are perhaps called once or twice a year to "touch base." Medium-sized customers will receive the catalog and a scheduled monthly call from an "order taker"–type salesperson. Large and important customers will receive a catalog, regular phone contact from the order taker, and personal sales calls on a regular basis.

Effective business marketers also utilize incoming phone lines for direct sales, making sure that each customer or prospect who calls is turned over to a qualified and well-informed inside salesperson.

Generally, then, for the business-to-business marketer the telephone serves as an important "middle ground" between the face-to-face contact of a sales call and the less personal catalog or price-sheet mailing.

12

BROADCAST MEDIA

Television and radio present exciting opportunities for some direct marketers, but in most cases these opportunities belong to established and well-financed operations. With estimates for the cost of a minimum television test ranging from $10,000 to $50,000 and more, it is clear that small-scale prospecting in space advertising and through the mail fits better with the budgets of most fledgling firms. Radio is less costly, especially if the marketer takes advantage of "P. I." or "per-inquiry" financial arrangements in which a set fee is paid for each inquiry received, but requires a great deal of administrative work to control if used on a widespread basis.

Because broadcast media are most likely to be explored by established firms—and because a full discussion of this field is beyond the scope of the book—this chapter will discuss only the basics of television and radio direct response marketing. For a good overview of direct response television today, read John Witek's *Response Television: Combat Advertising of the 1980's* (Crain Books).

Unless broadcast media are very familiar to you, plan to engage the help of a direct response broadcast specialist when you enter this field. The scripting, production, media planning, order processing, and evaluation of a television campaign require specialized knowledge which may be purchased from a good consultant or agency. In the long run, this approach is likely to save you considerable money and aggravation over "learning by doing."

CONSUMER BROADCAST MEDIA

More than 30 years ago, pioneers in television direct response advertising used this new broadcast medium with fine results. Today, one of the star attractions at direct marketing seminars is often the showing of the original ''Veg-a-matic'' commercial—about 15 minutes in length. Working without a script, a master salesman demonstrates this versatile product while explaining how Americans need the nutrition of fresh vegetables. In those days the TV commercials may well have been more interesting and involving than the programs. And television time was affordable—unlike today's six-figure rates for a 20-second prime-time network spot on a popular show or special.

As the television industry has grown and changed, direct response television has evolved as well. But the principles of selling merchandise by direct response, as exemplified by the Veg-a-matic commercial, still hold true. Here are some.

Television's prime benefit is as a medium for demonstration. Just as the old Veg-a-matic ad showed fruits and vegetables being diced, chopped, and pureed, today we see steam cookers and super-sharp knives demonstrated on direct response ads.

The product must have wide appeal or be of interest to a market segment that is reachable. The Veg-a-matic and other kitchen-related products appeal to a wide range of people. Phonograph-record offers may be aired during shows that appeal to specific groups—a country album ad during ''Hee-Haw,'' for instance, or a pitch for a rock album after ''Solid Gold.'' A set of books about World War II might be offered in conjunction with a classic war movie on a UHF station.

To overcome inertia and create action, your ad must be at least as interesting as the programming. Take a look at the direct response advertising on television and you'll see how this can be: most of the 90-to-120-second ads run late at night, early in the morning, or on cable channels or UHF stations with rerun programming or special-interest shows. This is done because the television buyer must be spurred into action. But unlike space ads and direct mail kits, which a prospective customer may read and reread at leisure, the television ad is on the air and then gone; the marketer thus has 90 to 120 seconds to run through the awareness-interest-desire-action formula. Prospects who see an ad as a welcome break in the monotony of the fiftieth rerun of "I Love Lucy" are much more likely to go to the phone and call a toll-free number, or get pencil and paper to write down an address. This also works out well for the direct response marketer because the time slots and programming in which his or her ads perform best are also the most affordable.

The product must be affordable. You will notice that most products sold on television are in the $9.95 to $29.95 range. This is the "comfort level" for most consumers. If you ask more than this for a product on TV you run the risk of eliminating a big part of your audience for economic reasons. However, you may use a two-step process to sell higher-priced items via TV: obtaining leads from your TV ad and then following them up by mail or phone. Veg-a-matic (now priced well above the "comfort level" of most consumers) recently used TV ads with exercise guru Richard Simmons to solicit leads for the product.

The spokesperson is crucial. Your salesperson may not be a celebrity like Richard Simmons, but he or she must be someone who speaks with authority yet is comforting to the television audience. Lead-generation campaigns for insurance have selected older, wise-looking celebrities such as Lorne Greene, Harry Morgan, and Art Linkletter.

It must be easy to respond. Offering a toll-free 800 number is an important enhancement to television marketing because it makes the viewer's response easier; you do not have the opportunity to provide a pre-addressed order form or Business Reply Envelope. Alternatively, you can offer the customer the opportunity to send in an order by mail.

The ordering information should take up one-fourth to one-third of the ad. The most common lengths for TV direct response ads that actually sell products are 90 and 120 seconds. Because of the fleeting nature of this method of promotion, 20 to 30 seconds of this time must be devoted to ordering instructions, repeated several times and superimposed on the screen as well as stated.

As cable and interactive television develop, direct marketers will find more—and more affordable—opportunities in the broadcast field. Cable television already offers a wide variety of specialized channels and programs, including the Cable News Network, ESPN (sports), MTV (music television), Nashville Network (country), and many more. And the salespeople for cable ad time are open to more creative time-buying arrangements than are most networks or local network affiliates. The per-inquiry and other special, affordable rate opportunities may be negotiated. Interactive television promises to provide opportunities for "television catalogs" whereby consumers read about merchandise on their TV screens and order by phone or directly over the television via computer modem. Even smaller direct marketers should keep an eye on the TV field for future affordable selling opportunities.

TELEVISION LEAD GENERATION

When your product is too costly or complex to sell directly on television, a two-step campaign may be appropriate. Because such a campaign is very costly, it usually isn't added to a media mix until a firm is well established in space or mail promotions or both. Large insurance marketers are regular users of two-step television marketing, as are trade and correspondence schools. The usual length of the lead-generating ads in the two-step system is 60 seconds, with a repetition of the ordering instructions both on-screen and verbally. A toll-free 800 number will enhance this type of campaign, although the option to write is usually also offered.

SUPPORT TELEVISION

In the last decade, support television has become an exciting new enhancement in the media mix of large direct marketers such as Reader's Digest, Publisher's Clearing House, Grolier, and various insurance firms. Support television does not sell directly, but rather takes advantage of the broad reach of television to alert prospects to an offer made elsewhere, such as in the mail, a newspaper, or a national magazine.

Support ads may be as short as 10 seconds or as long as 30 seconds. They should be placed at times when viewers are likely to be attentive—in contrast with the ads for direct response selling by TV. Support television should be used only in conjunction with campaigns that have already proven themselves independently; it is an enhancement, not a way to salvage a weak offer or poor direct mail kit or ad.

Support TV ads are mainly "sizzle," talking about the benefits of a new offer or sweepstakes and telling the prospect where to look for full information. To prove their worth, these ads must pay for themselves in terms of additional sales or qualified leads, as compared to a control campaign run without support TV.

Some advertisers have taken a clever step (which doubles as a broadcast "action device," see glossary) to try and determine how many of their customers have seen and remembered support TV ads. Prospects are told that they will receive a premium or additional product if they make a certain mark or circle a picture on the order form. This instruction is given only in the support TV ads, and people who do not see the ads therefore cannot respond in this special way.

SELLING BY RADIO

Because today's radio stations are beautifully segmented by interest area and demographics, direct marketers may be able to utilize radio cost-effectively for special-interest products. But since radio does not offer demonstration possibilities, its effectiveness is limited to those products that may be sold by means of "word pictures."

Two of the longest-running and most effective radio direct response campaigns are those of Earl Nightengale and of *Changing Times* magazine. Both are selling written material in the context of radio shows that establish the speaker as an expert on the topics discussed in the literature.

Even smaller direct marketers may be able to utilize radio by means of per-inquiry arrangements. Some experts advise that you obtain a list of radio stations from the Federal Communications Commission, and write to them inquiring about the availability of P. I. time. For the best potential coverage, look for "clear-channel" stations that may broadcast on an almost national basis late at night.

BROADCAST DIRECT RESPONSE FOR RETAILERS

Most television advertising done by retailers is of the traditional variety, providing information rather than selling merchandise directly. However, some creative thinking may provide local retailers with ideas for direct response broadcast possibilities, especially of the two-step variety. For instance, a retailer might solicit new customers by inviting them to call or write for a free catalog or sale flyer. And interactive television may provide great possibilities for retailers in the future. Reports are that Sears, Roebuck is in the forefront of this movement, with plans to put its catalog directly on the television screen for at-home, direct response buying.

BROADCAST DIRECT RESPONSE FOR BUSINESS-TO-BUSINESS MARKETERS

In most cases, the business-to-business marketer's target customer cannot be reached effectively via the broadcast media. But there are some exceptions.

Cable television business networks and shows, all-news radio stations, and even some sporting events such as golf tournaments may provide a fertile medium for your lead-solicitation activities. And even though such prospecting may be costly, keep the possibilities in mind as the cable- and interactive-television revolutions continue.

13

PUBLIC RELATIONS FOR THE DIRECT RESPONSE MARKETER

INTRODUCTION

Very little has been written on publicity and public relations specifically for the direct response marketer. But good public relations is an aspect of the overall direct marketing mix that deserves significant time and effort.

A basic definition of *publicity* is any non-paid editorial space or broadcast time devoted to your product or service. It is worth remembering, however, that publicity may be positive or negative—"non-paid" means that the firm forfeits control.

Public relations has to do with the overall image your firm communicates, not only to existing customers but also to the world at large.

A good customer service department, prompt deliveries, products that provide what your ads promise, and accurate order-processing clerks all contribute to your firm's public relations image with customers. But public relations programs aimed at your overall prospective buying universe may well help you win those customers in the first place.

And here's an aspect of public relations that may not have occurred to you: A well-planned publicity and public relations program can build you an impressive image that will gain your firm prestige with potential suppliers, joint-venture candidates, and other companies that can do you good.

What's more, a good relationship with the media representatives in your field or town can gain you a number of opportunities to speak out as an authority when issues come up that affect your industry. If a potentially damaging story should start brewing, those good relationships will mean you're called immediately for the "real story"— not kept in the dark while reporters seek second-hand information elsewhere.

CHOOSE THE WAY YOU'LL FORM YOUR CONTACTS

Many medium-to-large firms have public relations people on staff, and even some very small companies contract with freelance help to do this work. If you have such experts at your disposal, use this chapter to help you understand what kind of information they'll need from you to help enhance the image of the products or services you market.

If your firm has no public relations program, you have the option to do your own PR or hire a PR firm or freelancer to take care of the work. Although a novice can often write an acceptable press release with a few guidelines and pointers, it may well be easier and less expensive to hire a freelance writer to do at least this much for you. Your regular copywriter may be able to write press releases as well as direct response copy. If not, he or she is almost certain to know someone who can.

The follow-up function—working directly with the media to help encourage "pick up" (utilization) of your press releases and article ideas—may also be done by a freelancer or agency if you so choose. Stability is important here: your best bet in developing relationships with the media is to have the same person contact editors over a long period, so as to build a relationship of trust and reliance. Therefore, if you do not have a good, stable public relations firm to which you can commit for the long haul, the contact function may best be done by a member of your own staff.

FINDING THE CONTACTS YOU NEED

There is more specific information in the following sections on who can help you in consumer, retail, and business-to-business PR, but here is a general word about finding contacts: If you need a national list of newspaper city editors or the names of book-review editors at a score of different publications, a reference like *Bacon's Publicity Checker* can save you much time. The American and Canadian version of this two-volume reference set covers 5,100 business, trade, farm, and consumer magazines, and all 1,800 daily newspapers in the two countries, plus 7,300 weekly newspapers and publisher groups. The books are published annually in October and supplemented quarterly. Along with addresses for the publications it lists, the *Checker* gives current editors' names for general press releases and special-interest subjects. There are also codes to tell you which publications welcome news of new products, trade literature, personnel news, and so on. Beyond this, there is an international version of the *Publicity Checker* that covers 9,300 publications in fifteen Western European countries.

Both publications are available from Bacon's Publicity Checker, 332 South Michigan Avenue, Chicago, IL 60604. Recent prices were $123 for the United States and Canada version, and $133 for the international version, both including shipping and handling.

NEWS VERSUS FEATURES

The fledgling public relations liaison needs to understand how reporters perceive different types of stories, and how each type of story should be approached. The main distinction is between news and features.

Hard News

When you have what is known as a "hard news" story, there is no question of exclusivity involved. Information about new store openings, new product introductions, the introduction of a new catalog division, and other developments may be sent to all interested editors in general press-release form.

If you should send the same press release to several people at the same publication, do them the courtesy of marking the release with the names of the others who received it. This avoids duplication of effort and potential embarrassment at having two sections of the publication print the same story.

The Press Release

A press release is the best way to inform the media about your news. The idea of a press conference may seem glamorous and impressive, but it is impractical for all but the most earth-shattering news. It is difficult to get reporters to attend run-of-the-mill press conferences, and the conference allows a public forum for questions that may be potentially troublesome.

Here are some hints for preparing a good press release:

1. It should cover the journalistic basics: Who, What, Where, When, Why, and How.
2. It should be written in "inverted pyramid" form, with the most important information woven into the first few paragraphs. If your story has to be cut, editors will delete the bottom paragraphs, and if something important is buried there it may be lost in your write-up.
3. It should be as concise as possible. Try for no more than two 8½-by-11-inch pages, double spaced.
4. It should have an active, factual headline that will catch the editor's interest.
5. Even if the press release goes out on letterhead paper, it should list the specific contact person in your organization, and his or her phone number, to avoid confusion.
6. It should state "For Immediate Release" or, if that is not possible, should say specifically when the material may be released (e.g., "For Release After 12 Noon on Tuesday, June 3").
7. It should be dated so that an editor who picks it out of a miscellaneous pile will know how long it's been around.
8. It should carry its city and state of origin at the beginning of the body copy (e.g., "NEW YORK, New York—").

Use the sample press release on page 150 as a guide.

Feature Stories and "Pitch Letters"

A feature story is one that does not necessarily depend on today's news for relevance. It is likely to deal with a "trend" or "angle" on a story.

The classic way for public relations people to place feature stories is to approach editors or reporters with a feature concept. For instance, as a catalog marketer you might approach a magazine editor about doing a feature on Christmas shopping by catalog. As a business-to-business seller of office equipment, you might approach a trade publication about a feature on the latest trends in word-processing systems.

It is important that you share your specific feature ideas with only one editor or publication at a time, otherwise you will lose credibility. The key to good feature writing is a fresh angle. You can't "peddle"

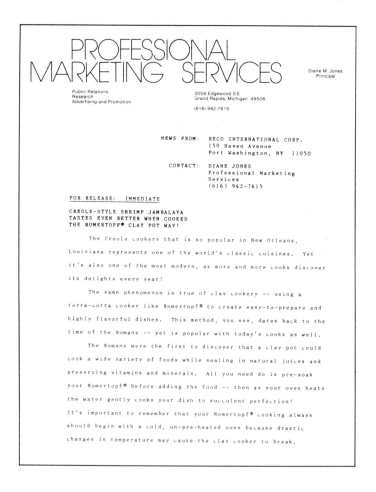

the same idea to two different magazines or you will be very unpopular when they come out with similar articles.

When you come up with a feature concept, you should try to interest your first-choice editor or writer in doing a story on it. If he or she turns you down, you may approach another editor in the same way, proceeding until you place the story. Then find another feature angle and work on that one until you find a publication that is interested.

The most effective way to place a feature story is to write what is called a "pitch letter" to your target editor. Include some "sizzle" about the feature concept you've come up with and an indication of the interviews and background information you can provide.

FOLLOW-UP FOR PRESS RELEASES AND PITCH LETTERS

Many firms simply send out their press releases by the bushel and hope that publications will pick them up. But with press releases and pitch letters alike, the chances for placement increase if you follow up by phone.

Except for hot, timely stories, allow the editor or writer a few days after its probable receipt to read over your release or letter. Then call him or her to see if you can provide more information, photographs, or other help. Here are some hints for that phone call.

1. Don't call when the writer has a deadline to meet. This is especially crucial when calling a daily newspaper. Generally, the last deadline for morning papers is early evening of the night before, for which reason it is good to call morning-paper writers in the morning. Afternoon papers finally "go to bed" at mid-morning, so try these people in the afternoon.
2. Don't start off by asking if the writer or editor is going to use your story. It is better to inquire if he or she has received your information, and to ask if you can provide more background or answer any questions. Be cooperative and helpful, and don't press.
3. Don't make a pest of yourself by calling back after that first contact. If the editor or writer is undecided when you first speak with him or her, ask *when* you should call back and wait until then for a second contact.

4. Never use your firm's advertising power as "bait" to obtain editorial space. Some periodicals, especially trade publications, may come after you with this "one hand washes the other" pitch, and you may end up making such an arrangement. But don't suggest it yourself or you risk losing a good media contact by compromising someone's journalistic standards.

5. Use each contact as an opportunity to build a good working relationship with the publication. Even if they don't pick up this particular piece of news or this feature idea, they will make a mental note that you are a helpful and available source of information in your field. Make sure they have your phone number for future reference, and before long you may be receiving calls soliciting your help with ideas they have.

INTERVIEWS WITH THE MEDIA

If you or another representative of your firm is called on for quotations or an interview on a subject related to your field, make sure you are prepared for the occasion. Here are some tips:

1. Never bluff, be honest. If you don't have an answer for the question posed, say that you don't know but will try to find out. If the question regards something you are not authorized to discuss, just say so; never come out with the deadly answer, "no comment." And even worse, don't give the answer "off the record." In making such statements you put the reporter in the awkward position of knowing something he can't use, and this may well backfire.

2. Don't try to make the interview a "commercial" for your company or product. Credits for you and your firm will develop in the context of the article. You are only too obvious if you try to work every question around to an answer that promotes your interests alone.

3. Don't ask to see a copy of the story before it goes to press. Few reporters take this request well, and in any case, many writers are forbidden by their editors to let you "censor" their work.

4. Be calm, friendly, and helpful. If you promise the reporter some back-up facts, literature, or photos, deliver them promptly. Remember that the reporter's deadline is firm.

PHOTOGRAPHY

Sometimes a handsome or intriguing photo can win you a place for a story that is not very intriguing on its own. But make sure that the photos you send along with your stories are good quality, black-and-white glossies, in focus, and as close-up to the subject as possible.

If you're doing a feature, don't send the publication a "stock" photo; do special ones if at all possible, and talk with the editor about what illustrations are desirable.

Once your photos are ready, provide a caption for each and attach it to the back of the photo itself. If you put it on separate paper you risk its being misplaced in a busy publication office.

And once again, remember those deadlines. Dailies and weeklies especially have no time to spare if they wish to tell your story in a timely way, so get those photos to them on time, even if you must pay your photography studio extra.

CONSUMER DIRECT RESPONSE PUBLIC RELATIONS

Objectives

If you are a consumer direct marketer, a public relations program may benefit you in the following ways:

- *Reinforcing and improving customer attitudes.* The customer who sees your spokesperson on television or reads an article quoting an expert from your firm gets an extra message that your firm is a leader in its field.
- *Exposing potential customers.* By the same token, potential customers may learn of your firm through periodicals or broadcast media and be intrigued enough to watch for your ads or write for your sales literature.
- *Spreading the news about important events and promotions.* An example of this is the way Neiman-Marcus promotes its famous Christmas catalog each year. National television shows, newspapers, and magazines all run simultaneous and often humorous pieces about the latest luxury items Neiman-Marcus has to offer.
- *Establishing your firm as a leader in its field.* By creating a relationship with local or national media people, or both, your

firm will come to mind when they need information about your field. Thus you may find yourself quoted as a "leading expert" in a national round-up article in *The New York Times, Ladies' Home Journal,* or *Sports Illustrated,* depending on the type of product you sell.

Whom to Approach for Consumer Public Relations

Here are some ideas on the type of media representatives you'll want to approach in the consumer field:

- *Daily newspapers.* Those in your area if you are a local or regional firm, plus perhaps top dailies in New York, Chicago, and Los Angeles if your company has aspects of national interest. A national firm may want to send press releases to dailies all over the country, or at least those in the top 100 metropolitan areas. This again will depend on your product: if your line has rural appeal, you may want to stick to smaller papers.
- *Weekly papers and local "shoppers."* Your interest in these papers will depend on the focus of your product. A firm that sells high-priced jewelry will probably pass them up, but if you market needlework kits by mail, these smaller, family-type publications may be a prime market for you.
- *Magazines.* If you were to advertise in magazines, which ones would you choose? These same publications will probably also be your best bets for news releases and feature stories. Your primary focus will be magazines that deal with your product's special interest area, and you may expand to general-interest publications from there.
- *Television and radio.* Some consumer direct marketers, such as Roger Horchow and Stanley Marcus, have become "media stars" in their own right. You may be able to do this for yourself or your product if you can devise an angle that interests the news or entertainment media.

Experts advise that you start by working with the network affiliates or local television stations in your town, and then move up to national contacts if the response merits. The person to contact is the assignment editor of a news show or the producer of a feature program. As for radio, it is today mainly a local medium, for which reason it is useful to contact area talk shows and the producers of feature segments who might be interested in your story ideas.

What Makes Good Public Relations for the Consumer Direct Marketer?

Here are some examples of the type of news or feature material you may want to submit to various media sources.

- New product introductions
- New features that make a familiar product better
- Interviews with designers, artists, or creators of products
- How-to ideas for your product and other products in its category
- New ways in which you plan to sell (e.g., a first-time catalog or continuity program)
- Survey of the field (the growth of your product category, reasons behind it, and other information)
- Human-interest stories showing your product in use or giving product related information
- Celebrity stories related to your product or firm
- The history of your product or product category with an angle of current interest
- Product price decreases or inflation-fighting policies in your firm or industry

RETAIL DIRECT RESPONSE PUBLIC RELATIONS

Objectives

Check the objectives listed in the preceding consumer public-relations section for a general list of the ways in which PR can help you. Here are a few more specifics on how a public relations program can benefit the retail direct response marketer—who is likely to operate on a local or regional basis:

- *Building a national image.* Some local or regional firms have a concept or a way of selling that is unique enough to give them national potential. A public relations campaign can make consumers all over the nation aware of such a firm's unique qualities; witness the awareness buyers have nationally for Bloomingdale's, Neiman-Marcus, Tiffany's, and other retailers who market by mail.

- *Supplementing direct mail traffic-building programs.* Features in local media about interesting in-store events make for a well-rounded promotional mix.
- *Reinforcing the local image.* Good relationships with local editors can mean "good press" when you are called on to provide products to be photographed as examples for features on fashion, sports, automotive stories, or whatever your product line may be.

Channels for Retail Public Relations

In general, your scope for retail public relations will be narrower than for consumer PR. If you are trying to build a national retail image for your firm, check the suggestions in the previous section on consumer public relations. For a local retailer, the following contacts should prove helpful:

- *Local and regional newspapers.* You may compile your own list of media contacts by calling the newspapers in your trading area. Determine what you need to know about each newspaper, such as the name of the editor who deals with your type of product line (fashion, automotive, business, or other) and possibly also the name of the city editor. You'll also want to check the correct mailing address. If the person you've called seems willing to talk, discuss deadline times and the types of press releases and other information that the publication welcomes. As a local retailer, you stand a good chance of becoming a regular source of information and help for the editor if you are friendly, low-key, and accessible.
- *Weekly papers and shoppers.* These smaller publications are often hungry for news, and if you believe that your customers read and are influenced by them, they may be worth pursuing. As a cooperative, idea-filled source, you could wind up with a great deal of editorial space.
- *Magazines.* If your business is local or regional in scope, the

national publications most likely are not worth pursuing unless your product or way of doing business is exceptional in some way. But you should approach your local "city" magazine, as well as any other local or regional periodicals, to see if your feature ideas might appeal to them.

- *Television and radio.* Depending upon the size of your town and your relative "clout" as a retailer, the electronic media may offer you good opportunities. In the fashion field, you might do style shows on television or offer advice on the radio about updating wardrobes. A car dealer could submit a feature idea about trends in new-model autos, or offer to speak on a radio talk show about winterizing cars, selecting accessories for a car, or other how-to information. If they are unique enough or have human-interest appeal, promotions at your place of business may attract the TV cameras, or persuade a radio station to do a live, remote broadcast.

What Makes Good Public Relations for the Retail Direct Response Marketer?

Here are some "handles" you might use for a public relations campaign to supplement direct mail:

- Introduction of a new product line
- A new type of catalog or by-mail promotion
- A feature angle about an in-store promotion with human-interest or unique appeal
- A special appearance by a well-known celebrity, artist, or designer at your place of business
- A report on consumer buying patterns, including the best-selling item in your catalog this year and why it is
- Seasonal features and how-to tie-ins

BUSINESS-TO-BUSINESS DIRECT RESPONSE PUBLIC RELATIONS

Objectives

The business-to-business marketer's public relations objectives are similar to those of consumer-oriented marketers, but he or she is seeking to reach business decision makers. Here are some of the ways PR can help:

- *Building prestige for the firm.* Having a top executive quoted or profiled in business publications can help gain prestige and exposure for your company.
- *Opening the door to new, potential customers.* The nature of the business buyer is fundamentally different from that of the personal buyer. It is his or her *vocation* to buy and to do a good job of it. Thus a good purchasing agent is always on the lookout for an effective source of supply. Your public relations efforts may expose prospective customers to your offerings.
- *Announcing new product lines: the look of an innovator.* Business buyers are sensitive to the research-and-development side of your firm. They want to buy from the company that is forward-looking so that they get the most up-to-date features and technology for their money. Your public relations efforts can help give you that innovative reputation.
- *Being a leader in the field.* Your company can have impact beyond its actual size if it is prominent in trade publications and community affairs. Publicity can give the appearance of prominence with much less investment than is needed for advertising.
- *Appearing as a public-service-oriented firm.* Don't underestimate the public relations value of your firm's community work. It can build good will and prominence for you in the minds of present and potential customers.
- *Coming across as a well-run company.* If the media quote your firm's executives on the business issues of the day, and if the business press reports your company's methods of operation as worth emulating, it will add to your standing in your field.

Whom to Approach

In business-to-business public relations you will work with the same media categories as consumer public relations specialists, but your focus will be different than theirs. Here are some tips on approaching various types of editors:

- *Daily newspapers.* News items of general interest may go to the city editor, while business-interest news should go to that department's editor. Feature stories will most likely be of interest to the business editor as well, but they may also be "pitched" to another department at the paper if there is a related angle.
- *Wire services.* If yours is a national concern, you may well have news of interest to United Press International and Associated Press. If there is no bureau for these services in your city, find a contact in your nearest big-city bureau. The business wire services are Dow-Jones and Reuters. If you have a sizeable firm, these wire services will want to hear from you with quarterly and year-end reports and news items.
- *Magazines and trade publications.* Unless yours is a sizable firm or a company with a unique story to tell, your industry's trade publications will probably be a more fertile field for you than the general business press. But don't hesitate to approach the business weeklies with an interesting feature angle. Trade publications can be among your best media friends in that they may well be "starved" for fresh news and feature angles. Another idea is to offer them ready-made articles authored by or ghost-written for one of your firm's executives. The trade press may pick these up verbatim, assuming they are informational and not purely and entirely commercial.
- *Television and radio.* Approach the producers of business programs with feature ideas, and send them your press releases so that they will think of you when they need a contact in your field. Many all-news radio stations have business-oriented programs as well.

What Makes Good Public Relations for the Business-to-Business Direct Marketer?

Here are some ideas on the type of news and feature material you might work up for your firm:

- New product introductions
- Personnel changes that will have an impact on your field
- Research and development breakthroughs
- Expansions in size and plant capacity

- New applications for business products
- Time- or money-saving ideas having to do with your product
- Surveys you have done in your field that will be of interest to buyers of your product
- How-to articles written by or ghosted for your execs or salespeople
- "State of the industry" articles in which your firm is quoted as an expert source
- Checklists of hints on buying your type of equipment
- The time- and money-saving aspects of buying your product via direct response

14

FULFILLMENT: AN OPERATIONS OVERVIEW

THE DYNAMICS OF FULFILLMENT OPERATIONS

Most marketers understand the significance of developing the right product and promoting it properly. Yet many managers fail to recognize the importance of an efficient fulfillment system until it is too late. All too often, fulfillment and customer service problems allow a crisis-management atmosphere to prevail throughout a firm's business operations. While no business ever fully avoids operational problems, the following sections on fulfillment functions will help you to develop a new system or improve an existing one.

Develop a Forecast Model

For effective fulfillment, you must devise a forecasting model that accurately reflects the flow of sales and products through your business system. Regardless of the size of your operation, your forecast should include: an estimate of the number of orders you expect to receive and when you expect to receive them; the estimated cost of each item; and your anticipated order-shipping dates. Coordinate your forecast closely with your planned purchasing and promotional activities to assure that your model portrays your business activity accurately.

THE DYNAMICS OF FULFILLMENT

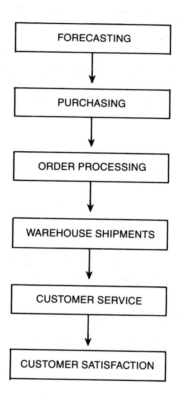

Establish a Strong Procurement Interface

In concert with your forecast model, you or your purchasing manager must coordinate closely to ensure that your product is produced and delivered on time. This may seem obvious, but it is not unusual to see a company's purchasing activity out of sync with its forecasted sales. Problems in this area will at best result in too much of a firm's money being tied up in inventory, and at worst in overbuys and writeoffs. It is absolutely essential that procurement be closely managed. Poor forecasting and poor purchasing procedures, or both, cause more serious financial problems than many managers realize.

Develop an Order-Processing System

If your operation is small and just getting started, you may want to consider using a service company to provide order processing for you. Organizations such as Epsilon Data Management of Burlington, Massachusetts, will open your mail, make deposits, complete order entries into a computer system, produce invoices, and ship them to the appropriate vendors for drop shipping, or to your warehouse for final disposition. The service-company approach allows the customer to take advantage of larger support services and technologies than a business could ordinarily afford. However, the service bureau's strength is in standardization, and problems can occur when a business requires special treatment of its transactions or customers. Many companies prefer to deal directly with their customers to ensure proper service.

Assuming that you have considered the service-bureau approach and decided to devise your own fulfillment system, it is best to establish a cashiering and caging (mail opening) procedure that complements your volume. If your mail can be opened by hand on a timely basis, do it by hand. Alternatively, you can acquire a mail opening and extraction machine that will do the job, but make sure you have sufficient volume before making a lease or purchase commitment for one of these.

Managing your mail once it is opened is particularly important for the timely processing of orders and prompt customer service. You should sort the mail along functional lines: payments, customer service correspondence, returns, and new orders. For new orders, you must establish a key-code-counting procedure so that you can tally your orders efficiently. This is essential for a "quick read" by you or your marketing staff. Your daily results report or "Order Flash" ultimately should be computerized, but because of the need to forecast sales promptly, a manual report will probably serve your immediate needs best. Finally, many companies color-code their Business Reply Envelopes by function in order to minimize their sorting time; thus, new promotions may have a blue bar code while payments returned have a pink bar code.

Should you decide to use a toll-free 800 number to receive orders, you must be prepared to provide this service seven days a week, twenty-four hours a day. Some companies feed their incoming 800-

calls directly to a computer terminal operator for on-line entry; others, because of seasonal volume savings, use such outside services as Ring America or Mardex to manage their calls. While using an outside service is probably the most cost-effective option for many organizations, it is important to devise a script that requires the operators to ask all the pertinent questions during the initial contact. If you're doing your entries directly "on-line"—as they come in—the computer can prompt the operator to make sure the order is complete. Handwritten orders will, of course, require editing, but a good script can minimize errors.

Batch processing allows you to process orders in groups of thirty or fifty with a control header form containing the date, batch number, and other control data. Batch totals are usually balanced against remittance batches, thereby providing a deposit and cash reconciliation control which you will need to ensure that you are not losing orders. You will, of course, want to make sure that you have established the necessary internal controls to avoid errors and the possibility of embezzlement. Deposit controls should be handled by different employees than batch controls, so that you have separate employees or employee groups checking each other. Credit-card orders are usually processed separately from cash orders since they require verification of the account number, expiration date, and other items. Subsequent to verification, the card companies must authorize the order. Most companies establish an authorization limit for charges over $60 so as to head off bad debts. We also recommend that your caging group keep a listing of fraud names; it is amazing how a good caging clerk will spot regular frauds.

Once your orders are prepared and ready for data entry, you should consider various entry options. (We assume that you are using a computer for processing, but the principle is the same if you use a typewriter.) First, entry at a computer terminal has become a fairly standard means of processing data, and has the advantage of allowing the computer to assist in making entry decisions and in cross-checking orders so that errors will be minimized. Second, optical scanners (OCR units) are becoming increasingly prevalent and increase order entry efficiency tremendously. But you must have a standardized input to benefit to any great degree from these.

We recommend the computer processing of orders on an on-line basis, since this speeds up shipping and immediately updates customer records and inventories. Furthermore, you can usually get on-line by leasing a computer or utilizing a service bureau.

Of course, not every business is large enough to warrant using a computer initially. For companies just beginning or for those with just a few thousand customers, the traditional ledger-card system is probably the most cost-effective for order processing. The card system is usually set up by posting the original order on a header card. After alphabetizing the customer header file, subsequent orders are posted manually to each account. While this system is usually cost effective and good for new start-ups, the manager should plan from the beginning to computerize as soon as the firm's order volume is sufficient.

Make the Warehouse Part of the Team

Many companies consider their fulfillment operation complete when the warehouse or drop shipper receives the invoices or shipping labels for a series of orders. The good mail-order companies know better. Your warehouse or shipper is not only a distribution point, but should be vitally involved in managing your inventory, inspecting and checking to make sure that quality control is maintained on your merchandise, and ensuring that incoming merchandise is counted correctly and put in the proper location. Further, the warehouse must keep your inventory secure.

Make Customer Service the Focal Point of Your Operation

Regardless of how good your merchandise is or how timely you are in fulfilling your commitments, you must be prepared to have a service area dedicated to answering a variety of customer inquiries and complaints. In fact, the customer-service department is one of the most important in your business, because it communicates with your customers—who are lifeblood—on a daily basis. If your customer-service people do nothing else, they must communicate effectively. You must require them to answer inquiries promptly, usually within a few days of their receipt in the case of routine inquiries. Urgent requests must be handled by phone. You must ensure that your representatives give precise answers whenever possible (for example, "a replacement product will be sent in two weeks"), and that your customer-service personnel follow through on all commitments made.

Many companies will also assign their credit and collections duties to their customer service representatives. This is a logical extension of the traditional customer service responsibilities of dealing with customers on a variety of issues, such as wrong credit-card numbers or bad checks. It also provides a good systems control for being sure that you are reporting credit problems accurately.

Because your customer-service department so often deals with your customer correspondence, you should also assign your list-maintenance function to this department. Timely maintenance of address corrections will reduce product returns, and adding the names of people who send in miscellaneous inquiries will improve promotional efficiency.

You might also want to develop form letters for use by your customer-service department. Letters addressing such standard issues as back-order notices, thirty-day shipment-delay letters, acknowledgments, late deliveries, and so on should all be approved by your top management. You must make policy decisions about returns and refunds, and make sure your customer-service personnel understand your refund guarantee policy and execute it properly.

It is very important to make the commitment to serve your customers well. It is easy to make the short-term decision to reduce service and increase profits. But remember that satisfied customers buy

Lew Magram sends customers whose merchandise was delayed an *apology* in the form of a $5 gift certificate coupon good on the next purchase.

Please accept our sincerest apologies for the delay in sending you the enclosed merchandise. An extended delay such as the one you have experienced   is indeed a rare occurrence.

Sorry for the delay...

At Lew Magram, we pride ourselves on our prompt and reliable service. The $5.00 certificate attached is our gift to you. We hope that in the near future you will give us a chance to prove how good we really are. Many thanks for your patience and understanding.

Just Detach
This Coupon and Enclose It
with Your Next Order

**IT'S WORTH $5
TOWARD ANY PURCHASE.**

try us again

lew magram

more, and if you service them well they will buy more from you than from your competition.

DYNAMICS OF FULFILLMENT

Each element of the fulfillment cycle is clearly interdependent, and it is vital to keep each element in cadence with the needs of your business. If you forecast accurately, buy efficiently, process orders on a timely basis, ship regularly, assure quality control, and institute a customer-service approach that is dedicated to total customer satisfaction, your business will be poised to grow and prosper as you execute your marketing plan.

Using Fulfillment Tools

Regardless of your operating decisions—to use your own computer, a service bureau, or operate manually—there are a number of reporting functions necessary for monitoring and managing your business. First, you must have a *sales report* showing sales by product, and a *sales tax report* to document the taxes you have collected. Depending upon your audit requirements, you will also need a *cash-management report* for cash receipts, and a *charge report* to document charges made against shipments as well as those pending approval. You will need an *inventory-control report* which shows your item-by-item costs and inventory levels at any given time, as well as a *return-goods report* to document the flow of inventory back into your firm. Many companies require *employee-performance reports* which document productivity on an hourly or daily basis, using criteria such as products picked or shipped per day or customer inquiries answered per day. If you have a club or continuity business, you will need an *attrition* report to follow the flow of customers through each campaign. A *bad-debt or collections report* is usually used to document write-offs and focus on problem areas. A *customer-status report* is helpful for monitoring customers who have been put on a pending status until problems are resolved. Finally, you should have the standard *accounts payable and general-ledger report,* which will be used to calculate your overall operations cost.

If you are already in business, you have probably devised a reporting scheme that serves you well. If you are starting up a new business, review this list with your financial and operations personnel.

15

BACK-END MARKETING

"Front end" is a direct marketing term that means promoting to a new customer. "Back-end" marketing is the important set of tactics used to convert, keep, trade-up, and resell to these customers once you have their names.

In nearly all sales situations, the initial customer relationship is expensive to develop. Direct marketers often must invest a great deal of money to obtain a new customer or lead. For this reason, the way in which that person is handled on the "back end" is crucial.

Here are some of the functions of back-end marketing:

- To convert a lead into a buyer
- To cut returns and reinforce wisdom of original purchases
- To promote good will for the firm
- To build long-term customer loyalty
- To sell products with better profit margins than those sold by front-end marketing
- To insure continued sales to the new customer
- To pay for necessary mailings, such as premium notices, by offering additional merchandise for sale
- To collect funds owed or to gain subscription renewals

The specific "how-to's" for these functions are explained below in the sections on consumer, retail, and business-to-business back-end marketing.

CONSUMER BACK-END MARKETING

Converting Leads

Often the sole objective of a front-end promotion is to obtain a lead for a salesperson or for a direct mail follow-up. When the follow-up must be done by direct mail these follow-ups are considered back-end promotions.

The lead itself may come to you through any of the following:

- Space advertising
- Direct mail solicitation
- Telephone solicitation
- Inquiry from a publicity story
- Unsolicited inquiry
- Customer referral

Most important to remember is that the moment the potential customer "raises his hand" by sending in a lead to say that he or she is interested, that same customer begins to "cool off." If you don't answer the lead in good time, the potential customer may cool off completely and not even remember asking about your offer.

It is therefore imperative that you respond to a lead quickly. Two weeks is about the maximum any lead or inquiry should have to wait before you reply. If for some reason your formal "conversion package" is not ready on time, send your leads a "keep warm" letter. This should thank them for their interest, give them a few teasers about the exciting information to come, and let them know that the information they requested is on the way.

The Extent of the Follow-up Depends on Your Product

If you are following up on a request for information about a $30 book, the cost and effort you'll want to expend will be significantly less than if you are answering leads for a $2,500 home computer. The cost-per-sale factor is obviously quite different in the two cases.

Many marketers try both one- and two-step programs on a given offer, and for responding to leads, in a two-step program, simply modify their one-step direct mail package. Typical modifications include:

- An envelope teaser stating "Here is the information you requested."
- A revised letter acknowledging that the person has requested this information.
- Special wording on other pieces of the mail package, which the lead-generation piece may have referred to, such as a premium slip, special-offer order form, and so on.

If you are selling a high-ticket item by means of a direct mail follow-up, however, one simply modified front-end package is generally not enough.

Let's take the example of the $2,500 personal computer. You may well be able to spend hundreds of advertising dollars to convert just one sale on such an item, especially if you plan to follow up with later offers of software, accessory equipment, and other items with high margins. Thus, to stop after one follow-up package would be foolish. You can "balance out" the inexpensive sales (in terms of low mailing costs) you make on the first go-round with some harder-won sales generated by later efforts directed at the same leads. (One note of caution: before investing this much money and effort in leads, make sure they are tight enough to warrant your attention. See Chapter 5, on offers, for information about loose versus tight leads.)

It is not enough simply to re-mail the same package time and again to leads, hoping that they will eventually notice your mailing. Instead, come up with a series of mailings with varied appearances, appeals, and premium offers, using modular components that you can print in quantity to save money. Here's an example:

CONVERSION CAMPAIGN FOR PERSONAL COMPUTER

Standard Components

1. 6-by-9 inch decorated outer envelope
2. #10 decorated outer envelope
3. Basic selling letter
4. Four-color brochure which can be folded for either envelope
5. Premium slip
6. Order form
7. Business Reply Envelope

Extra Components

A. Testimonial letter
B. Letter from the engineer who designed the computer
C. Extra premium slip
D. Last-chance slip
E. Telegram-format letter

Mailing	Time	Contents
#1	One week after receipt of lead	"Keep warm" letters with "sizzle" about package to come
#2	Two weeks after receipt of lead	1, 3, 4, 5, 6, 7 (Outer envelope is stamped "Here Is the Information You Requested")
#3	Six weeks after receipt of lead	2, A, 4, 5, 6, 7
#4	Ten weeks after receipt of lead	1, B, 4, 5, 6, 7 (Outer envelope is stamped "Inside: Special News from the Designer of the XYZ Home Computer")
#5	Fourteen weeks after receipt of lead	2, 3, 4, 5, 6, 7, C (Outer envelope is stamped *"Two* Free Gifts: See Inside for Details"; letter has a handwritten message about the extra premium)
#6	Eighteen weeks after receipt of lead	2, E, 4, 5, 6, 7, D (Outer envelope is stamped "Last Chance!")

Even after all of these mailings, you might follow up again with a telephone call to try to get a commitment from the customer. Such a final effort may be warranted on a high-ticket item. And don't simply delete the customer from your files even after all these efforts. He or she may be a valuable potential customer for another offer you'll make in the near future.

Reinforcing the Original Purchase

Put yourself in the place of your customer for a moment, and imagine your product has just been delivered to your home. You open the package and find the product inside. There it is: the radio or suit of clothing or decor item you ordered several weeks ago, all by itself, without the "sizzle" that was provided on the front end when you made the decision to buy it. Kind of a letdown, isn't it?

But this doesn't have to happen if you, as the direct marketer, provide your customer with some "purchase reinforcing material." It won't cost you more than ten cents or so per package to do this, although some marketers spend considerably more to reinforce high-ticket purchases. Here are some ideas on what you could include in the package to make customers feel good about their purchases on receipt.

- *Restatement of the reasons for buying.* Include a short letter or promotional piece that re-tells the story of the product and reminds customers of all the features and benefits that convinced them to buy it in the first place.
- *Restatement of the guarantee and other terms of the offer.* Remind customers of their opportunity to put the item to use before deciding whether to keep it.
- *Testimonials.* Include a few quotes from satisfied customers, especially those who have re-ordered the product many times. Each testimonal might discuss a different reason why the purchaser has found the product a big hit.
- *How-to information in easy-to-use form.* Even if it seems completely obvious how to put the product to use, remember that your customer is not as familiar with it as you are. A few step-by-step instructions, even on a simple item, will move the customer to start using the product right away. If your item is more complex, how-to information is essential. Don't trust this vital writing job to a nonprofessional; have a good copywriter do your how-to instructions for you, and then test them out on people who cut across your customer profile to make sure the instructions are helpful, not intimidating, and usable.

Certificates and other documentation that the customer can save. This could be a Certificate of Authenticity for a limited-edition col-

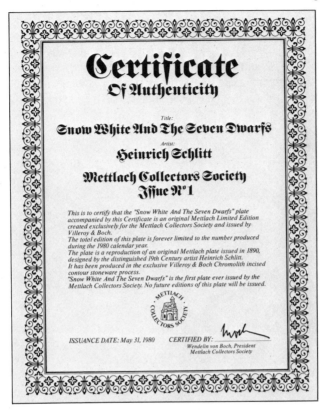

Certificate
Of Authenticity

Title:
Snow White And The Seven Dwarfs

Artist:
Heinrich Schlitt

Mettlach Collectors Society
Issue N° 1

This is to certify that the "Snow White And The Seven Dwarfs" plate
accompanied by this Certificate is an original Mettlach Limited Edition
created exclusively for the Mettlach Collectors Society and issued by
Villeroy & Boch.
The total edition of this plate is forever limited to the number produced
during the 1980 calendar year.
The plate is a reproduction of an original Mettlach plate issued in 1890,
designed by the distinguished 19th Century artist Heinrich Schlitt.
It has been produced in the exclusive Villeroy & Boch Chromolith incised
contour stoneware process.
"Snow White And The Seven Dwarfs" is the first plate ever issued by the
Mettlach Collectors Society. No future editions of this plate will be issued.

ISSUANCE DATE: May 31, 1980   CERTIFIED BY:
                                Wendelin von Boch, President
                                Mettlach Collectors Society

This *Certificate of Authenticity* helps reinforce the purchase of a collector plate
from Mettlach Collectors Society. It is shipped to the buyer along with the plate.

lectible, a warranty statement for an appliance, or a small flyer providing an interesting historical background on the product.

Creating Goodwill/Building Long-Term Loyalty

If the customer gets a bad taste in his or her mouth when the product
is delivered, your expensive front-end efforts may go right down the
drain when your follow-up selling efforts begin. Good will activities
take many forms, from the restatement of the guarantee to the maintenance of a helpful, knowledgeable customer-service staff. But here
are some ideas on what you can do to reinforce the customer's positive impression on the back end:

Don't make it difficult to return goods. Because clothing merchants traditionally have very high direct-response return rates, you might think they would shy away from telling customers directly how to send back unsuitable merchandise. But to get customers to buy something as personalized as sized clothing by mail, it is essential that they feel no obligation to keep an unsuitable item. Thus, sellers of clothing

A small *portfolio* is supplied to Hamilton Collection subscribers to a series of collector plates. This piece, printed on coated stock, holds certificates, flyers, and other materials that help reinforce the significance of this purchase.

have learned to make it easy for their customers to make a return or exchange. They may include a return-shipment label in the package or offer a step-by-step guide to returning the item. A simple form for the customer to fill out will also help, and enable you to find out the customer's reason for returning the item, which is valuable market research in the long run.

Provide a customer-service number, address, or both. Don't make the customer who has a problem hunt too hard to find you. He or she can shop with plenty of other direct marketers who are highly accessible and responsive, and therefore you will also have to be. The ultimate in customer service is a toll-free 800 number for such calls; however, many marketers find that it is much less costly to provide an 800 number for ordering only, and a regular, pay-call number for customer-service questions.

Give the customer a "thank you" gift or discount. With every order over $100, you might, as an example, provide a surprise thank-you gift tucked into the package with a note. Or include another offer in the package with a very special discount for preferred customers only.

Send a newsletter or other chatty correspondence. Make the customer feel like a preferred member of your "family" with a newsletter in the product package announcing special offers or discounts for preferred customers only. This may be a great way to clear out small-inventory items and please your customers at the same time.

It is essential that customers feel confident making purchases by mail. This *return goods form* from American Express® explains exactly how to return unsatisfactory items.

Provide "preferred-customers-only" benefits. These might include advance mailings when sales or special values are available; a special, extra-helpful telephone salesperson whom only your regular customers know is available; monthly discounts on various items available only to customers who are sent special coupons; quantity discounts; free gift wrapping; or some other "extra" that you offer and deliver only to persons on your present-customer list. Don't make the mistake of offering any of these extra services on the front end— at least not free or at the same discount your preferred people are getting. The service or item must be an exclusive, special-treatment one that makes customers want to continue being considered part of your firm's "in crowd."

Send a thank-you letter at year's end. Thanks are appreciated any time of year, but a letter to preferred customers on a yearly basis is a nice gesture. If you can computerize the letter so that it mentions items the customer purchased, so much the better. If you're a smaller firm, you may be able to do this without computerization. A thank-you gift for customers at certain purchase levels is a nice gesture too.

Achieving Better Margins on Sales

Unless you have a new or exceptionally popular direct mail product to sell, you may well have to invest money to gain a new customer on the front end. It is therefore important that your back-end efforts yield a profit from that customer as early as possible, so as to make your front-end efforts worthwhile.

This can be achieved via back-end efforts in a number of excellent ways. Here are some.

Sell an accessory. You've seen this gambit when you've bought an automobile: you make the deal on the car of your choice and may pay as little as $50 to $100 over the factory-invoice price. But ask to add a stereo radio or roof rack after the deal is struck, and the dealer will gain a hefty margin for that accessory. You can do the same on a direct mail sale, and much of your extra margin can come from your making the add-on sale right in the package you're sending to your customers. For instance, send them the personal radio with headphones they've ordered, and include an offer for a set of small speakers to go with it. The speaker offer "rides free" with the package, which you have to send to the customer anyway. The accessory item couldn't be offered to better prospects than customers with new stereo sets who are excited about this product concept. Convince even one-tenth of your stereo buyers to buy the speakers also and you'll make an appreciable move toward profitability with this new group of customers.

Sell more, or sell better quality items. This tactic is best used on items that are used up quickly. For instance, when you send the invoice for a magazine subscription, you can offer customers a bargain rate if they will pay for two years right away instead of one. If you're delivering custom stationery, offer the customer a special deal on a larger quantity re-order, or a better quality item.

Sell something else in the package. Even if you offer customers something totally unrelated to the item they have bought, you stand to do well if this second item is appealing. When you have just delivered the main item the customer wanted, the timing and atmosphere for such a second item are tops—your customer has a good feeling about your firm, and an offer of another item or items from your product line should be well received. Many direct marketers help pay another marketer's cost of shipping merchandise by buying package-insert space, on a per-thousand or per-sale basis, with the latter's shipped goods. One note of caution here: make sure the items being sold in your package are noncompetitive with your own merchandise, and that they do not damage your image with your customer. A good example of a package insert is one seen in Grolier's children's book club packages, offering a series of Mickey Mouse collector's plates. A poor example would be an offer for "seconds" on nylon panty-hose in a package delivering a $300 dress to an upmarket clothing-catalog customer.

Ask for referrals. Getting a referral from a current customer won't help the margin you make on sales to him or her, but it may gain you a new customer very inexpensively. In fact you might offer your current customers an incentive for referring potential new customers: record and book clubs give free merchandise to members who deliver friends or relatives as new, paying customers. Other firms use a lower key approach, not offering any incentive other than the opportunity to share a good buying source with a like-minded friend.

Ensuring Continued Sales to Customers

After the sale and delivery of a first package to a customer, you'll need a way to keep up communications and sales with him or her. You'll want to set up a schedule of mailings to the customers on your list to keep your name on their minds and—more importantly—to keep bringing in more and bigger sales from them.

The more complete the information you can record about each of your customers, the better the job you can do at targeting future promotions to them. Send high-ticket offers to high-ticket buyers, for instance, and book offers to previous book buyers. People who have bought collector's plates on the subject of sailing ships are good prospects both for future plate offers and for sailing-related merchandise.

Often you can help insure continued sales by means of the offer you make on the front end. Here are some front-end offers you can make to win ''guaranteed'' sales on a continuing basis.

Continuity series. Offer the first of a series of books, records, collector plates, food items, and so on on a front-end basis, with the promise of more to come in future mailings. You'll find that obligating customers to buy a number of items later on will probably cut

The friends, relatives, or business associates of your customers are likely to be good prospects for you. This *referral form* from The Hamilton Collection requests the name of someone who might be interested in the firm's products.

★ ★

Do you have a friend who may wish to know of this offering?
(Please fill in the coupon below and return it with your order.)

Name _____

Address _____

City _____ State _____ Zip _____

HC-338-X
9949

The Hamilton Collection
1 Charter Plaza, P.O. Box 2567, Jacksonville, FL 32203

the percentage of your original responses, but will also help avoid attrition as the program continues. Testing will help you determine whether a tight or loose continuity pitch brings you the most net dollars over the life of the program. A tight continuity pitch would explain very specifically to given customers that they are expected to purchase x number of items over a given period. A loose pitch would tell them of the existence of the additional items, but give them the option of continuing or not as they please. If you want to gain the greatest possible number of new customers but still have a continuity series over which to spread your cost of customer acquisition, try a loose front-end sale followed by a load-up offer, or a strong follow-up or "efforting" program on the back end.

A load-up offer. This comes after the customer has received the book, record, or other item he or she originally ordered. You offer the customer the opportunity to receive *all* of the books, records, or whatever you're selling in the series, but to pay for them in convenient monthly installments over a given period of time. This cuts your shipping costs, since you'll send all of the remaining items in a single shipment. If you opt for this system, provide your customers with a coupon book so that they can make their monthly payments easily, or send them a monthly invoice/reminder. Also, test the offer to make sure you aren't stuck with too many uncollectible accounts. For many book marketers and others in the business of continuity selling, however, the load-up technique works well.

An efforting program. This is another way to bring in additional sales from customers who were offered products on a continuity basis but with no obligation to buy. This is usually a multi-step correspondence plan. Here is how a typical efforting program might work:

1. With the original shipment, send the customer a selling letter, a small brochure with a picture of the next product, and an ordering device.
2. After several weeks, mail again to those who have not ordered the product. Send a different letter, the same or a different brochure or picture, and once again an ordering device.
3. After several more weeks, send a more urgent message to those who have not yet responded. A telegram format with a "last-chance" order form is a good bet.

Weekly Reader Books   1250 Fairwood Avenue, P.O. Box 16556, Columbus, Ohio 43216

**Get the expert advice you need to help
your child grow up right...
at a surprisingly low cost to you!**

Dear MRS. JONES,

Congratulations to you...MRS. JONES!
Your full set of READY-SET-GROW
books are enclosed for you and SHANNON
to read and enjoy!

As a concerned parent, you've proven that you want
to take an active role in helping SHANNON
succeed in life...and become a self-confident,
responsible person. I'm sure SHANNON
will thank you later for making this superb series
available -- right in your GRAND RAPIDS
home -- to use whenever your child wants to!

And in choosing READY-SET-GROW,
you demonstrate your awarness that SHANNON
needs the added advantages of this unique reference
to meet the challenges of growing up and learning
in the complex world of the 1980's.

Now that you have the full set in front of you, take
a few minutes to consider these special features...

. Each lively volume is packed with easy-to-follow
   help that is applied to everyday situations!

. You can use these books over and over as your
   child grows and matures!

(over, please)

to all of childhood's
-- right at your
fingertips -- at times when SHANNON
needs them most!

. The bouncy, colorful illustrations and short,
   snappy examples make these books fun to read!

. And...you get practical, step-by-step solutions
   to difficult parenting problems!

There's no risk to you, MRS. JONES!

The enclosed 18 volumes are sent to you strictly on
approval! If you are not satisfied, you may return
them within 15 days at our expense (via 4th-class
book rate) and owe nothing!

If you decide to keep them, MRS. JONES,
you may pay in convenient monthly installments --
while your child enjoys the entire set in your
home -- at the same low price of just $4.95
each, plus shipping, handling and sales tax. And,
as a preferred customer, you'll never have to pay
a finance charge for the privilege of paying in
installments.

In addition, you will also be entitled to receive
future READY-SET-GROW volumes as they are developed,
to keep your set up-to-date.

So, please take a moment now to examine these books
and to share them with SHANNON!

Sincerely,

William R. Tynan
Publisher

P.S. Remember -- You are entitled to examine these
     books for 15 full days -- absolutely FREE!

180

The number of mailings in your efforting program will depend on their relative effectiveness and the price of the item you're selling. A high-ticket item may still yield acceptable results with a fourth or even a fifth effort, while a low-end product may merit only one or two efforts.

Negative option. Many book and record clubs are run on a negative-option basis: customers agree to receive the monthly selection unless they make the effort to return a card with an alternate purchase, or direct the club to send nothing at all this month. This is a proven way to gain new customers and make them pay over a given period. Customers are brought in under a "Four-Books-for-$1" type of offer, with the direct marketer making an investment to gain the customer's name and his or her promise to make future purchases. The customer agrees to buy x number of books over a given period and also has the option to buy a number of other items via monthly mailings. The key here is to learn by testing how loose or tight the front-end offer must be to yield acceptable sales per customer in the long run.

Ship-' til-forbid. This is the ultimate in a continuity series: the customer gives the direct marketer the right to continue shipping products on a monthly, bimonthly, or other basis unless the customer expressly tells the marketer to cease. This can be a smooth way of obtaining nearly guaranteed sales, especially if customers provide their charge-card numbers so that the marketer simply ships the product at regular intervals and puts the charge on the customer's account. Another option is to ship the item with an invoice enclosed or sent separately; but here the marketer must keep careful records to make sure an acceptable number of items are paid for before additional shipments are made.

In the case of all of these offers for ensuring continued sales, it is important to make sure that the offer and follow-up sales information are carefully worded. The services of an experienced direct mail copywriter, followed by a careful reading by a lawyer with experience in direct mail, will avoid problems later.

Weekly Reader Books uses the *load-up* technique, sending an entire set of books with this explanatory letter and asking for monthly payments to complete the sale.

Pay for Necessary Mailings with "Ride-Along" Offers

Whenever you send an invoice or other communication to a customer, why not include some type of offer to help pay for the mailing? The premium-due notices of insurance companies, for instance, often include stuffers offering information about other policies. An invoice on a continuity program could have a brochure of seasonal merchandise "riding along" with it. Customer-service notices, order acknowledgements, and other correspondence often allow space for a selling message within the one-ounce limit for the lowest rate on first-class mail.

Collection Letters

A well-written series of collection letters is a "necessity of life" for many direct marketers who send out merchandise before it is paid for. This "back-end" function is often neglected, put off, or given half-attention, when it can be taken care of very simply.

Direct your copywriter to create a series of collection letters for you, beginning with a gentle reminder and building to a "last chance" notice promising to turn the matter over to a collection agency. Depending upon the dollar amounts involved, your collection series might range from two letters to six or more. Include an invoice and a Business Reply Envelope with each letter. But don't spend too much time and effort on this function. Engage the services of a good collection agency and *do* turn over delinquent accounts if your own efforts don't yield results within a reasonable period. It's not wise for you to write harsh or threatening letters to customers who may once again become valued buyers at a later date.

If you wish to put together your own collection series, check one of the standard business-letter reference books for ideas.

Gaining Renewals for Periodicals and Clubs

The big money in selling periodicals or club concepts by direct response is in renewals. The $12 or $25 paid the first time around is unlikely to cover both the cost of obtaining the name of a customer and a year's order-fulfillment activities. For each additional year for which the customer can be persuaded to remain a reader or club mem-

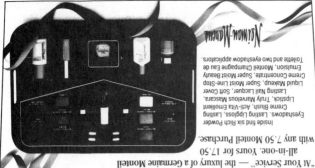

"At Your Service" — the luxury of a Germaine Monteil all-in-one. Yours for 7.50 with any 7.50 Monteil Purchase.

Inside find six Rich Powder Eyeshadows, Lasting Lipgloss, Lasting Creme Blush, Acti-Vita Emollient Lipstick, Truly Marvelous Mascara, Lasting Nail Lacquer, Soft Cover Liquid Makeup, Super Moist Line-Stop Creme Concentrate, Super Moist Beauty Emulsion, Monteil Champagne Eau de Toilette and two eyeshadow applicators.

M _____

_____

PLACE
STAMP
HERE

Neiman-Marcus

P.O. BOX 2142
DALLAS, TEXAS 75262

Please send me "At Your Service" with the following Monteil purchases:

___a. Truly Marvelous Mascara 8.50.
___ 1a Black Brown___2a Black
___b. Super Moist Beauty Emulsion, 2-oz. 1
___c. Super Moist Line Stop Creme Concentr 1-oz. 17.50.
___d. Rewiance, 1.8-oz. 65.00.
___e. Perfect Texture Powder (Sheer Moonlig 12.50.
___f. Super Moist Night Creme, 1¼-oz. 17.0
___g. Galore Cologne Spray Concentrate, 2-o 16.00.
___h. Monteil Champagne Eau de Toilette Sp 1.7-oz. 16.50.
___j. Galore Milk Bath, 8-oz. 12.00.
___k. Royal Secret Cologne Spray concentrat 2-oz. 15.00.
___m. Royal Secret Luxury Lotion, 8-oz. 15.0

___ Check
___ Charge to my N-M account num

□□□□ □□□□ □

Name_____
Address_____
City_____ State_____ Zip._____

In our N-M delivery areas of Dallas, Fort Worth, and Houston there is a 1.50 charge per delivery. For all other orders, please add 2.50 for each item ordered. Please add applicable tax on all merchandise delivered into the following states: Arizona, California, Florida, Georgia, Illinois, Missouri, Nevada, New York, Texas, Washington, D.C.

Germain Monteil available in the following N-M locations: Dallas, Fort Worth, Houston and Chicago.

ORDER TOLL FREE (Neiman-Marcus credit card purchases only in continental U.S. dial 1-800-NEIMANS. Place calls from 8.00 a.m. to 8.00 p.m. CDT Monday through Saturday. For inquiries on orders already placed dial 1-800-322-INFO.

MOISTEN AND SEAL

Please enter your N-M account number on your check and return with the top portion of the statement.

□ *Please check here if change of address*
N-M account number: □□□□ □□□□ □
Name_____
Address_____
City_____ State_____ Zip._____
New telephone number:_____

184

ber, the profit of dealing with him or her improves. Thus it is wo
while to prepare and implement an aggressive subscription or m
bership renewal program—one with four, six, or even eight step
all.

Most renewal series begin several months before the renewal d
with a special incentive for renewing early. This might be a disco
a premium, or several free issues of a record or publication. On
other hand, some marketers hold off on special offers until later
series because they have found that a good percentage of their
tomers will respond to a straight offer right away. The marketer
therefore save the more costly offers for the purpose of convin
the less eager segments of their customer lists to respond.

Over the series of mailings, a number of formats may be u
Here are some.

- A simple, double postcard with a tear-off half for the
  tomer to return by business reply mail. All the customer
  has to do is check off "Yes," and he or she will be bille
  the subscription or membership.
- A telegram-type letter warning that the customer may
  valuable issues or membership benefits unless he or sh
  sponds in time.
- A traditional envelope mailing with a feature/benefit l
  brochure, premium slip, and reply card.
- A contest offer, giving those who respond either "yes
  "no" an equal opportunity to win. (Human nature tell
  customer that he'll have a better chance of winning if he
  "yes," even though by law this isn't the case.)
- An "action device" tipped into the letter, such as a st
  that looks like the cover of the magazine, to be transfer
  the order form and sent back with the order.
- For membership pitches, a temporary membership
  which the customer can keep until the permanent card i
  after the customer sends in the renewal.

RETAIL BACK-END MARKETING

A great many examples of consumer back-end marketing me
can be applied to retail situations. However, several back-en
mats have very specific applications for retailers.

Statement Stuffers

Long ago, retailers realized that it was a waste of valuable postage to send out monthly statements alone when they could "stuff" them with solicitations for more merchandise at the same postage cost.

Most retailers with charge accounts use some sort of statement stuffer plan, whether this employs specially prepared pieces done by the retailer, offers prepared by vendors and stamped with the retailer's name, or syndicated merchandise offers for which the retailer will obtain a royalty based on sales.

Statement stuffers can generate store traffic, sell off small quantities of items left in stock, or amplify sales for a high-volume item such as nylon stockings. The retailer using statement stuffers for the first time will want to keep close track of sales (both in-store and via coupon and telephone) of the items offered, to make sure that the cost of the stuffer is justified by additional sales. But considering that most statement stuffers are small and simple in format (albeit with four-color illustration), they are likely to result in extra sales and profit.

Bangtail Envelopes

The bangtail envelope is a very efficient form of statement stuffer. It serves a double purpose, incorporating the Business Reply Envelope for return of the customer's invoice as well as a tear-off "bangtail" which serves as a solicitation and order form for additional merchandise. Weighing only slightly more than a Business Reply Envelope alone, the bangtail makes excellent use of space. What's more, since customers are very likely to take advantage of the postpaid Business Reply Envelope in returning their payments, it is virtually certain that they will at least glance at the offer being made.

Some bangtails have a simple, removable flap with a very small copy space and picture area, while others have double flaps with plenty of space for explanatory copy and ordering information. Ask your printer or envelope supplier for samples of bangtail formats.

Retailers often utilize *bangtail envelopes* in billings to charge customers. This bangtail sells a beauty kit on one side and provides an order form on the other.

Bangtail envelopes are also an excellent way for vendors or syndicators to promote merchandise via your statement program.

Package Inserts

Once a customer has purchased from you, you will want to bounce back another offer to take advantage of the customer's new allegiance to you. A current catalog that you can insert in the package makes an excellent bounce-back. Even if the customer has already seen it, a fresh copy may spur an additional or repeat purchase. Merchandise similar to what the customer bought is another good bet. Or you can supply a coupon for x amount off the customer's next purchase from the catalog or another merchandise selection as a "thank you." Seasonal bounce-backs are another good idea: Christmas offers in the fall, and for Mother's Day and Easter in the spring, for example.

Co-op Mailings

If your business is part of a shopping center, you may wish to work with other stores and services to create a joint mailing highlighting special events, telling of holiday special sales, "cross-pollinating," such as by offering a free dessert at the center's restaurant with a purchase at the sporting goods store, and so on. This can spread mailing costs among a group of retailers and bring in more traffic and goodwill for all of you.

Reactivating Dormant Charge Accounts

Those charge-account customers on your rolls who haven't purchased in six months or a year or more may just need a little push to get back into the store and start buying again. Send them a letter with a "we've missed you" theme and a premium offer if they'll visit the store or make a charge purchase. Some offers simply ask the customer to stop by at a store's credit office to pick up some premium, figuring that that is enough to get the customer back on the premises and buying. Others require the customer to present proof of a new charge purchase to receive the free gift.

BUSINESS-TO-BUSINESS BACK-END MARKETING

Many of the consumer back-end concepts apply to business-to-business marketers as well, and a reading of that section is therefore a good "idea starter" for the following discussion. But here are a few other concepts that apply specifically to the business/industrial community.

Converting leads. In a great number of business situations, leads are converted by personal sales, although some rather high-ticket items may be sold in a two-step routine. The personal-computer example described in the section on consumer back-end marketing (see pp. 170–71) is an example of a complete conversion series on a high-ticket item.

Maintaining an image. Business and industrial sellers may take advantage of available space on package inserts and invoice stuffers with communications that create and maintain a positive image for their firm. One way to do this is with a chatty newsletter that serves both company employees and customers. The newsletter might contain information about the firm's recent activities and promotions, focus on the functions of a different department each issue, and so forth. General-interest feature material could also be included, as well as how-to articles related to the firm's field of endeavor.

Large business and industrial marketers who underwrite television programs and sports events might stuff their customer correspondence with reminders to watch upcoming shows under their firm's sponsorship. Local businesses that sponsor parades, sports teams, regional television shows, and the like can take advantage of this same stuffer concept.

Another "image builder" is the suggestion-box idea, asking customers to return requests, criticism, ideas, and other data along with their monthly payments.

Selling affinity products. Careful segmentation may help business and industrial marketers approach current customers with further products that make special sense to each type of buyer. Among such products are accessory items for equipment the customer already owns. Replacement parts, service contracts, service check-ups, and free audits of existing systems are other possibilities.

SECTION III

16

THE MATHEMATICS OF DIRECT MARKETING

One of the most attractive aspects of direct response marketing is the efficiency the marketer gains in evaluating each advertising expenditure against specific profit objectives. This enables the marketer to run each promotion as a separate business entity. If the results of a promotion are good, the marketer can invest more cash in the product line to achieve greater profitability. If the results are poor, the executive can cut losses by phasing out a product line. It is, therefore, absolutely essential to understand the basic mathematical tools required for assessing results and subsequently making the proper decisions.

ESTABLISH REALISTIC FINANCIAL CRITERIA

To begin with the obvious, it is important to classify the revenues and costs and to establish the profit-margin criteria for a promotion. You must make realistic assumptions about your net sales, cost of goods, and overhead to make sure that your marketing expectations are realistic and that you are controlling each promotion properly. To provide an example of this, let's assume that Jack Kramer is starting a new gourmet-products catalog and has used the following assumptions as a basis for determining the profitability of this new venture:

188

Gross sales	103%
Less returns and cancellations	3%
Net sales	100%
Cost of goods sold	46%
Overbuy reserve	1%
Advertising expense	35%
Overhead	10%
Pretax profit	8%

By buying merchandise and making advertising expenditures against this financial model, Mr. Kramer can assess each promotion and determine if the business is on target. We strongly recommend constructing a model of this type before launching a promotion. If the proposed offer does not seem viable, perhaps it deserves to be rethought or discarded. As you may recall from your economics classes, the classical definition of break-even is the point at which marginal revenues equal marginal costs. For example, suppose you are selling for $30 a diamond pendant, costing $10, and that you have an advertising budget of $10,000. A simple formula for computing the number of orders you need to break even would be:

$$\frac{\text{Total advertising expenditure}}{\text{Unit contribution before advertising}}$$

Your break-even would be 500 orders for the campaign. Net sales of $15,000 would let you recover the $5,000 cost of your goods and your $10,000 spent in advertising. If your results exceed 500 orders, your profits increase incrementally. For example, if you sold 1,200 pendants, you would have made $14,000 in this campaign, or an average incremental profit of $20 per unit for every unit sold above the 500-unit break-even figure. It is essential that you understand this concept and apply it to each campaign.

UTILIZING ASSESSMENT TOOLS

Now is the time to focus on the various tools you can use for assessing each of your promotion campaigns. One of these, the *profit per response* or PPR method, is a simple way of rating the profitability of responses. To determine the PPR, deduct your advertising costs, cost of your goods, and overhead from your net sales and divide the proceeds by the total number of responses. This is particularly useful for assessing the relative profitability of sales made through selected media and from lists with cost variances.

Return on investment is probably one of the most common standards for evaluating the results of a mailing. Here you simply divide the profit per response by the dollars you have invested to produce the profit. This will give you the percentage return on your investment.

For *contribution* as a percentage of sales, deduct C of G S (cost of goods sold), and advertising cost, including lists or media from net sales.

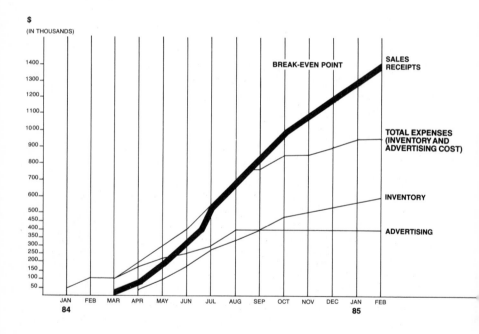

CASH FLOW CHART

These assessment tools will help you establish the appropriate criteria for each of your promotions. They are simple and provide the basic guidelines for the small to medium-sized company with limited cash resources. Larger organizations with greater financial resources may extend these criteria to include the relative value of new customers both for additional new purchases and for list rentals.

ADHERE TO ROLLOUT ANALYSIS

One of the most common mistakes made when assessing marketing test results is the failure to compare apples with apples. Your current control package may cost $300 per thousand while your test package costs $420 per thousand. Assuming that your sales are the same, many people would assume that staying with the control package would be the better decision. However, only after computing the rollout cost of your test package and comparing with the control package can you be sure you are making the correct comparisons. Also make sure that your creative costs (photography, separations, and so on) are deducted to assure an accurate comparison.

DEVELOP PROFIT-AND-LOSS CRITERIA
FOR EACH PROMOTION

After you have established the criteria for each of your promotions and understand how to analyze each, you should develop a profit statement for each. The following is a sample worksheet:

Profit-and-Loss Worksheet

	Unit	No. of Units	Total
Sales price	$30.00	1,000	$30,000
Shipping and handling			1,750
Gross sales			31,750
Less returns and allowances (3.3%)			1,052
Net sales			30,694
Cost of goods sold	7.00	1,000	7,000
Advertising cost	10.00	1,000	10,000
Gross margin			$13,694

Overhead charges:

Order processing charges	4.00	1,000	$4,000
Credit-card charge @ 3%	.90	1,000	900
Shipping and handling	1.50	1,000	1,500
Bad debt @ 4%	1.20	1,000	1,200
Returns and cancellations	.30	1,000	300
Overhead allocation	.30	1,000	3,000
			10,900
Pretax tax operating income			$3,594

By applying the principles presented in this chapter, you will be able to assess the initial feasibility of various offers, rate their performance relative to the financial criteria of your organization, and ultimately forecast sales and profitability upon rollout.

17

WORKING WITH AGENCIES AND DOING IN-HOUSE STAFFING FOR DIRECT RESPONSE PROMOTIONS

The saga of the direct response genius who "did it all"— developed products, wrote about them, selected media, and managed the business as well—is a romantic one indeed. In a few cases, it is true. There *are* some very smart, very dedicated people with a flair for marketing and writing that matches their business sense: men and women who have "taught themselves the business" and can handle or supervise every part of a direct response operation with a minimum of outside help.

Joe Sugarman of JS&A, for instance, is said to write all his own copy and to have directed every important aspect of his company's development. The husband-and-wife team, Donna and Claude Jeanloz, from *Renovator's Supply*, a firm that sells home-improvement materials by catalog, is another example of such success. And every once in a while some lucky person who starts in his or her garage or back room will come up with a good product, read everything he or she can find about direct marketing techniques, start out with a few small space ads, and build up a thriving business, "learning by doing."

Even many direct marketers in large companies retain a special "hands-on" interest in their firms' direct marketing efforts. One company president we know looks forward to the absences of his very competent vice-president of direct response marketing. The president used to hold that job, and he enjoys having a legitimate reason to "get his hands dirty" with day-to-day marketing tasks from time to time.

193

However, it is only realistic to note that eventually, the direct response marketer will need some outside help, even if only on an irregular basis. And if you are planning to run a large direct response program alone, or to do some direct response advertising in addition to carrying other business responsibilities, you may find outside help necessary from the very beginning.

The array of direct response service options can be confusing to the novice. Should you hire a consultant or a full-service agency? Should the agency work on a project basis or should you discuss a retainer? Should you plan to do most work in-house or farm it out as needed? Should you use your agency for creative work only or allow it to coordinate entire mailings and media campaigns for you? There is no one right answer. In this chapter we will weigh the pros and cons of the various options and give you some guidance on how to obtain the help you need at a cost you can afford.

IF YOU'VE DECIDED TO GO IT ALONE

Teaching yourself the "ropes" of direct response marketing is a challenging task, but not an impossible one. If you are alone and starting from scratch, you might consider learning by trial and error. You needn't just "stab into the dark," though. There are sources of information and help. This book and those listed in the Appendix should be your first sources of information. You'll learn hard-won facts about what works in direct response marketing and what doesn't: how to find products, select media, write ads, develop order-processing and shipping systems, "trade up" your customers and keep them buying, and so on.

Most people who go this route start with one product, and contract for some small space ads to sell it "off the kitchen table." As the business grows they may expand into direct mail testing, and eventually go to a catalog and other more costly and sophisticated methods of selling. Attending seminars, trading experiences with direct response professionals, and reading trade publications as well as books may help such a person—if he or she is also smart and lucky—to build a lucrative and successful business.

However, most firms and individuals who hope to grow smoothly and quickly in the direct response field feel more confident with expert help from the very beginning; and that's where this advice on working with consultants, agencies, or an in-house staff comes in.

WORKING WITH A CONSULTANT

When you have a fledgling direct response operation, you may be frustrated to learn that the agencies you approach are not interested in your business. Unless you can promise a sizeable retainer, even a medium-sized agency may find your account too "iffy" or too small to handle. In this case, a consultant or one-person agency may be your best bet, at least to start.

Many direct marketing consultants have a specialty, such as copy, production, or account work; and an overall understanding of the field that permits them to provide you with marketing guidance and sources for all of the other services you will need, including creative, list-distribution, color-separation, print-production, mailing, and fulfillment services.

The plus side of such a consultancy relationship is that you will be able to work on a project-by-project basis with little or no commitment to a monthly retainer. The minus side is that without the glue of an agency structure, your consultant will have to be a strong and detail-minded individual to keep all the independent contractors involved in your account working smoothly, effectively, and on time.

Another plus for using consultants is that you may hire one to create a marketing or feasibility plan with no further strings attached. An individual consultant can do this—without having the overhead worries of an agency—partly for his or her own profit and partly with an eye toward future business from you.

But don't "hook up" with the first consultant you meet or see advertised in a trade publication or speaking at a convention. Ask for references, and check them carefully. Find out if the consultant has experience with your particular type of product or with similar products. Get an idea of the consultant's fee structure. Find out whether the consultant marks up the outside services he or she would help you acquire—and how much extra you'd be paying for the consultant's coordination services. Try a sample job, much as you would with a first-time copywriter: a small marketing-concept assignment, perhaps, or the creation and placement of a single ad in several publications. If all goes well, you can develop a close business relationship with a good consultant that serves your needs for years of growth.

IF YOU WANT TO WORK WITH AN AGENCY

The array of direct marketing agencies, boutiques, and copy/art teams may be confusing. Your best defense against confusion is to approach any new agency relationship with your homework done and with an understanding of what you want the agency to do and what and how you expect to pay for it.

Check out "networking" opportunities at trade organization functions, and comb trade publications for leads on agencies you'll want to talk to. Once you've found some good sources of information, learn all you can about the prospective agency and its past work, and about its payment record and specialties and reputation, before approaching the account-services manager to express your interest in discussing an association.

Why Work with an Agency?

There are several reasons why you may decide to work with an advertising agency for your direct marketing efforts. Among these are:

- *Overall help and guidance.* With an agency you can assume the role of manager and supervisor of your campaigns, and delegate a great deal of creative and administrative work without giving up the decision-making function.
- *Direct marketing experience.* Even if you are somewhat seasoned in direct marketing, you probably don't have the broad background that the staff of an agency can offer you, including knowledge about what works and what doesn't, and experience in getting mailings, ads, and other promotions done on time and effectively.
- *Unbiased feedback.* The agency is an outsider, with the ability to give you a fresh view of your objectives, your product, your promotions, and your results. You don't have to work in a vacuum or rely strictly on the opinions of your own staff.
- *A constant idea supply.* Assuming you have found a good agency, you won't be stuck in a rut in terms of your product or promotions. The stimulation of seeing what works and

what "bombs" for other clients will keep your agency alive to new possibilities for you.

The Other Side of the Agency Coin

Despite the unquestionable "pros," you owe it to yourself to examine the "con" side of the ledger before you sign on with an agency. Here are some of the negative aspects of working with a direct response agency:

- *Expense.* The bigger the agency, the bigger its overhead. Whether you use them or not, you'll be helping to support the agency's media department, production staff, and other facilities. So think hard about going with a full-service agency unless you need all or most of its services.
- *Ongoing costs.* Most direct response agencies want to work on a retainer basis only; very few will do more than a single introductory job on a project basis. This makes sense from the agencies' viewpoint, since the time and energy they must invest to win a new client and learn his or her business is quite large. But you must ask yourself if your business is year-round and constant enough to justify the payment of a monthly retainer. Perhaps you'd be better off calling in a consultant or "one-person agency" when you need help, with no strings attached.
- *The education process.* If your product, proposition, or way of doing business are quite complex, you may be better off training people to do your direct response work for you—at least the marketing planning and creative work—on an "in-house" basis. With an agency you run the risk of getting the agency copywriter "where you want him" in terms of product knowledge of your product, and suddenly having him transferred to another client or account group.
- *Your size/their size.* Perhaps you've read about some of the agency "giants" of the direct response field and would like to have them work for you. If you're a division of a Fortune 500 company with a sizeable budget, you may have no problem getting this. But if you're beginning with more enthusi-

asm than money, you may have a problem finding even a small agency that's willing to gamble the time it will take to help you get your "iffy" (to them) program off the ground.

How Advertising Agencies Are Paid

As you may know, the concept of the advertising agency grew out of the space brokerage business, in which an agent bought space from a publication and resold it to advertisers for a commission. These agents added services over the years to make their space more enticing to their clients, and eventually the modern advertising-agency structure evolved. As a result of this historical pattern, many advertising agencies still receive a commission on the sale of space, time, and other media units. The traditional commission is 15 percent. The client pays the agency the full charge for a given ad, and the agency then pays the publication, television station, or other medium the space or time fee less the 15 percent commission.

Today, this traditional system is under challenge in many quarters, with many agencies abandoning it completely to work on a fee basis. It is especially unworkable in the case of industrial accounts, where thousands of dollars' worth of work may go into the creation of a very impressive ad campaign that is run in trade publications with very small circulations—and thus with low ad rates that yield tiny commissions for the agency.

The commission system is especially unworkable for direct marketers, whose stocks-in-trade are direct mailings and small space (low commission) ads. As a direct marketer, you should work out a payment structure with your agency that includes fees for services rendered. Any space commissions will be considered when fees are set, but are unlikely to be sufficient to compensate for the volume of service the agency provides in its other areas. In addition, you will be paying a mark-up on the outside services your agency contracts in your behalf. The standard mark-up is 17.65 percent.

And if you set up an in-house operation, don't automatically assume that you can "pocket" the 15 percent agency commission. Publications differ in the stringency of their policies, but you may find that unless you use an outside media-placement service, your "agency" will not be recognized as eligible to receive the commissions since you own it.

Types of Agencies

It will help you in evaluating possible agency candidates to understand a few of the types of advertising agencies that may be able to
help with your direct response efforts.

The full-service direct response agency. There are several of these
firms in Chicago, New York, and other large cities, but if you're in
a smaller locale, you may also be lucky enough to find one near you.
However, the big names in the direct response field serve clients all
over the map, so don't let distance itself be a stumbling block in your
quest for an agency. A full-service agency provides a broad range of
services, and if this is not a *complete* range, the agency most often
can contract for the type of extra work you need. The full array of
direct marketing services includes:

- Marketing research and planning
- Account service
- Product development, planning, and packaging
- Merchandising (i.e., for catalogs)
- Art and layouts
- Copy
- Media planning and placement
- List planning and brokerage
- Print, television, and radio production
- Publicity
- Sales promotion
- Analysis of results and forecasting
- Telephone marketing
- Related services (Point-of-purchase, collateral literature,
  etc.)

The modular or à la carte agency. This agency is distinguished from
the full-service agency in that the client may opt for certain services
while not taking advantage of others. Thus, the client may have his
or her own source for the creation of ads, but need help with media
placement. It is up to the client to determine if this is an effective and
economical way to proceed, considering that a modular agency offering a full-service array must carry the overhead for these services

whether they are used or not. The client should compare the cost of hiring an agency to do piecemeal work with the cost of hiring someone to do it in-house or hiring a service which specializes in media, lists, or whatever help is desired.

Creative boutiques. This term is most often associated with traditional advertising, but the direct response field also has boutique-type firms that offer strictly creative help. The boutique may be so small and simple as to comprise only a copywriter who has "hooked up" with an art director to present both copy and layouts to clients or the boutique may go so far as to present camera-ready art or a finished direct response TV spot while playing no administrative role. Such a service may be ideal for the direct marketer who prefers to handle his or her own business functions (such as media placement, mailings, planning, and results analysis) in-house but does not wish to keep high-priced creative talent on the payroll.

Collateral services. Some direct marketers hand their programs over to a full-service agency that handles all the details of list selection, merge/purge, production, mailing, media buying, and so on. They believe that the mark-up they pay for in using an agency is offset by the coordinative help the agency provides. But the direct response marketer also has the option to "pick and choose" the services he or she wants an agency to provide, and can also elect to deal on a one-to-one basis with collateral services such as media buying firms, printers, research organizations, telephone marketing firms, list brokers, lettershops, computer firms, and many more.

What Type of Agency Is Your Best Bet?

As we have already mentioned, many a small direct marketer would like to stride into one of the ten biggest direct response agencies and sign on as a client. But considering that such agencies most often quote minimum monthly retainers in the $10,000-to-$20,000-or-more range, many direct marketers—and especially smaller ones—must find alternative help.

If you need a full array of services but are not large enough to require this on a monthly basis, seek out a smaller full-service agency with direct response experience. If your business is seasonal, or if you work in definite "on again, off again" cycles, look for an agency that will work with you on a project-by-project basis. (As a rule of thumb, the smaller the agency the more likely it will consider this type of arrangement.)

If you have some staff to cover administrative and business functions, or to place ads in the media or write copy, look for à la carte services or collateral firms to fill in your missing needs, and consider coordinating your own overall program. Many larger direct marketers do just this, hiring a creative boutique or freelance help to put together a mailing or other campaign for them, and then planning and coordinating the campaign in-house. If this sounds appealing but you don't currently have the in-house staff for it, consider hiring an experienced direct marketer to join your staff and implement such a program for you. This person (and his or her staff, if more than one employee is needed) can also serve as liaison to the agency or outside-service organizations you use. See the section of this chapter on in-house agencies for more on this.

Working with the Agency

Once you have located a direct response agency that seems suited to your needs, you must set up a working relationship with it. No two client-agency relationships are exactly alike, but the following are some general guidelines that will help you keep your agency well informed:

Make your goals clear. Explain what you expect from the agency and what you hope to achieve from the campaign it's undertaking for you.

Agree on time frames. Try not to cry "Wolf!" when you don't have to meet an overnight deadline. You will usually be gratified when you give your agency enough time to fulfill your requests. Then, when you do have a crisis, it will be treated as such, and not as just another "client panic call."

Keep an open mind. Part of the fee you're paying your agency is to have its personnel be creative for you. If all you want is someone who follows your commands, you may be better off buying your services piecemeal. Listen to your agency's ideas and alternative plans. The agency may be more objective than you are, and its experience with a range of similar and different clients allows it to offer you a fresh outlook.

Make the agency part of your team. A little bit of "them-and-us" feeling is natural when working with an agency, since it is a separate firm from yours. But the more your agency account person feels part of your team, the more he or she can do for you. To help foster this relationship, you should share background material freely with your agency personnel, kick ideas around with them, and explain your hopes and fears without putting on an overly optimistic "front" all the time. If you fear the vulnerability of sharing so freely with your agency, you may have the wrong agency! Confidentiality is a hallmark of a good, successful direct marketing service.

Discuss the best division of labor. If you have some in-house staff, you may not wish to have your agency use all of its possible services for you. But discuss this with the agency so that there is no duplication of effort. A failure to communicate could result in frustration for your staffers and an inflated agency bill for you.

Be frank about money matters. When you evaluate an agency, one of your concerns will be to determine whether it pays its bills on time, since it may well buy services in your name, pay for them itself, and then bill them to you, along with its own agency fees and mark-ups. And since the agency will also be concerned about your payment policies, it's smart to be "up front" about your terms, and to live up to them. This is especially true if you are a small or new client whom the agency is accepting on a speculative basis so as to help you explore your possibilities. Many agencies will agree to somewhat liberal payment terms if they are confident of being paid within the time limit of an advance agreement.

THE IN-HOUSE AGENCY

A number of direct marketers, large and small, prefer to develop an in-house staff to handle all or most of their promotional needs. The reasons for this seldom revolve around saving money, although this may be a consideration for smaller firms whose personnel can serve double duty as direct marketing administrators while also handling other aspects of the business.

An in-house agency is one that is owned by the advertiser. Its functions are quite similar to those of an outside advertising agency, and the job titles at an in-house agency may be quite similar to those at independent advertising firms. However, the account-executive function will probably be handled by a *project manager*. The project manager acts in a rather entrepreneurial way, with responsibility for the profit or loss of his or her own programs and the implementation of all parts of a direct marketing plan. He or she works with creative people, media planners and placement people, list experts, printers, and other specialists, any of whom may be either in-house or with an outside vendor.

If yours is a small or fledgling operation, you (or a person hired by you) may serve as project manager, media-placement administrator, mailing expeditor, and in any number of other functions. As your firm grows, you may add more project managers, service people, or both to your staff.

There are three main "pluses" of in-house agencies. They are:

The in-house agency can develop experts and keep them. If the product is complex or the method of selling unique, it may be easier for a firm to develop its own talent than to teach its business over and over again to outsiders.

Work can be turned around quickly. Since the in-house agency seldom has clients other than its parent firm and possibly including various divisions of the firm, it can meet the firm's advertising priorities on a daily basis. Often an outside agency can get away with longer lead times simply because the advertiser is not fully aware of the mechanics of getting a job done. With the in-house agency, these mechanics are much more open to scrutiny, and built-in contingency time is therefore harder to obtain.

The advertiser has more control. For an in-house agency, company philosophies are easier to get across and keep in mind. There is more day-to-day supervision of the agency's work, and more give-and-take between the agency and the advertiser's personnel.

There are, however, some harsh critics of the in-house agency concept. Here are a few of their negative comments:

Work from an in-house agency tends to lose freshness. Lacking the stimulation of people working on a variety of accounts, and who see different ways of marketing succeed on a daily basis, the in-house agency may turn out less innovative work than outsiders would.

The firm with an in-house agency takes on a good deal of overhead. Rather than treating advertising help as an expense, the in-house agency owner must pay advertising support costs as part of the regular corporate payroll. He or she must be sure that this continuing cost of doing business will be warranted by the results.

Bureaucratic or inner-directed thinking. The in-house agency is usually much less sales oriented than an outside agency would be. It is not so much a vendor as a service department, and may be categorized as such along with the data-processing, customer-service, fulfillment, and other departments. Thus it tends to be more "inner directed," and concerned with office politics and corporate problems than with finding the best way to interest the consumer in buying a product.

THE EVOLUTION PROCESS

As your direct marketing business grows, you may find that your way of handling the consultant/agency/in-house question changes. Perhaps your small, rather unexciting account has grown to the point where top agencies are calling you for the opportunity to pitch your account. Or maybe you've come across a person with all the qualifications to set up and run an in-house agency for you, and all of a sudden the concept seems workable, where it didn't before.

The best advice is to keep an open mind and periodically re-evaluate your situation to make sure your way of producing advertising is really the best way for your current circumstances and prospects. With the wide array of options available to the direct marketer, it should be possible to implement any change once you're convinced that it will improve the quality and effectiveness of your direct marketing program.

18

SCHEDULING AND CRITICAL DATES FOR DIRECT MAIL AND SPACE

Success in direct marketing has much to do with proper timing. Seasonal and competitive factors are important, as is the phasing of tests and rollouts within your own program.

Sometimes the optimum promotional schedule is fairly straightforward, as in the case of a Christmas-theme product or an item tied to a national holiday or Super Bowl. And even when there is no obvious "season" for your product or service, the dynamics of the marketplace may make it better for you to mail or promote during some weeks or months than during others.

So before we present a way of scheduling your promotions so that they come out on time, we need to outline the timing factors that will help you choose dates for your mailings, ad insertions, and other direct marketing programs.

SEASONALITY

Direct Mail

General "rules of thumb" for the best and worst direct mail months are a helpful starting point for your efforts in the industry. But you must find out for yourself if January is truly the best month for you.

Take a look at the following chart, which was offered by direct marketing expert Bob Stone of Stone & Adler in his book, *Successful*

Direct Marketing Methods. This information was generated by a three-year test program for a non-seasonal item. You might try this yourself if you have a non-seasonal offer: mail the same number of direct mail kits to random groups from a homogeneous list at the beginning of each month of the year. Here is what happened in the test that Stone ran, where a rating of 100 is the top score:

Month	Rating
January	100.0
February	96.3
March	71.0
April	71.5
May	71.5
June	67.0
July	73.3
August	87.0
September	79.0
October	89.9
November	81.0
December	79.0

Reprinted with permission from *Successful Direct Marketing Methods* by Bob Stone, published by Crain Books, division of Crain Communications, Inc. Copyright © 1984 Bob Stone.

According to this study, June is the worst month for mailings, yielding only two-thirds as well as the "top" month of January. But if your offer is transitional such as women's clothing (e.g., summer/fall), June might be a fine month for you despite the "rule of thumb." And obviously, if your offer is Christmas-related you won't let the 79.0 in September or the 81.0 in November scare you away. Your firm's scores naturally will differ dramatically from the average for non-seasonal items.

If you are entering the test phase of a campaign, experts agree that you should run your first test in the strongest season for your product. You can then factor in the seasonality component for later tests simply by considering your best month's results as 100 percent and multiplying the new test-month rating by the number of orders in your best month figure for the number of orders in the new month. Here is an example, assuming the same number of pieces mailed to equal portions of a homogeneous list:

January rating:	100.00	January results:	90 orders
June rating:	67.00	Anticipated June results:	
		$(90 \times .67 =)$	60 orders

Business/Industrial Mailings

Although factors like the Christmas holidays and other "time off" (vacation) periods have some effect on business and industrial direct marketing schedules, the seasonality factor here depends much more upon the industry in question. School supplies sold to school districts have a demand based on the school calendar. And if you are mailing to landscapers, your prime time will differ dramatically from that of snowmobile parts suppliers. But if your seasonality factor isn't so obvious, some testing to determine what months spark better lead and sales responses with the same offer could provide you with profit-building information—or at least some explanation of what may be disturbing "slides" in response from time to time.

Periodicals

Non-seasonal propositions for magazines and newspapers do best when not pitted against the heavy ad schedules that ordinarily exist at holiday time. Also, advertising readership is down in the summer, or at least attention levels suffer at this time, because many people are on vacation. So the best times for direct response space advertising are generally January through the beginning of spring and Labor Day through Thanksgiving.

If you're selling summer products, of course, you mustn't take this warning too seriously. You can begin testing in the early spring to determine your own "response curve" by month or week. And if your product is Christmas-related, you may safely promote up until the time when you cannot promise delivery by Christmas (or—and perhaps more importantly—until the time when your consumer no longer *believes* you can deliver, even if you know you can).

THE CRITICAL DATE SCHEDULE

The first step in establishing a schedule for any direct response medium is to *determine the optimum date for the message to reach the prospect.* In direct mail, for instance, it is not enough to schedule only up to the date your message is mailed. If you are doing a bulk mailing, it may take as much as 10 days or more before all of your prospects receive the piece you've mailed. And in space advertising, don't take the cover date of a publication as a "given" for the arrival of the publication at the prospect's door; check out the delivery date specifically, and then choose the proper issue for the impact you seek. Then work back from the optimum delivery date to determine a schedule that will accomplish your goal. You may still be able to make a date that seems uncomfortably close, but only with a firm schedule and much vigilance. Following are some of the checklist factors in critical-date schedules for direct mail and space advertising.

Direct Mail

There are as many direct mail critical date schedules as there are firms in the business, and very little agreement about how long it takes to get certain things done. Where there are many parties involved, and a computerized letter operation is being used, a direct mail program may require a six-month schedule. On the other hand, firms whose approval processes are swift and whose suppliers are accommodating may be able to take a mailing campaign from the concept stage to the prospect's hands in a matter of a few weeks.

Naturally, each link in the "chain" of such an operation considers his or her timing needs to be paramount. A prototype schedule from a printer, for instance, allows a month for printing but only three days for copywriting. You can imagine that the writer's schedule would be quite different. We will therefore list the factors important in a mail-campaign schedule, in the basic order in which they are done. You can adjust these as needed to determine a workable schedule for your own campaign.

Critical Date Factors

1. Approve marketing plan
2. Create rough layouts and copy (this is often necessary for list owners to approve rentals to you)
3. Select and order lists (obtaining the lists for a campaign takes several weeks, and a merge/purge may take a week or longer to complete)
4. Obtain price quotes for color separations, printing, lettershop work, and other necessary production services; award jobs to vendors; make vendors aware of time schedules so they can make available the proper amount of time for your job
5. Approve rough layouts and copy, and proceed to comprehensive layouts and final copy
6. Order envelopes; in most cases they take longer to produce than other printed materials (three weeks or more)
7. Arrange for photography and have product shots and other necessary photography completed
8. Approve final layouts and copy and proceed to typesetting, keylining and paste-up
9. Receive lists from broker and expedite merge/purge operation so that it can be completed in time for lettershop work
10. Approve keylined boards and send four-color work to separator
11. Approve color separations by means of chromalin or press proofs
12. Send boards and separations to printer(s)
13. Approve blueline proofs from printer(s)
14. Supervise press approvals at printer(s)
15. Send mailing instructions to lettershop, including list of all materials that will be delivered to the shop
16. Expedite folding and binding of printed pieces
17. Coordinate arrival of envelopes, printed pieces, and labels (product of list merge/purge operation) at lettershop
18. Expedite lettershop work (labeling, materials insertion and mailing)
19. Ascertain exact mail date (national penetration will be approximately 10 days later)

Space

The critical-date schedule for a space-advertising campaign is simpler than for a direct mail campaign in that there is no involvement with printers, lettershops or lists. However, a space advertising campaign has the added factor of your having to meet a publication's closing dates for space reservations and materials, which vary by publication. Check the consumer or business *Standard Rate and Data Services (SRDS)* books for magazines to determine these dates for publications in which you wish to place ads. There you will also find the specifications for the types of boards or film each publication needs, so that you can direct your production people accordingly. For newspaper ads, *SRDS* has a newspaper rate and data book that provides the same helpful information.

19

POSTAL AND LETTERSHOP
COORDINATION

One of the most important practical considerations for any direct mailer is the timely distribution of promotional material to its proper destination. Additionally, the mailer must receive return mail promptly—often, as a customer service, at his or her own expense. To achieve this, careful planning, coordination, and communication with both the post office and the lettershop are crucial. Your local post office and the lettershop of your choice should be able to give invaluable information about the mailings that you have planned.

THE POST OFFICE

The U.S. Postal Service recognizes direct mailers as a huge and growing market, and one that it can serve by allowing and encouraging a wide variety of acceptable formats and mailing rates. On the other hand, direct mailers must observe a very specific set of postal rules and regulations.

One of the most valuable relationships for any direct mailer is an ongoing communication with the post office or bulk mail center from which most of his or her mailings will take place. Your postmaster has printed "how to" materials that will save you considerable time in creating mailing pieces. What's more, it is essential that you understand exactly how your local postmaster enforces certain regulations that may be open to various interpretations. It goes without saying that a cordial relationship with your postmaster may be very helpful if a critical matter ever comes up.

Most experienced direct marketers can recount at least one tale of post office woe. One of these involved an insurance marketer who prepared a direct mail kit which, according to his scale, weighed a shade under the basic maximum weight for a bulk rate mailing (currently 3.87 ounces). More than a million kits were printed and prepared at the lettershop before it was discovered that according to the post office scale, the kit weighed a shade *over* the maximum bulk-weight weight. With many thousands of dollars in extra postage due, the marketer decided to open the envelopes and trim each piece in the kit. All of this could have been avoided if a dummy kit had been carefully prepared and weighed on the "ultimate scale" at the post office in the first place!

The moral of this story is: If in doubt, ask your postmaster. A few minutes spent on the phone or in a face-to-face visit may save you a great deal of money and time.

Mailing Classes

Postage rates and regulations change frequently, and therefore the most specific advice this book can provide is that you obtain current rate charts and regulatory materials from your post office. There are several frequently used direct mail classes of which you should be aware:

First-class mail. The simplest to use but most expensive, first class theoretically provides mail "penetration" to all parts of the continental United States within three days. There are no special sorting requirements, although mailers may obtain a discount for first-class mail sorted in zip-code order. This is only practical when large quantities of mail are involved, since the cost of pre-sorting by zip code may outweigh the savings for small to medium quantities. The pre-sort option is often used by local department stores, banks, and other firms that have large numbers of customers in only a few zip codes. Discuss the feasibility of this option, for your situation, with the computer service that handles your list requirements.

Most direct mailers consider first-class mail too expensive for mass mailings. In the testing phase they may, because of its fast penetration, use first-class to provide quick answers about the viability of their offer; it carries more immediacy than bulk-rate mail and appears less like advertising to most consumers. First-class mail may well be used for mailings to existing customers, both for a prompt turnaround and because the volume of these customers' orders makes the more expensive mailing rate cost-effective.

Another reason for mailing first class, at least periodically, is to take advantage of automatic mail forwarding and the return of undeliverable mail to the sender. This is an inexpensive means of helping to keep your list clean.

Postcards. Currently, postcards not smaller than $3^1/2$ by 5 inches and not larger than $4^1/2$ by 6 inches are eligible for the special postcard rate. The cards must also be at least 0.007 inches thick. Because there are color regulations and maximum-thickness regulations as well, it is advisable to check with the post office if you plan to use a nonstandard postcard format.

Direct mailers use postcards for reminder mailings, traffic builders, and special events, or for straightforward one-item offers (especially fold-over postcards).

Third-class mail. Most direct mail is third-class mail. This category includes mailings at single-piece-rates and bulk mailings. Single-piece rates apply to mailings of less than 200 pieces or of less than 50 pounds. The real savings for mailers are to be had in third-class bulk-rate mailings, in which a piece weighing up to 3.87 ounces can be mailed for approximately one-half the first class rate for a one-ounce piece of mail.

A bulk mailing requires the mailer to acquire a bulk-rate permit at the post office where he or she will drop the mail. There is a fee involved. In addition, the mailer must present the mail in zip-code sequence, bundled or bagged according to post-office regulations. There are facing (labeling) requirements and other regulations to be followed in order to obtain the substantial bulk-rate savings. Your post office and your lettershop will be able to help you conform to proper bulk mail procedures and your postmaster can give you current rates and application information.

Even greater savings may be obtained by additional computer coding, which saves the post office time in sorting and distributing mail. The nine-digit zip-code (carrier-route code) system allows mailers to sort and bundle their mail down to the level of the individual mail carrier's route. Larger mailers often save money at the post office in this way, since their mail quantities are large enough, and their computer programs sophisticated enough even to computer-generate mailbag tags for carrier-route coding. Smaller mailers may well find the basic third-class bulk rate to be the most cost-effective, since additional sorting is most likely to involve considerable computer time and cost. To determine the right formula for your firm, compare the additional computer and lettershop costs of preparing your mail for carrier-route coding against the potential savings at the post office.

A further point about the bulk-mail permit is that you will need a separate permit for each town from which you mail, unless you qualify for and obtain a "universal indicia." If you mail or plan to mail from various locations, talk to your post office about obtaining such an indicia. It will save you money and time, and will allow you to preprint outer envelopes for use at any and all locations.

Nonprofit bulk rate. Nonprofit organizations may take advantage of additional savings when they prepare mail according to third-class bulk-rate regulations. A post-office bulk-rate fee must be paid. Check your post office for more details and information about whether your organization is eligible for these extra savings.

Business Reply Envelopes and Cards

Most tests show that mailers who pay return postage for their customers get a higher level of response than those who require the customer to pay his or her own postage. Because of this, most front-end mailings are accompanied by Business Reply Envelopes or Cards.

To qualify for this service, the mailer must obtain a First-Class Permit from the post office that will be receiving the incoming mail from customers. In addition, the mailer must provide postage money in the permit account to pay for incoming mail at first-class rates plus a service fee. It is essential to keep sufficient funds in this account; otherwise the mailer's incoming mail will be held until he or she has properly funded the account. Besides holding up the receipt of orders, having mail held in this manner destroys the mailer's ability to forecast on the basis of numbers of orders received each day.

Business Reply Envelopes and Cards must be prepared according to a special set of regulations. The accompanying sample shows the proper business reply format.

THE LETTERSHOP

Not so long ago, many lettershops were mainly "envelope stuffing services," with row upon row of individuals inserting materials into envelopes before mailing. In recent years, the science of preparing the mail has advanced at an astounding rate. Today most mailings are prepared so that all of the pieces may be inserted by machine and the envelopes labeled in zip-code sequence by machine, sealed, and bundled for mailing, all with a minimum of human intervention.

Some lettershops still provide hand-insertion services for mailings that are not machine-insertable, and there are still cost-effective services available for small mailers who do not need seven-station inserters and other sophisticated equipment. On the other hand, the range of lettershop services available to today's larger mailers is quite broad, and includes folding, collating, trimming, autotyping, laser printing, and many more.

There is a specific format for business reply mail that must be followed. See your post office or lettershop for more details.

To select your lettershop, do a bit of detective work. Ask for the recommendations of other mailers whose volume and type of mailings are similar to your own. Visit the booths of lettershop services at trade shows and read their literature to learn about their capacity, specialties, and extra services. Then select several lettershops and visit their premises personally. Here are some questions you may use as a basis of comparing different shops.

1. Did the lettershop seem to run smoothly? Were the offices neat and well organized?
2. How many machines were "down" during your visit? How many employees were standing around idle?
3. Did the machines run smoothly, and were there service people available to promptly fix any breakdowns?
4. Check the warehouse. Was the inventory stacked neatly? How clean was the warehouse area? Would your material have stayed there in mint condition until inserted?
5. Does the lettershop have a good relationship with the post office? Is there a postal official on site? If not, how far is the lettershop from the post office?
6. Did the lettershop provide you with a list of the things they need to know from you to make your mailing run smoothly: sources of material, insertion order, codes, and so on?

Working with the Lettershop

There are three things that are essential for any mailer who will be dealing directly with a lettershop. First, to provide materials that are in good condition and properly packed. Second, to provide a complete record of what will arrive at the lettershop and how it is to be prepared. Third, to keep in communication with the lettershop so as to make sure that things proceed in a timely manner. Here is more information about each piece of advice:

Provide materials in good condition. Your printer and computer house will probably provide materials directly to the lettershop according to your orders. Check with the lettershop for instructions about how they prefer to receive materials: how boxes should be labeled, the preferred sizes for cartons, how materials should be stacked, and so on. Improperly boxed and shipped material may become curled, damp, or otherwise uninsertable while in storage at the shop, and this extra care may therefore well yield you much in time and money saved.

The computer house may provide labels, tapes, or other materials to the lettershop. Since labels may be generated 1-up, 4-up (one or four in a row, respectively), or in any number of other configurations, you have to know the configuration your lettershop needs for smooth machine operation. Also make sure the computer house knows whether you want Cheshire labels, pressure-sensitive labels, or some other type of label to fit the lettershop's needs.

A form such as this from ARC Graphics in Novato, California will help provide your lettershop with the information it needs to insert and mail your packages.

```
                        aRCGraphics

          10 SHANKLIN COURT   NOVATO, CALIFORNIA 94947
                      MAILING INSTRUCTIONS
  _____
  CLIENT:_____   INSERTION ORDER NUMBER:_____

  MAIL DATE:_____   LETTERSHOP:_____

  JOB DESCRIPTION:_____
                  _____
                  _____
  LABELLING:         _____

                     _____
  TOTAL QUANTITY: _____
  LIST CODE   QUANTITY   | LIST CODE   QUANTITY   | LIST CODE   QUANTITY
  _____    _____   | _____    _____   | _____    _____
  _____    _____   | _____    _____   | _____    _____
  _____    _____   | _____    _____   | _____    _____
  _____    _____   | _____    _____   | _____    _____
  _____    _____   | _____    _____   | _____    _____

              MATERIALS:                          CODE:
              1._____   _____
              2._____   _____
              3._____   _____
              4._____   _____
              5._____   _____
              6._____   _____
  SPECIAL INSTRUCTIONS:
                 _____
                 _____
              Pull _____ production run samples and send to _____
              Advise _____ of exact counts by code within 48 hrs.
              POSTAGE AMOUNT DUE $_____.
  CLASS OF MAIL:  ___FIRST    ___SECOND    ___THIRD   ___BULK    ___FOURTH
  TYPE OF POSTAGE: __PERMIT    ___METER    ___PRE-CANCELLED STAMPS ___STAMPS

  AUTHORIZED SIGNATURE:_____   DATE:_____
```

If you are providing a computer tape of names, specify exactly what kind of computer tape to avoid any extra cost and time spent in transferring names from one format to another.

Provide proper documentation. The lettershop business requires precise attention to a number of tiny details. If you give your lettershop a letter or form which tells what they will be receiving, how it will be marked, where it will come from, and what to do with it, your mailing will be off to a good start. Here are formats that may help you provide documentation to your lettershop. One is a letter and the other is a form that may be filled in with information for each individual mailing.

Keep communicating. Your documentation will tell the lettershop what is to arrive and when; but if it does not arrive on time, do not trust the lettershop, no matter how efficient it seems, to let you know this. It is up to you to follow up on a daily basis and check with the lettershop to make sure things are proceeding smoothly. If they are not, *you* will have to prompt the printer, envelope company, computer house, or other source of a problem to get things back on schedule.

This is especially important because mail dates, for the most part, must remain firm. Your list rentals are protected only for a certain mail date, and you cannot make a casual decision to delay a mailing. The larger your firm grows and the more often you mail, the more essential prompt mailing will become.

20

LEGAL CONCERNS OF
THE DIRECT MARKETER

In this chapter we pinpoint areas of legal responsibility for the direct marketer that will often require consulting an attorney to help you make the right policy and operational decisions. We are not attorneys, and we can only give a brief overview of possible areas of legal concern. If you have any questions, be sure to seek competent legal advice.

FEDERAL TRADE COMMISSION MAIL-ORDER DELIVERY REQUIREMENTS

Whether you are an industrial, retail, or consumer marketer, there are several legal requirements that affect your promotional and fulfillment responsibilities.

First, your advertisements must be specific about a shipping date for the merchandise your customers order. If no shipping date is specified, the legal implication is that the merchandise will be shipped within thirty days. Therefore, if you cannot deliver within thirty days, it is essential that your advertising material (preferably your order device) clearly state your planned delivery time. Many direct marketers state "Please allow six weeks for delivery."

Second, regardless of how good you are at purchasing or production, you must be prepared to notify customers of unexpected late deliveries. Assume, for example, that your fall catalog has advertised delivery of a product within six weeks of your receipt of it, and that you suddenly learn that deliveries from your factory or vendor will be delayed by one month. You must notify each customer who is on back-order status of the delay, via first class mail, before the expiration of your original six-week commitment. Your notification should include a postpaid reply form for the buyer, offering the options of accepting the extension of the shipping date or requesting a refund. Cash refunds should be sent to the customer seven working days after a cancellation request, while credit-card adjustments should be posted within one billing cycle following your notification. This requirement is not only legally significant, it is absolutely essential to establishing an ongoing direct marketing business. Communication with your customers will maintain their confidence that you are aware of their order and will fulfill your commitment at the earliest possible moment.

YOUR WARRANTY OR GUARANTEE COMMITMENTS

Commitments on warranties and guarantees are usually more of a policy decision than a legal matter, unless you also are the manufacturer or you add value to an existing "core" product. However, competitive factors, rather than federal or state requirements, will often dictate the warranty and guarantee commitments you must make. Survey your competitors to determine what you should discuss with your attorney before making final decisions about warranties. Again, if you want to develop a customer franchise, recognizing that the better satisfied your customers are the more they will buy from you in the future, you should strive to develop liberal policies that reflect your interest in serving your customers' needs.

LEGAL REVIEW OF PROMOTIONAL COPY

Sometimes you, your copywriter, or your marketing manager may become overzealous in the effort to convince a prospect that the latest product or service is the greatest. You want to communicate enthusiasm but, at the same time, you must ensure that your promotional package and the included offers and claims adhere to appropriate legal guidelines. To do such, have all of your materials reviewed in their initial draft stage by your attorney to be sure that they meet the proper legal standards for TV, in print, or mail with promotions. For example, if you had decided to sell via direct response promotion a series of limited-edition prints honoring the 1984 Olympic Games without the endorsement of the U.S. Olympic Committee, you would have found upon legal review that there were severe copy limitations on the use of the phrase "Olympic Games," because the Olympic Committee has trademarked this usage. Without a licensing arrangement in such a case, a few casual references in your copy could result in an infringement suit. While this is perhaps an unusual circumstance, it clearly documents the rationale for reviewing all of your promotional copy before it is used.

CONDUCTING THE TRADEMARK SEARCH

Whether you are a new or an experienced marketer, make sure your attorney does a trademark search when you introduce new product lines, catalogs, or trade-names. This search is done to ensure that your newest addition does not conflict with an existing trademark or trade-name. This is often a complicated question which involves classifications of products and their formal registration. While you do not need to understand all of the legal ramifications of this, it is extremely important that you establish this procedure on a regular basis to avoid infringement problems.

PRODUCT LIABILITY CONCERNS

Beyond your obvious need to have product liability insurance, there are several common-sense things you can do to minimize your risks. First, make sure that you label your product, specifying its contents, any harmful components, and the directions to follow in case of any emergency. Second, issue an owners manual, care and handling brochure, or some other form of "how to use this product" instructional material. Make sure that you clearly state guidelines that will maximize benefits and minimize the risk of misunderstanding. Make sure your attorney carefully reviews these documents. Finally, your product must be packed properly. One direct marketer with twenty-five years of experience sold beautiful barometers. Once shipped, however, the barometers leaked mercury. The direct marketer received complaints from everywhere: United Parcel Service, the airlines, and most importantly, from his customers, who were furious. Had he taken time to test his packaging thoroughly, many problems could have been avoided. So give yourself time to test your packaging concept.

DISCUSS PROMOTION CONCEPTS WITH POSTAL AUTHORITIES

Your local postal officials can be invaluable in helping you to answer questions about a proposed promotion concept. If you're considering using an unusual size mailer, a colored Business Reply Envelope, or an innovative indicia, you should have the postal officials review a prototype to ensure that you are adhering to the various postal regulations before making production commitments. If your local officials cannot provide an answer, they will usually refer you to the appropriate postal officials in Washington, D.C.

MORE INFORMATION

For more information on legal concerns, contact your attorney or the Direct Marketing Association in New York City, which offers seminars and publications on the subject of legal matters affecting direct marketing.

21

ART/LAYOUT/DESIGN

Some direct marketers claim that "copy is king," but even they must admit that there is a big difference in reader perception between an ill-designed direct mail piece and a masterful job by an art director. Better to proclaim that the product is king and that both copywriters and art directors should work to enhance it, forsaking "art for art's sake." Selecting the right art director, giving him or her a proper input, and producing a well-designed direct marketing presentation are crucial ingredients in your overall success.

Just as it is beyond the scope of this book to teach you to become a copywriter, we won't attempt to make you an art director in "ten easy lessons." Rather, we'll give you some guidance in selecting and working with art directors, finding the other services you need to produce finished boards or film, and evaluating the work these people do for you. We will also give you some tips on good design and on prior planning which may save you time and money in the long run.

THE ART DIRECTOR

The term "art director" is one that people new to the advertising field find somewhat confusing. It sounds like a higher title than "copywriter," but it may describe any job from layout artist to vice president of an agency's creative division, depending on where it is used. Basically, the art director is the person who handles the visual side of the direct response creative process. He or she works with the copywriter, client, and account executives to determine the "direction" or "feel" of the graphic presentation of a promotion, creates or supervises the design of rough layouts, final layouts, and camera-ready boards, and in many cases assists with production all the way through printing—at least to the extent of attending photography sessions, critiquing color separations, and presiding at press approvals.

If your direct marketing efforts at this point will consist of a few small, black-and-white space ads, involving an art director may not yet be necessary. You may be well served simply by working with the publications in which you buy space, and having them typeset your copy and headings.

But if you plan to do anything more sophisticated than small print ads, the help of an art director will be well worth its cost in terms of appearance and possibly even money-saving shortcuts. The following sections give some ideas on finding and working with art directors.

Who Will Your Art Director Be?

If you are working with a direct response agency, your art director will be assigned to you. In fact, you may never see your art director. The art director's work may be brought to you by the account executive, along with that of your "invisible" copywriter.

Suggest to your agency that at least once, however, your art director would benefit from a face-to-face meeting with you, on your premises. This will give the art director a valuable "feel" for the sights and atmosphere of your business—experience that will help him or her convey your message visually. What's more, this will give you an opportunity to become a living, breathing person whom the art director is working with: not just "the client," well hidden by layers of account executives.

If you have opted to hire your own outside talent, you'll want to read the section in the following chapter on selecting a copywriter. This will give you some specific ideas on how to locate, meet, test, and evaluate a creative person, whether he or she is a copywriter or an art director.

If you have already located a good copywriter, he or she may be your best source for an art director, for two reasons. First, if the copywriter's work is pleasing to you, you are likely to be impressed by the work of an art director whom he or she recommends. Second, if the copywriter is used to working with this art director, their "rapport" may well work in your favor.

In many cases, copywriters and art directors may be as much "natural adversaries" as cats and dogs. The copywriter fights for another paragraph of copy space and complains that the art director "really didn't try" to arrange for the location shots that would have been perfect for a particular brochure. The art director complains about long copy (anything over thirty words) and insists on breaking up a block of type that needs to be read in sequence because it "looks better" that way.

But if the copywriter and art director respect each other's work and understand how much each can do to make the other "look good," their cooperative efforts will be a joy to behold. The art director may suggest the headline while the copywriter sifts through background colors to find the best complement to your product, the art director offers more copy space to explain a sticky point while the copywriter sits down with a blue pencil to edit an over-long subhead. True, this is an ideal, but if you work with a copywriter who knows and recommends a certain art director, by all means give that art director a try.

Another source for your art direction may be an art studio, which may or may not function as a full advertising agency. Some art studios are merely alliances of artists so that they can share overhead costs, while others are much more complex and may include account executives who act as liaisons between you and the artist. Such a studio may be quite helpful if you have more money than time, because it probably will be able to handle your job from thumbnail layouts to rough layouts and printing. But if you want a more "hands-on" approach, or if you fear the overhead costs associated with such a full-service studio, look to the individual freelance art director for help.

A very inexpensive and surprisingly viable alternative for art direction for your work is a local art school. This could be especially good if you are just getting started and have more time than money. Your program could become a class or individual student project, with your layouts and boards created under the guidance of an experienced professional teacher. Of course, the quality of artwork varies among schools and students, so try this alternative only after you have checked the students' previous samples. Also, allow plenty of time in case your student art director "misses the boat." This route carries a lot of "ifs," but we wouldn't even mention it if it hadn't proven highly effective for scores of small businesses and nonprofit organizations.

What Does Your Art Director Need to Know?

Once again, check chapter 22 for the kinds of information your creative sources will find beneficial. If you're working with a copy/art team, your copywriter may be able to share what he or she has learned from you when meeting with the art director. But if you're bringing two creative sources together, try to arrange for a three-way meeting among you, the copywriter, and the art director. This will give you the opportunity to observe the "chemistry" between these two important creative people. And you'll only have to go through your "song and dance" once to provide them with input.

Your art director does need to know some things that are not directly related to copy. You'll want to discuss with him or her the sizes and types of materials you want to have created, whether small space ads, direct mail kits with certain components, or other pieces. You may want to wait for this phase of the meeting until you and the copywriter have agreed on the copywriter's rough layouts, but assuming good rapport among the three of you, the art director's input at this point can be most helpful. For instance, he or she may be able to steer you and the copywriter away from brochure sizes that do not utilize paper to best advantage. If you're looking for a "Wild West" look, the art director may be able to suggest papers, colors, and typefaces that will get the theme started for you. And if you're planning a space ad campaign, the artist may be able to help you plan a few "modular" ad sizes that will fit most all publications without undue revisions.

Put together a file of the competitive samples and copy which you admire for your art director, just as you will do for your copywriter. Sit down with the art director and go through some of these samples, pointing out the typefaces, papers, color combinations, and "looks" that you prefer. Give the art director full information about the "corporate image" that your firm already projects and which must be adhered to. If there is not yet such an "image," consider asking the art director to create an "image package," including a letterhead, outer envelope, business cards, logo, and so on, so that you present a consistent image to the public in all your mail and advertising correspondence.

Let your art director know how far you expect him or her to take the project before getting back to you: thumbnail layouts (small, preliminary sketches), rough layouts (which are usually actual size), or comprehensive layouts (which are complete as to color, typesize, headline and photo placement, and other elements). Discuss price, whether by the hour or by the job. If by the hour, ask for an estimate of the hours needed to complete the job, so that you have some idea of the amount you'll be paying. And don't forget to discuss timing: let the art director know the deadline for layouts and for finished boards, if you wish him or her to go that far.

THE BASICS OF ART, LAYOUT, AND DESIGN

To be an intelligent consumer of graphic services, there are certain "basics" that you will need to know. Here is an outline of these basics, and guidelines for evaluating the work that is presented to you.

The Steps in the Creation of an Ad or Brochure

From thumbnail layout to camera-ready boards, your ad or brochure will go through various processes beginning with tiny sketches and progressing through rough layouts and comprehensives to the final boards or keylines. As the layout progresses, your art director will select typefaces, arrange for photography or the creation of drawings to accent the layout, and determine the colors and processes that will be used for a particular piece of work. Once these decisions have been made and type has been set and approved, the keylines will be created, approved, and turned over to the people responsible for separations, film, and printing. These production functions will be discussed in the chapter on printing and production, but here we will "zero in" on the stages from layout through final boards.

The Layout Process

There are several distinct layout stages, and in many cases you and your art director will progress from one to the next without skipping over any. However, it is quite common to skip directly from thumbnail to comprehensive layouts if the art director and client trust each other and the job is fairly straightforward. This is also necessary when timing prohibits an extra step. It is never advisable to skip directly from a thumbnail layout to camera-ready art, however, or even from rough layouts to boards. The comprehensive layout is the "road map" for the typesetter and for the keyliner, and its importance should not be underestimated.

Thumbnail layouts. You, your art director, or your copywriter may create thumbnail layouts. These small sketches indicate the general shape and proportion of the piece being created, and the placement of basic elements such as headlines, photographs, borders, boxes, and so on. Thumbnails are valuable because they give the parties involved something to look at and evaluate, beyond a verbal description of how the layout should be done. Because they are small and rough, they allow everyone to explore many different ideas without an undue investment of time.

Rough layouts. Sometimes called "pencil roughs," these layouts are done to actual size, but are not exacting as to color, type sizes, photograph and drawing sizes, and so forth. They help everyone involved to visualize the finished product, the "flow" of the material, and the impact of an ad or brochure of that size. They may incorporate actual headings and subheads, if possible, since this again helps in the evaluation of flow and effectiveness. Roughs may be done by the copywriter or by the artist, or as a cooperative effort for presentation to the client.

Comprehensive layouts. Just as its name implies, the comprehensive layout or "comp" covers all the bases. It indicates color areas and suggests the colors that will be used, exact copy areas, the sizes of headings and of photos, where borders will appear, and so on. The art director will often attach color samples to such a layout to indicate background hues, and he or she may indicate type sizes right on the layout. The "comp" serves not only to help the client and artist visualize the final product, but also as a "blueprint" for the keyliner.

Keylines or camera-ready art. Also called "boards" or "mechanicals," keylines are the final layout step in preparing for offset printing. Basically, a keyline is piece of white art board on which the exact size of a brochure or ad is drawn up in blue pencil. Light blue pencil is not picked up in the offset reproduction process, and thus will not show up on the final product. Using a T-square, ruler, or both, the paste-up artist puts all type, borders, photos, and drawings in place on the keyline board with rubber cement. On an overlay, colors to be printed other than black are so indicated, and a sample of these extra colors is attached for the printer's use. If the piece is to be done by a four-color process, boards are sent to the separator along with color transparencies of the photos to be separated. If it is to become an advertisement for a magazine, the art director must proceed to create what the magazine requires in terms of screens, color work, and other elements. The best two sources for a magazine's requirements are the advertising space representative and *Standard Rate and Data Service.*

Evaluating Layouts

When your art director presents you with comprehensive layouts or even fairly well-done roughs, it is up to you to evaluate them. Here are a few guidelines that will help even a novice take a constructive look at layouts as they are presented:

Is the product the star? Even experienced art directors occasionally get carried away with typefaces, background colors, or special-effect shots that are gratifying to work on but in fact do very little to enhance a product. When evaluating the layout, ask yourself whether the product is the star or whether it is buried in "art for art's sake." Ways to "star" the product include showing it as large as possible, depicting it in use, and giving it a flattering background that conjures up positive associations.

What is the point of the layout? Try to look at the layout as a customer would. What is it that the art director is trying to get across? The main focus or point of the ad should be your product's prime features and benefits. What's more, the layout also needs reworking if you cannot quickly discern a point from it. A layout that tries to cover all points equally is destined to confuse or turn off the reader. Remember that your prospect is likely to give your piece only a few seconds' glance before deciding whether to read on. Does this layout have a "grabber" of a point that will encourage the reader's involvement?

Does the layout look inviting and readable? Some printed pieces are so busy or so poorly typeset that reading them is literally hurtful to the eyes. Others are open, airy, and inviting. To make sure that your layouts are of the latter kind, check to see if your headings and body copy are large enough to be readable. Make sure there are no stumbling blocks to the flow of the copy, such as a two-column picture that breaks up a body of related copy for no important reason. Even though long copy is one characteristic of direct response pieces, make sure that the copy area does not look like a "sea of small print." See that the artist breaks up the copy with subheads, small illustrations, and so on.

How does a space-ad layout look in its editorial environment? Take your comprehensive layout and place it randomly in the publication in which it will run. Does it seem to blend into the background, or is it a stand-out? Being a standout is of course more desirable, but the ad should shine because of its superiority and not because it seems incongruous in a specific publication. Ways to make an ad stand out include:

- Running a short ad reversed in white out of black in a publication that has lots of black-on-white ads (be careful with this, as too much reverse copy is difficult to read)
- Running a long-copy, editorial format ad in a publication that carries mostly big picture/short copy ads
- Running a big picture/short copy ad in a publication that normally features editorial ads
- Using a bind-in card that pops up between the pages instead of a clip-out coupon
- Running a full-color ad in a publication where this is a rarity

How does a direct mail piece look in a dummy kit? Looking at an unfolded layout is one thing, but seeing the piece as it will appear when folded for an envelope—and actually inserting it along with a letter and order form in the envelope—is a very valuable exercise. You can perceive the kit as your recipient will, and you may catch the little problems that may go unnoticed until it's too late: an order form that does not fit easily into a Business Reply Envelope, or a brochure that is too bulky when folded down for a #10 envelope.

In this same context, always fold down a brochure layout as it will appear when mailed, to be sure that the recipient's first view of the brochure is an appealing one. You wouldn't want the fold to cut your main headline in half, for instance.

Your dummy kit also serves two other purposes. First, because you create it with paper of the same weights and sizes that will go into the real kit, you can determine the weight of your kit to make sure it falls within the postal category you seek (one ounce or less for first-class mail; 3.87 ounces or less for the bulk rate on the lowest rate schedule). Second, the dummy kit helps you to get proper quotes from your printer and lettershop. Your print salesperson and lettershop representative may also be able to point out cost savings on the basis of your dummy—slight modifications that will cut your paper costs or make inserting and labeling less expensive.

Is the layout in a standard size, or is there a good reason for custom sizing? Sometimes a product calls for special treatment: an odd-sized outer envelope to give the kit a European look, for instance, or an ad that runs in three parts, diagonally down and across the magazine page, to create reader interest. But unless such a special effect is part of your stated plan, you'll probably want to stick with standard sizes for envelopes, brochures, letters, and ads. This will save you money and time and allow you to take advantage of stock envelopes and standard printing configurations. Standard sizing is discussed further in chapter 23, on print production.

Is the use of color and bleeds appropriate for this job? Since the first color ad ran in 1937, the conventional wisdom has held that color is superior to black-and-white when it comes to readership and impact. The 1967 Daniel Starch (an advertising research company) "noted" scores show that in magazines, half-page color ads are almost twice as often noted as half-page black-and-white ads. Yet in some cases, a full-color treatment just isn't necessary. Compare the selling of ladies' dresses by mail, for instance, with the promotion of men's white underwear. In the first case, color is almost a necessity. In the second, it may be a luxury. And in some instances, a black-and-white presentation may make an even bigger impact than full color (see the Edward Marshall Boehm ballet figurines brochure in the accompanying illustration).The white bisque product is presented most dramatically through black-and-white photography: the firm decided to spend its money on superior photography and an oversized brochure rather than on color separations and four-color printing.

You needn't go all the way from black-and-white to a full-color process to make an extra impact, either. By the addition of another, accent color, or by printing in a second dark color besides black on a light-colored stock, you can achieve a multicolored look at a lower cost than with full color. Work with your layout artist to find the color treatment that enhances your product best, while keeping you within your budget.

Bleeds, in which the color "runs off the page" instead of stopping at a white border, can offer a luxury look or a special impact. But because bleeds are more expensive than non-bleeds in printing (they require more paper for trimming), it is worth questioning the need for them when your layout artist presents it. You might have your printed piece quoted for bleed and non-bleed prices, or you can check a mag-

azine's rates for bleed versus non-bleed rates, to make sure the extra cost is justified in your mind.

Some other nuts-and-bolts considerations for layouts. Ask yourself whether a layout presents the personality and tone you imagined for it: casual, sophisticated, elegant, family-oriented, hard-sell, or whatever. Are the color combinations pleasing? Does the presentation make your product or service easy to order (with an accessible coupon at the lower right of the ad, or an order form that fits well into a Business Reply Envelope for example). Put the layout away for a day if you can afford the time, and then approach it as if you were a prospect. Is it pleasing and effective? If not, go back to the drawing board with your layout artist.

What You Need to Know about Type and Typesetting

Your layout artist will take care of the type specifications and selection for your work, but it will pay you to be an "informed consumer." In some cases the artist may unwittingly select a typeface that conjures up the wrong association for your product or company, or which is hard to read or just not pleasing. And if you're a real "hands-on" direct marketer, you may find yourself reading proof galleys for a job well before you see the final boards. The following hints will help you deal effectively with the question of type.

Type styles. Serif typefaces are those that have fine lines at the top, bottom, and corners, while sans serif faces are plain and modern in appearance. Serif faces are easier to read in long copy blocks, and give a more traditional appearance. Some studies also show that serif faces lend more credibility to a presentation. Sans serif faces give a contemporary look and are easy enough to read in all but extremely long-copy, small-type situations.

There are hundreds of different type styles, some used with great frequency and others reserved for special applications. Use the specialty typefaces with care: they are not familiar to your reader and may "put him off." A good rule is to use that Oriental-look typeface or the Circus-style one for headings and perhaps for subheads, but to use a more traditional face for body copy. Another good rule is not to use a specialty typeface unless there is a good reason for it, such as an Oriental typeface for headings about a new Japanese garment line.

You may wish to select a typeface that reflects your corporate iden- tity, or you may mix typestyles depending upon the product you're selling. But don't use more than one or two typestyles at a time unless you're in the care of an experienced typographer with a good "track record" at such mix-and-match routines. Otherwise the results may be a confusing mish-mash.

With a given typeface, you have the option of using regular type, a bold (darker and thicker) version, or a light version. There are also italic versions of most faces. And of course you have the option of using all capital letters, although this cuts readership if used for copy of any length.

Type sizes. Type sizes are expressed in "points." Generally, it is considered difficult to read any type smaller than 8-point, although in a small-type publication like *TV Guide* you might be able to get away with 6- or 7-point type. The type sizes for promotional body copy range from 6-point to about 14-point, depending on the overall size of the piece and the impression you wish to make. Headings and subheads generally range from about 12-point up to 48-point or even 72-point type.

Youngsters and senior citizens may not admit it, but it is best to user larger type when approaching them. And for any reader, the leading between lines as well as proper word spacing are necessary for easy readership. Leading is the spacing between lines of type; the larger the type, the more leading is necessary for good appearance and readability. With one point of leading added, an 8-point type for- mat would be expressed as "8 on 9" or "9 on 10," where the second number refers to the leading. If type is set "solid" with no leading, this is expressed as "8 on 8" or "9 on 9." Several points of leading might be added to 14-point copy.

Reading proof. You or your layout artist and copywriter will need to check a "reader proof" of your promotion piece for the accuracy and fit of all of its elements. The artist will have specified typefaces and sizes which, when typeset, should fit into the layout he or she has created. The first question when the proof is presented, then, is "Does it fit?" If not, the layout may be revised or the copy cut, or some combination of the two. Any such changes should reflect co- operation between the layout artist and copywriter so that the final product does not suffer.

SERIF TYPE:
abcdefghijklmnopqrstuvwxyz

SAN SERIF TYPE:
abcdefghijklmnopqrstuvwxyz

1 POINT LEADING:
Language is a systematic means of communicating ideas or feelings by the use of conventionalized signs, sounds, gestures, or marks having understood meanings.

2 POINTS LEADING:
Language is a systematic means of communicating ideas or feelings by the use of conventionalized signs, sounds, gestures, or marks having understood meanings.

6 POINT:
abcdefghijklmnopqrstuvwxyz

9 POINT:
abcdefghijklmnopqrstuvwxyz

12 POINT:
abcdefghijklmnopqrstuvwxyz

20 POINT:
abcdefghijklmnopqrstuvwxyz

30 POINT:
abcdefghijklmnopqrs

48 POINT:
abcdefghijklm

72 POINT:
abcdefgh

Assuming that the copy fits, you will check the proof for any broken or fuzzy type, as well as for spelling, "breaks" from line to line, word spacing, proper leading, and overall readability. Make sure that any columns of type are not too wide for easy reading, or paragraphs too long. Then proofread everything again carefully when it is presented on boards, and have a "disinterested party" read the proof as well, if you can. You may get "too close" to the project to see the errors.

Saving money on typesetting. Make sure your art director checks around for the prices on typesetting; the cost range is phenomenal, especially in large cities like New York or Chicago. One way to economize, and enhance your presentation at the same time, is to use regular typewriter type for your selling letters. Such letters are more credible than typeset letters, and can be typed up by your own secretary (be sure you get perfect copy, of course) or spun out on a word processor, then keylined into position on a board. Another cost-saving move is to have the publication in which you're advertising set your space ads, assuming the copy and layout are simple enough that you can trust the publication's judgment.

What You Need to Know about Photography and Art

Just as color generally gets more attention than black-and-white, photography gets more attention than drawings. Thus, if you can afford it, and if photography fits into your promotional scheme, add one or more photos to your layout plan, preferably of the product itself or of someone using it.

Selecting a photographer is similar to selecting a copywriter or layout artist: ask for referrals, check the work of the photographers you're referred to, and even check the Yellow Pages if necessary. Talk with each photographer to try and establish a rapport and see if he or she has a "feel" for your merchandise and what you're trying to achieve.

Make sure your photography setup conveys the proper image. Your models should not merely be pretty or handsome, but should be of the age and lifestyle-look that your customers will relate to. The surroundings for your product shot are also important. You wouldn't show power tools in a game room, for instance; you'd set them up in an "ideal home shop" to which your customer could aspire.

Don't give up on the idea of "product in use" illustrations if you're selling an intangible service like insurance. Your "in use" shot can show a happy, secure family or a person receiving a check in the mail while recuperating in the hospital. It doesn't have to be merely a "mug shot" of the insurance policy.

When photography is presented to you, make sure that the shots will "work" in the size you're using. An 8-by-10-inch print, for example, comes across very differently than a two-column product shot in an ad. If cropping is to be done, check it carefully to make sure the composition of the photo is not destroyed. Check all product shots very carefully at every stage for fidelity to your product: remember that this is the customer's entire perception of your product, and that if it's bright red in the picture, it had better be bright red when it's delivered!

Rely on your art director for help in this very important area, but do try to develop a sense of color and composition so that you are evaluating photography on the basis of more than your "gut reaction." Talk with your art director about what he or she looks for in photography, and start a clip file of pleasing ad shots. These self-teaching tools will help you develop a flair for what works and what is appealing.

If the cost of professional, custom photography is beyond your budget, consider sources for free photography that has already been done. This probably won't apply for your product or product-in-use shots, but you can get a wide variety good general shots free from the U.S. Government, just for the asking. Try trade organizations, Chambers of Commerce, and other sources of free photos that may suit your needs. You can find stock photo services in the Yellow Pages of any good-sized city, and these organizations will supply you with photos to suit many purposes at a fee which should be considerably less than for comparable custom photography.

Sometimes photography doesn't suit your purpose, or it isn't possible to shoot the visuals you'd like to put forth for your prospective customer. In this case you might commission illustrations or line drawings to enhance your layout. Your layout artist may also be an illustrator, and if not he or she can probably recommend one. In addition, you may want to subscribe to a "clip art" service—a firm that supplies you with a steady stream of non-copyrighted artwork that you can use to illustrate your pieces as you see fit.

22

COPY/WORKING WITH
COPYWRITERS

One of the most dangerous mistakes a fledgling direct marketer can make is to try to become an "overnight expert" in various specialties such as copy, art direction, telephone scripting, lists, or space placement. This is often done in the hope of saving money, but is more likely to lead to costly mistakes.

What seems perfectly logical to you as a business person or traditional marketer/advertiser may well prove totally contrary to the hard-won direct response test experience your agency or freelance copywriter can provide you with. On the other hand, leaving your copy totally to the "pros" isn't advisable either. You need to know what makes good selling copy and how to work fruitfully with your copywriter(s).

Therefore, this chapter will not attempt to teach you "how to write winning direct response copy in 10 easy lessons." Rather it will give you sound advice on selecting the right copywriter(s), giving them proper input and direction, and evaluating and critiquing their work. Further, it will provide some of the basic "shoulds" for direct marketing copy, so that you will have some basis for evaluating copy and making revisions in it.

To begin with, many new direct marketing clients feel that some of the tried and true "tricks of the trade" recommended by copywriters are unworthy of their consideration. "Nobody would ever believe that I hand-wrote a note on every letter I sent out, so don't try that technique with my direct mail letter," is one often-heard protest.

But whether the customer believes that the phrase is handwritten or not, the special note may well draw attention to the point being made, and that handwritten blurb or P.S. may well be worth a test on your next direct mail letter no matter how "upscale" the audience.

Other proven techniques which new direct marketers may mistakenly seek to avoid, with an eye to making their presentations "classy," are action devices, envelope teasers, "folksy-friendly" letters, and hard-selling response television copy in the style of the classic "Veg-a-matic" commercials.

WHO WILL WRITE YOUR COPY?

If you elect to retain a direct marketing agency, your copywriter or writers will probably be assigned to you. Some agencies try to keep their copywriters hidden from view; you may be expected to deal only with an account executive who relays information back and forth to the writer for you. If at all possible, do not accept this arrangement. The closer your copywriter is to the "scene of the action," the more he or she understands the sights, smells, and excitement of your business, the better job that person will do for you. What's more, it only stands to reason that second-hand information will be interpreted or "watered down." For these and other reasons, it is important to get that copywriter into your presence, preferably on your own turf.

If you do not hire a direct marketing agency, but have instead chosen to subcontract for various services, you'll have to find your own copywriter (or do the writing yourself, which we do not advise for those without an advertising-writing background). If you already have a list broker or art director whom you trust, you can ask them to refer you to copywriters. You might also discuss your requirements with colleagues who do direct marketing, to see if they know a freelancer who might suit your needs. Checking the classified ads in publications like *Direct Marketing* or *Zip* is a third option. And if you are a member of a local direct marketing club, its roster should provide you with a list of the copy services in your area.

Once you've located a likely candidate, call him or her on the phone and introduce yourself. Explain the kinds of products you're going to be marketing and any ideas you have about media and themes for your campaign. If the information is confidential, say so to the writer right away. Direct marketing freelancers who expect to stay in business know that confidentiality is nearly as important in their profession as it is for the clergy and for doctors.

Listen carefully to the reactions of the copywriter to your product and your ideas. Does he or she sound enthusiastic about your proposition? Does the copywriter know what you're talking about, or does your field seem foreign to his or her experience? If he or she has heard of your firm and starts mentioning your previous efforts and those of competitors in a knowledgeable way, you may have found yourself a gem. But you might also ask the copywriter to verify his or her experience in your own or a related area—work on other lead-generation programs, for instance, if that's what you're planning. Some direct marketing writers have sufficiently broad backgrounds and interests to sell almost any type of product if they get a complete input, while others choose to specialize in consumer or industrial goods, retail clients, or even something as specific as collectibles or insurance.

Don't talk only about the product, though; make sure the writer knows whether you're considering a mail program or space-advertising, television, business-to-business, or telephone-marketing plan. It's a rare writer who is equally proficient in all these areas, and an honest one who will tell you where his or her specialties lie. A ''well-connected'' writer may be able to help you find a colleague who can do television scripting or phone-marketing writing for you, while he or she handles your direct mail kits, space ads, and catalog writing.

If the phone contact goes well, invite the writer to send you some work samples. The promptness of the response and presentation of the materials will be good indicators of the way in which the writer will handle your account. Are the samples ''keyed in'' to your expressed interests in terms of product and media? Or do they look like a ''canned'' package of samples that would be sent to any prospective client? Does the style of writing please you? Is the copy meaty and specific or vague and general? Is it clear and interesting to read? Do your best to separate the graphics presentation from the copy itself when evaluating the work, since the writer often has no ''say'' about how the work is produced, especially if he or she is a freelancer.

Once you have evaluated the samples, a face-to-face meeting is the next step. Make sure you have an advance understanding of whether the meeting will be done on a speculative basis or whether you will be charged for the writer's consultation. A good way to get started is to give the copywriter a straightforward, simple assignment such as a one-column space ad or a direct mail flyer. But to "indoctrinate" the writer, you will have to provide plenty of background information. It's unfair to expect him or her to "wing it" on a first assignment, and you'll have to invest some time and effort in explaining the basics of your business and the particular assignment at hand. See the "input" section that follows (pp. 241–244) in this chapter for more information.

Before giving the writer an initial assignment, keep in mind that you are asking him or her to do research on your firm and its products that will continue to "pay off" if you give the writer more writing in the future. A flat fee is probably safer than an hourly rate at this point, because writers work at greatly varying speeds and you may be faced with a bill for twenty hours' work when you expected ten. But do inquire about the writer's usual rates and whether he or she normally works on the basis of hourly rates, a fee schedule, or by agreement.

To establish trust from the beginning, you should provide the writer with a purchase order (P.O.) number. Also state your policy about payment (net within thirty days, payment on receipt, payment when your material appears in print, or whatever). Clients who are candid about their payment arrangements and keep their word are rewarded with loyal and swift service by grateful copywriters.

WHAT DOES THE WRITER NEED TO KNOW?

Everyone has heard the old saw about computers: "garbage in, garbage out." Well, the same holds true in the relationship between client and copywriter: the better (or worse) the input, the better (or worse) the written product. This refers less to grammar, sentence structure, and flow than to the selling message and "thrust" of a direct marketing piece.

Before you meet the writer, then, it is wise for you to do your homework. You'll either have to provide the type of information described below or point the writer in the direction in which to obtain it. (Keep in mind that the more research you expect the writer to do, the more the assignment is likely to cost you.)

If the writer has worked with you before, he or she may already know about your company, product, and market. But even so, you'll need to talk about objectives, copy points, and the plans that have been made for this particular promotion. Here, then, is a list of the information your copywriter should have:

What is the company behind your product? Has your firm been in-volved in direct response advertising before? How long has it been in business? What is its reputation? What kind of people and busi-nesses form its present customer base?

What is the competitive environment for this product? Who are your competitors and how do their products differ from yours? What fea-tures of your product, if any, excel theirs? Do you have a lower price or a better overall benefit package? How have the competitors been promoting their products as compared to your efforts?

What is the product? Unless the product is the size of an eighteen-wheel tractor-trailer, try to provide a product sample for the copy-writer. If your product is a service, let the writer participate in the service—including all collateral materials, "how-to" instructions, and other aspects—if at all possible. Let the writer live with the prod-uct during the research process, to "soak up" all of its real benefits and drawbacks. Put the writer in touch with the buyer or developer of the product, if the latter is someone other than yourself. Let the writer ask questions about how the product works and what it can do for the customer. Provide library research, articles, books, and any-thing else that will help the writer understand the product and its ben-efits.

Who is the customer? To the best of your ability, describe the likely buyer of your product to the writer. Some of the best direct response writers visualize a typical customer while they write, someone they know who fits the customer profile, whether it be the chief executive officer of a corporation or a sixty-five-year-old grandmother who col-lects thimbles. If the product is a new one and you don't yet have a customer profile, sharing with the writer your plans for lists and me-dia will give him or her an idea of your prospective buyer. If you have testimonials from previous buyers of this or similar products, show them to the writer as background material and for possible inclusion in the copy.

How will we sell the product? Give the writer your thoughts about the medium or media that will be used to sell your product, whether direct mail, space advertising, or something else. Explain your rea-sons for using these media, and then listen to the writer's ideas. If he or she believes that the offer will not work in the one-column ad you had planned, listen to the reasoning for this and you may find that you'd be better off going to a larger ad. Or the writer may tell you that an 11-by-17-inch brochure is "overkill" for a particular product, and suggest that you scale down to an 8½-by-11 size. Make sure that the writer understands your budgetary restrictions and media plans so that he or she doesn't construct a jumbo spectacular brochure when your budget calls for a black-and-white small space ad.

How have we sold the product in the past? One of the best sources of research for your writer will be your past efforts for a product. Don't mention only the winners. The writer can learn as much from what didn't work as what did. If the product is new, any materials from your past efforts on other products can be supplemented by competitors' advertising samples.

What are your objectives? Make it very clear to the writer what your campaign is meant to accomplish. If it is a lead-generation campaign, are you looking for loose leads (people willing to raise their hands in interest but who have not made any type of commitment) or tight leads (people who are already somewhat pre-qualified)? In a retail campaign, are you looking to generate traffic, direct mail sales, or both? In every case, make sure the writer knows where you are headed or the copy may point you in the wrong direction, creating costly delays while extensive rewriting takes place.

What are the copy points for the product? The copywriter will have his or her own ideas about this, but your input will be most helpful. Make a list of what you want the advertising to get across about the product, starting with the chief benefit and working down. Include the important specifications: price, size, shipping information, guarantee, and so on.

What other creative work has so far been done for the product? If you have rough or comprehensive layouts already, show them to the copywriter and provide at least photocopies of them. If at all possible, get the writer together with your art director so that they can work together on the campaign. If you have given some thought to the "tone" you want in your copy, share that information with the writer. You might also provide samples of advertising you admire, and explain what you like about it.

What is the writer's immediate assignment? Some clients ask their copywriters first for roughed-in subheads and a short concept piece.

Others request a full-copy treatment in rough form, while still others ask the writer to go to complete copy right away. Whatever your preference, make sure the writer understands what you're expecting next, and what your time frame is.

HOW TO CRITIQUE THE COPY

Working with a copywriter to achieve a fine direct response effort is an art. It requires a combination of marketing skills, communication prowess, tact, and experience.

The first thing a new direct marketer should do is become a voracious "consumer" of direct response advertising. Read ads and direct mail kits and catalogs from cover to cover. Watch late-night and cable television for the direct response ads. "Hear out" the telephone marketers who call on the phone. Read books for professional or would-be copywriters on how to write copy. (A few good examples are *Tested Advertising Methods* by John Caples, *How to Write a Good Advertisement* by Victor O. Schwab, the copy sections of *Direct Marketing: Strategy, Planning and Execution* by Edward L. Nash, and the *Direct Mail and Mail Order Handbook* by Richard S. Hodgson.)

Be especially aware of your competitors' efforts, and "decoy" their mailings and other solicitations not just to see the products but to see how their strategy plays itself out in collateral materials and later offers. Watch for the ads and direct mail "pitches" that appear month after month, year after year. Cut them out and save them. Unless the marketer has some motive other than the profit motive, they are practically guaranteed winners. Learn what you can from the appeals and benefits these ads "push."

In another step, fill out coupons and order forms and see which ones are easy to use and which are confusing. Put your own past direct marketing efforts in a stack of mail—or leaf through a magazine in which you have advertised until you come upon your ad—and try to read them the way a prospect would. How do they stack up against the competition, not just in your product area but against the other messages which your prospect is likely to receive?

BASIC "SHOULDS" OF DIRECT MARKETING COPY

There are as many different formulae for direct marketing copy success as there are copywriters, and some of the big names in the field have become well-known for their "ten-point checklists" and "how-to" guides. The following is a distillation of many of these "shoulds." Rather than use a checklist of all the good and bad points of copy that are presented to you from various sources, keep the following hard-won direct response concepts in mind when reviewing and critiquing copy.

Headlines

In print media, the headlines and subheads you use are important as attention-getters. They also serve to lead readers into the body copy of your material, where they will get a better idea of the benefits of your offer. The least effective headings, such as "Summer Outerwear" or "Tools for the Home Workshop," are merely labels; the most effective offer benefits, rewards, and promises.

In his book, *Building a Mail Order Business—A Complete Manual for Success,* direct marketer William A. Cohen offers these words as some of those that psychologists have found to intrigue readers:[*]

advice to	magic
amazing	miracle
announcing	new
at last	now
bargain	power
challenge	powerful
compare	quick
easy	remarkable
found	revolutionary
free	secret
how	sensational
how to	startling
hurry	success
important	suddenly
improvement	wanted
introducing	who else
it's here	why
just arrived	which
last chance	when

[*]Permission to reprint granted by John Wiley & Sons, Inc. ©John Wiley & Sons, Inc.

246 SELLING BY MAIL

Some of the "how-to-write-copy" books mentioned above list hundreds of successful headings that utilize these words and others that are full of excitement or appeal to human wants and needs.

One successful case history of headlines is that of Bradford Galleries Exchange (now The Bradford Exchange). This marketer of limited-edition collector plates built a list of hundreds of thousands of names in the mid-1970s via editorial-style ads in newspapers across America. A listing of just a few of their oft-repeated headings will give you an indication of how "teaser" words and phrases can spur readership.

Know Your P's and Q's About Plate Collecting?

(A test and a challenge—who can resist reading on?)

Should Your Wife Collect Rare Plates?

(The reader wonders if she should, and reads on.)

Cash in on the Boom in Rare Plates

("Shaking the money tree," as copy great Tom Brady often advises, is a powerful inducement to readership.)

The "You" Approach

Some copywriters and clients fall into the trap of simply counting how many times the word "you" is used in a direct response solicitation. But that is not the point: it's the overall "you" approach that counts. Make sure the copy doesn't talk only of how your product is made or what its features are; customers also want to know "what's in it" for them.

When you read through your copywriter's work, keep product benefits firmly in mind. The copy should address the customer's wants, needs, hopes, aspirations, lifestyle, and interests. Do your best to evaluate the copy in terms of the market, not your own biases and beliefs. You may be a target for your own product, but as often as not you won't be; so you shouldn't make the mistake of slanting your copy toward what pleases you and your own (non-target) type of person.

Copy Length

There is no reliable rule for copy length. Nothing says that a four-page letter is inherently better than a two-page letter, or that a 120-second spot is inherently better than a 90-second spot on direct response television.

Copy great David Ogilvy states firmly that long copy sells more than short copy, and in general, direct response ads carry much more verbiage than regular advertising does. But the best advice is to have your copywriter write until the story is told; revise, edit, cut the copy until it is clear and strong; and then quit writing. Resist the impulse to assign a direct mail kit as a ''four-page letter, 8½-by-11 inch brochure, monarch-size publisher's letter printed one side only, 8½-by-3⅜-inch order form.'' Leave your options on copy length open until you see a rough draft of the copy; then decide whether you need more or less space than you'd planned.

Another guideline is that the more complex the proposition, or the higher the price, the more explanation your customer will expect before buying. Therefore, for an offer of a free booklet at no obligation, your copy would normally be considerably shorter than what you would need to sell a $495 stereo set via mail or space advertising.

Feature/Benefit/Value

It isn't enough to point out the features or characteristics of your product. It is more important to make sure the customer perceives the benefits of the product, in personal or corporate terms. In other words, you wouldn't say simply that a toaster ''has light, medium, and dark settings.'' Rather, you would say that the toaster ''has light, medium, and dark settings'' (feature) ''so that every member of the family may dial the toast of his or her choice'' (benefit).

The features and benefits presented should add up to a value that your prospects can perceive and which will lead them to become customers. The best way to make sure your copywriter presents meaty, benefit-oriented copy is to help him or her know your product completely. As that old saw of direct marketing goes, ''sell the sizzle . . . not the steak.'' Make sure that you and the writer get across what your product will add to the customer's life.

It's also vital to make sure that benefits are presented in the order of their magnitude, with the most important given first according to your customer's perceptions and not your own.

Success Stories

If possible, give some success stories of your product in use. One graphic way to do this is via testimonials or endorsements. Testimonials and endorsements should be believable. They should be in the words of real people or representatives of organizations with expertise in your product line. They should be as specific as possible, spelling out results in dollars and cents, pounds lost, compliments received, or whatever the success story comprises.

Another way of showing your success story is to give proof of effectiveness. This may take the form of a notarized statement by an expert, a demonstration on television, or something else.

The Call to Action

The goal of every component of a direct response advertising campaign is to induce action, whether writing in, calling, agreeing to buy, or coming in to the store. This action must be spurred by copy, but without coming on too strong. Read the "call to action" copy of some direct response advertising you admire, and of your competitors to learn how they induce a response. Here are some possibilities:

1. Offer a premium for a response by a given date.
2. Set a time limit on the offer, either because of a "subscription block," a "limited edition," "manufacturing capacity," a "charter subscriber or member offer," or some other reason.
3. Give a seasonal reason to order now: such as "order by November 15 to assure Christmas delivery."
4. Offer a discount for an "early bird" response.
5. Use the old "be the first on your block" pitch, but in a more carefully phrased manner.

The P.S.

Some direct marketers swear that a letter without a P.S. is as incomplete as a cat without whiskers. We won't go so far as to say that *every* letter needs a P.S., but considering the benefits of adding a P.S., and the versatility of this little technique, it definitely should be considered for every letter.

Studies show that readers look almost immediately to see who the sender of a letter is, and are therefore likely to glance at a P.S. before practically anything else in your direct mail kit. You may use your P.S. to guide readers to the buying decision in any number of ways. For instance, a hand-written P.S. from you could give "last-minute news" or be a personal pitch with a top benefit or reason to buy your product. Other uses for the P.S. include:

1. Referring the reader to another part of the kit that is very important, whether testimonials from satisfied users, a color picture in the brochure, an easy-to-use order form, or something else.
2. Reinforcing the urgency of the matter at hand and calling for immediate action before it is too late.
3. Reminding the customer of the premium that will be his or hers for free with a response.
4. Summarizing quickly the reasons why this product is right for the customer.

Copy Characteristics

It may help you in evaluating copy to ask yourself if it lives up to the ideals of good copy. Is the copy clear? Is the language simple without being simplistic? (Copy great Maxwell C. Ross said that for every 100 words of copy, 70 to 80 should comprise only one syllable.) Is the copy in the present tense and the active voice? Is it friendly—not patronizing or self-important? Does it flow well and have good transitions? Are there connecting phrases such as "what's more" and "in addition"? Did you have to force yourself to read it, or were you drawn in from the beginning? Check these things yourself, and then have a layman read the copy and answer the same questions.

Specificity

Take the copy that has been written about your product and read it through, substituting some other, similar product as subject. How much of the copy still works? If much of it works for another product, your copy has flunked the specificity test. The cure for copy with this problem is to zero in on your product's *specific* attributes and benefits, making sure that the copy points these out in specific and descriptive terms. Don't just say "large, economy size"; say "six pounds—enough to feed two parakeets for three months." Don't simply say "complements any decor"; say "the classic, clean lines of this table complement both traditional and contemporary homes."

Sales Sense

The direct response copywriter is first and foremost a personal salesman or -woman. His or her copy should do everything a personal salesman does—but (with the exception of telephone marketing) in a two-dimensional format. Thus the sales writer must anticipate objections from customers, lead them to positive responses, and then "close" the deal. Compare the copy you're evaluating with a verbal sales presentation, and see how it rates.

Appearance

If you're at the point of a rough layout, see how your piece "comes across" visually. Letters should have plenty of margin space to enhance their readability. Brochures should be broken up with subheads. Strive for a paragraph length of little more than six lines whenever possible. The key is readability and appeal. The art director can do a lot with typefaces, leading, illustrations, colors, and so on—but the copy itself must also draw the reader in visually.

Ease of Ordering

As a next step, let someone else read your direct response copy—and preferably several people not directly involved in your business. Have them go through the steps to order your product and see if they have any trouble with the ordering device as it is presented. Can they find the price? Color choices? Address to mail to? Ask them what they think the copy is trying to get across, and see if your benefits come back to you in some semblance of your own order of importance. Ask them which parts of the copy they find interesting, dull, easy to understand, and hard to understand. Then go back and work on the "rough spots" with your copywriter.

REVISING COPY WITH YOUR COPYWRITER'S HELP

The best advice we have seen on revising copy comes from ''Murder by Rewrite'' by Joyce Thomas, in the February/March 1982 issue of *The Creative Forum,* the newsletter of the Direct Marketing Creative Guild:

FOR THOSE WHO REQUEST COPY CHANGES: 5 WAYS TO GET BETTER REWRITES

1. *Remember you are the copy reviewer, not the copywriter.* You'll end up with a much stronger ad if you let the copywriter be the rewriter. *Your* role as a copy reviewer is to make suggestions and recommendations, *not* the actual copy changes. Leave them up to the person whose job it is to write and who has already poured a lot of time, thought, and words into the creation of the copy. One of the copywriter's earlier drafts may very well incorporate the ideas you want, stated exactly as you want.

   If for any reason you don't trust your copywriter to be your rewriter, you have more than a copy problem; you have a personnel problem. If you don't trust your copywriter as the rewriter, why do you trust him or her at all?

2. *Don't use time as an excuse.* Time is always an enemy in the direct response business . . . and rarely a more deadly one than during the copy review and rewrite stages. By that point in the project, the snowballing effect of delayed approvals and missed deadlines has generally reached avalanche proportions. All the more reason to let the professional wordsmith do the rewrite. Since your writer's stock-in-trade is words, he or she should be able to turn around a rewrite or revision quicker than anyone else.

   If the copywriter is on vacation, location, or medication, and is unavailable to ''reenter'' the job, that's still no excuse to do it yourself. When your dry cleaner is away, do you do your own cleaning? Do you give up wearing clothes? Or do you find an interim cleaner? Well . . . find an interim writer.

3. *Take a big-picture approach to copy review.* When you first review the copy, try to read it the way your prospects would. Don't read every word, scan the copy instead. Make sure the

headline grabs your interest and attention. Read the copy quickly. Does it flow? Do important points stop you and scream out "pay attention to me"? Do you believe what you are reading? Is there something you want to know about the product or service that the copy hasn't told you?

To ensure that your first reading is a big-picture one, keep your pen and pencil out of hand and out of reach. This discipline will help you avoid the all-too-easy trap of crossing "t's" and dotting "i's" instead of focusing on the general mood and flavor of the copy. Why waste time changing the nits at first, when they may not even be there if your initial reading results in major deletions, additions, or reshufflings?

4. *When you meet with the copywriters, be sensitive but be honest.* Go into your discussions open-mindedly and remembering that copywriting is an art, not a science, and that there is consequently no one "right" way in which to do it. Keep the meeting friendly and give the copywriter every opportunity to explain and defend the copy. This phase of your meeting could unearth a wealth of ideas for use both in the rewrite and in subsequent campaigns.

If after hearing all sides you still feel that your changes are in order, say so. Don't confuse evasion with sensitivity. Don't waste valuable rewrite time pussyfooting around and speaking in euphemisms. Ask the writer to take another crack at the copy, and back up your requests with the specific reasons why you want each change made. If you can't explain why you want a change, you don't deserve to have it made.

5. *Restate the revisions.* First-round rewrites are harrowing for everyone involved, therefore you want to do everything in your power to avoid a second go-round. One technique for this is to make sure you have clearly spelled out the changes you want. Reiterate them at the end of your meeting, summarizing them in point-by-point order.

Be extra safe—and this is especially important if your deadline is tight or if the meeting goes badly—issue a post-meeting report that lists each copy change individually. This will allow the copywriter to check off the changes as he or she makes them.

23

PRINT PRODUCTION

Even if you elect to work with a full-service agency that carries your direct marketing efforts clear through printing to mailing and evaluation, it is important that you understand enough about print production to monitor your agency's activities. And if you're like many direct marketers both large and small, you'll find that it pays to handle most of your print production chores in-house, even if you use an outside agency for the creative process. This is because agencies routinely add the standard 17.65 percent or some other fee to any printing or other outside services they handle for you. And besides it being cheaper, you may also find that it is less worrisome to handle the expediting of such services yourself. Either way, study the following hints on working with vendors, knowing your options, and saving costs.

WORKING WITH VENDORS

Involve your vendors early in the planning process. Don't call them in after you've invested hundreds or even thousands of dollars in layouts and artwork, only to learn that your prospective printed piece is totally cost-inefficient. And don't let your art director sell you on a brochure with lots of strip-ins and outlines without consulting your color separator to find out how much these special effects are going to cost. The help of a knowledgeable vendor can be especially crucial if you are new to the production process and tend to make costly mistakes due to ignorance. Many fledgling direct marketers are clever enough to seek out a group of dependable, experienced suppliers to rely on until they learn enough about production to fly on their own.

Use your vendors' expertise in your planning, timing, and even "blue sky" sessions to find new ways to promote your products more effectively. If you do, you'll stay abreast of the latest applications in the field and your vendors will earn their commissions for more than quoting the price of your job and delivering your samples.

If you don't know any good printers, separators, or other suppliers to call upon, ask other direct marketers for referrals. Or check the Yellow Pages, the member listings of direct marketing association handbooks, or ads in trade publications. Attend conventions given by groups such as the DMA and local associations, and talk with the vendors who have booths at these shows. And rest assured that once word gets out that you are a new direct marketer with money to spend, the vendors will find *you*.

When you have your first session with a vendor, ask to see some samples of his or her firm's work. This will give you some idea of the quality of the company's output as well as the specialties it is proud of. And you may get some ideas for your own marketing planning, since vendors are likely to show you the most innovative applications they've done.

If you're starting from scratch, ask your vendors for referrals: ask a printer to recommend a color separator, for instance, or vice-versa. The vendor you ask is most likely to refer you to a source he or she has worked with smoothly in the past. You'll receive as good a referral as possible; after all, the vendor wants to impress you and win your continuing business.

Finding sources that work well together will also pay off; there are few things more frustrating than listening to a separator complain about a printer or vice-versa. One of your goals should be to put together your own little production team of vendors who work well with you and with each other to produce a quality product. Things won't always go smoothly; that's too much to expect. But when you have vendors who respect each other, you'll face much less wrangling over who gets the "blame" for a late delivery or a color job that doesn't quite match the product sample.

This is not to say that you will stay forever with one printer and one separator, one photographer and one envelope supplier. At least periodically you will want to get competitive bids for the jobs you award. Here is some information on how to solicit and use vendors' quotes:

VENDOR QUOTES

Especially when you are just getting started, you will want to solicit quotes from various vendors to learn the range of prices and services available to you for your direct marketing efforts. Some new direct marketers are surprised to learn that one printer cannot handle all their needs, or that they may need a different source to get their color work prepared before it goes to the printer. That is one reason why obtaining some wide-ranging quotes can be highly instructive.

For instance, assume that you wish to print 50,000 two-page letters. You take your job request to three suppliers: a "speedy printer" doing fast-turnover offset work in your neighborhood, a medium-sized printer who specializes in sheet-fed, non-four-color work, and a large printer with the most sophisticated color web presses and computer capabilities.

The range of prices quoted to you by these suppliers may well be phenomenal, for a very simple reason. The "speedy printer" is likely to be too small to do 50,000 pieces of anything economically. His optimum runs are much smaller, and his prices are set accordingly. The large, four-color printer prices his jobs on "press time per hour," and his firm is geared to producing hundreds of thousands of printed pieces in a short time frame. Thus a job of 50,000 letters is too small to be run cost-efficiently at his shop. The medium-sized printer, however, is likely to find that your letter job is right for him: not too large nor too small, and not involving any color work. So his quote will probably be by far the best.

Don't take this quote as proof that this is the only printer for you, however. If you have a print job of 200,000 color brochures, for instance, it may be over the head of your medium-sized printer. He may try to give you a price quote for running your four-color process twice through his two-color press, and sometimes this can be done effectively with good quality control and care. But on a job like this, the large web printer is probably your best bet.

When dealing in color work, some of your printers may offer color separations as part of their service. But don't neglect to check the printer's separation price against that of independent color houses, or you may find yourself paying a large mark-up for having all the work done under one roof.

The "do's" and "don't's" of selecting suppliers could fill a book of their own, but suffice it to say that you learn by doing. Don't hesitate to invest the time and effort to obtain at least three quotes on each job you do, especially in the early stages of your direct marketing endeavors. And make sure your agency is doing the same if it's handling printing work for you.

Later on, unless you have a production staff to handle the expediting and cost/volume/time comparisons involved in obtaining a wide range of quotes, you may cut back on competitive bidding, and award jobs according to your experience of the vendor whose price is generally best for various types of jobs. But never let your suppliers think that you belong to them. Do go through the quote process on a periodic basis to make sure your sense of competitive prices is still sound.

And when evaluating quotes, don't feel that you have to bargain excessively with the vendor. This is detrimental to the establishment of a strong, long-term relationship in which the vendor will do everything possible to assure your success (and his own). On the other hand, don't accept quotes without some questions; and it doesn't hurt to bargain some, especially when you feel the vendor might not have understood your request properly.

PHOTOGRAPHY QUOTES

One of the most common misperceptions among new direct marketers is that it is always the printer's fault if a printed piece does not look as good as anticipated. On the contrary, the source of a problem on a job that doesn't measure up may be anywhere along the line: going as far back as the photography or even the layout.

Good, sharp photography is essential to a fine printing job. Color fidelity in photography is the first key to color fidelity in printing. It's up to you to work with your photographer at the quote stage to make sure he or she understands the kind of quality you're looking for.

When requesting quotes from photographers, show them something similar to the kind of photo job you're visualizing. Otherwise you may get quotes on the type of high-style, high-price shot you'd see in *Town and Country* magazine, when you're looking for something more like the J.C. Penney catalog.

And here's a hint that will save you money at the color-separation stage: Try to have your photographer shoot your product against the background you'll actually be using for your printed piece. Stripping products into position or outlining around them is expensive.

COLOR SEPARATIONS

When you plan to print with a four-color process, you'll have to obtain color separations to complete the job. The four colors in the process are red, yellow, blue, and black. Every color consists of some combination of red, yellow, and blue; the black adds detail and grey tones to a picture.

The separation process involves photography through filters: red is photographed through a green filter; yellow through a violet filter; and blue through an orange filter. With the addition of a specialized filter for black, four separate negatives, called "color separations," are obtained.

At this point the separations are corrected to match the look that you wish to obtain. When this correction process is complete, the separations are photographed through a halftone screen. This produces four halftone plates: red, yellow, blue, and black.

When the separations are photographed, each of the four color plates is rotated slightly away from the others so that when the four plates are superimposed in printing, the dots generated in the halftone process do not completely overlap. The result is that instead of "mud," you get a good reproduction of the original colors. Transparent inks are used, and the plates are printed one by one, usually in the sequence of yellow, red, blue, and black.

QUOTES ON SEPARATIONS

Color separation is one of the most difficult processes on which to get price quotes, because there are so many variables. Even some rather sophisticated marketers bring their transparencies for catalogs to the separator in a "bushel basket" of shots of different size, focus, and other qualities. Some clients want to see press proofs of the separation work done for them before approving it, while others will approve chromalins (a proof that shows how the four colors appear when laid on top of one another).

To get the most accurate possible quote on separations, tell your separator all about the job you want done. If possible, get the separator involved at the photography stage. Have the separator look over the comprehensive layouts to pinpoint areas that may make for expensive stripping, touch-up work, or other problems.

Because the separator will want to know many of the same things your printer will, share with him or her the print quote specification information discussed on sizes, number of photos, paper quality, etc. The separator will also need to know your time frame, how he or she will receive material from you, whether you are looking for pleasing color or 100 percent accuracy, and what type of proofs you want on the job.

You can save money by having your art department or studio create the pages of your materials with everything in position. This requires that your photography all be shot in the same focus, so that the separator does not have a registration problem, which requires costly alterations. If full pages are presented in complete form, the color separator can use a laser-type process to separate the work, keeping hand work and its attendant costs to a minimum. You will also save money if you cut down on the color corrections you do. One way to do this is to make sure the photography on your job is right, so that all the separator has to do is match the photography—not adjust colors to match the product.

Chromalin proofs are less costly than press proofs, and they also save time. But if your color work is very exacting, you may need press proofs. Your printer will then have something very accurate to use for a guideline at the press-approval stage, assuming the press proofs have been done on the proper kind of paper. The colors in chromalin proofs will be slightly "off" from those in your actual press run, if only because these proof are not printed on paper, but merely indicate what the color-on-color appearance of a printed piece will be. Chromalins usually show colors more vividly and detail sharper than what you will obtain in a press run. If you do need press proofs of your work, check with your color separator and find out if it is possible to print your job on the proofing press. If your quantity is not too large, this may be less expensive than going elsewhere for your press run.

There are just a few of the "basics" for dealing with separators; as with other aspects of direct response production, most managers will have to learn by doing. But because of the technicality of this area, you should rely on your art director or production specialist for help, especially regarding color fidelity. He or she will know how to request your color corrections, being able to point out where there is too much yellow, for instance, and too little red. As a layman, you may be at a loss to describe what is wrong with the separations you are shown, and will thus have a hard time getting the look you want. At least until you feel comfortable with the terminology and capabilities of your separator, take your art director along when approving chromalins or press proofs.

PRINTING QUOTES

The printed pieces you mail to customers or prospective customers are all they have by which to judge your firm. Therefore, good printing is very important, especially if you wish to establish a quality image in the marketplace. On the other hand, there are plenty of applications for simple, one-color printing jobs, and times when the image you wish to project will be simple, low-cost, and low-key. Before you invest in a fancy, full-color, broadside brochure, or economize with a small black-and-white folder, think about the image you need to project, and model your printing accordingly.

When approaching printers for quotes, you will want to know a few of the basics of their field. First, most direct mail printing these days is offset printing—a process that is based on photography. In years past, some marketers believed that offset could not produce excellent quality printing, but thanks to new printing technology, that problem has long since disappeared.

You may still come across some applications for letterpress printing, which is very sharp and clear but generally more expensive than offset. And if you plan to do catalogs in very large quantities (such as half a million or more), gravure printing may be a good process for you to investigate. Generally, though, your printing will be done via offset, on either a sheet-fed or web printing press.

The sheet-fed press prints on paper on a sheet-by-sheet basis. It is slower than web printing, and in many cases allows for somewhat better quality printing and color fidelity. However, sheet-fed printing is not cost-effective in higher quantity ranges (50,000 and up, generally), and you should therefore look into web printing if your quantities are this large. The web press is fed its paper from a continuous roll. There are small web presses meant for one- and two-color work (such as letters) and large presses that are as long as a bowling lane. Generally, a printer prices the work done on these presses by the hour of press time used, so be sure to check what type of press the printer's quote is based on. This is one reason why competitive quotes are so important: one printer may quote you a price based only on the use of his or her most effective press for your job, whereas another may have the ideal press for your application, and save you quite a bit of money.

When you ask a printer for a quote, he will need quite a bit of information to bid accurately on your job. Make sure that all of your bidders get all of this information, so that you are comparing "apples with apples" when all your quotes are in.

Below is a short list of the type of information your printer will want from you before making a price quotation. You should devise a "quote sheet" that you can use to fill out this information whenever you need to get quotes. This worksheet can then become the basis for a comprehensive purchase order once you award the job.

Print Quote Specifications to
Present to Printers

- Quantity (you will want to indicate any changes within the total quantity for different prices, dates, and so on).
- Flat size, folded size, number of folds (you should do a diagram if folds are unusual or could be misconstrued).
- Paper stock (weight, finish, color, brand name if known. If you can't describe the paper by its specifications, attach a sample).
- Number of colors on each side (expressed as 4 over 4 for four colors on both sides of a single sheet, and 4 over 2 for a four-color front and two-color back).
- Use of process color (separations).
- Colors other than black (indicate specific colors, such as PMS [Pantone Matching System] color, if known, or have your art director indicate this on the boards).
- Number of halftones (if any).
- Bleed or non-bleed.
- Type of proof you require, whether bluelines, chromalins, on-site press approval (which you or your art director or production person attend).
- Type of binding, if any (for booklets, etc.).
- Embossing, if required.

- How to pack and label printed material.
- Where to deliver material, when required, and to whose attention.
- Number of overrun copies you will accept and pay for (this normally ranges from 3 to 10 percent depending on your policy).

If you are unsure about how to specify your job for the printer, enlist his or her help and that of your art director. Describe the look you are seeking, work with these graphic experts to achieve it, and obtain accurate quotes.

PRESS APPROVALS

Whether you or a representative of your firm attends the press approval meeting for your job depends on the complexity of the job and the importance to it of color fidelity. Some clients put so much trust in their printing sales representatives that they allow these people to give press approval for runs of millions of color brochures. Others, perhaps no less trusting but more cautious, routinely send one of their own representatives to all press approvals except those for the simplest one- and two-color jobs.

With simple jobs such as letters and order cards, it is routine for the direct mailer to request a blueline proof, which will be delivered to his or her office. This proof allows you to make a final check for typographic errors, to see that all halftones and other art is in the right place, and to watch for specks and broken type that might mar the printing job. Once the blueline is approved, your job will be run and you will receive proofs off the press.

With color printing, there are more factors to check, and usually more money involved. You'll want to make sure the color is accurate to the chromalins or press proofs provided, and that it is in register. You may not be able to make an accurate judgment on these matters, so you should send your art director or production person to the approval. But go along if you can; the more experience you have in evaluating color work, the more informed a customer you will be. One word of warning: press approvals arrive like babies. The time seldom comes at 9:00 A.M., when you're wide awake and raring to go. Most color presses run 24 hours a day, and when it's time for a new job to go on press, that's when the press approval must take place. So you'll need to be on call for a possible middle-of-the-night trip to the printer if you wish to see your big color job go to press.

ENVELOPE QUOTES

When planning your mailing, the envelopes are among the first things you will have to order. This is because the most cost-effective way to buy envelopes is to custom-order them early enough to have them made specifically for you, instead of having them made by overprinting on stock envelope bodies. What's more, if you order envelopes to suit your mailing, you can specify the type of paper and printing you want, and even ask for bleeds and special window positions. If you use stock envelopes, you'll probably be limited to a few simple paper choices and standard window positions, and the type of art you can overprint will also be limited.

When planning your job, however, try to employ standard envelope sizes. Envelope manufacturers are "geared" for these regulation sizes, and if you request something different, you may lose time and money. Standard outer envelopes are #10 ($4^1/8$ by $9^1/2$ inches), 6-by-9 inch, and 9-by-12 inches. Standard Business Reply Envelopes are #$6^1/4$ ($3^1/2$ by 6 inches), #$6^3/4$ ($3^5/8$ by $6^1/2$ inches), and #9 ($3^7/8$ by $8^7/8$ inches).

Standard envelope papers are bond or wove. Bond papers are less textured than wove ones. Standard paper weights are expressed as 13, 20, 24, and 28, with the most common being 20.

When asking for quotes on envelopes, you will have to let the supplier's sales representative know the size you want, the window position and type (open or with glassine), the paper weight, quantity, and type of inside pattern if any, the number of printed colors front and back, whether any halftones or screens will appear on the envelope and of what kind, and your delivery schedule. Also tell the sales representative where you wish to have the envelopes shipped, and make sure you know whether shipping charges are included in the "per thousand" price.

You may also want to talk with your sales representative about promotional envelope ideas such as die-cuts, plastic see-through envelopes, side-openings, and so on. But remember that in small quantities, these special features will be quite expensive.

Try to order standard envelopes such as Business Reply Envelopes in quantity, because it will save you a great deal of money. Some envelope houses will let you print a year's worth of a certain envelope at a quantity discount, and then ship the envelopes as you need them, allowing you to pay as the envelopes are shipped. But don't get yourself in a creative bind simply for the sake of having standard envelopes. Often a new look or a special envelope teaser can make a difference in the way your package performs.

One last word about envelopes: Before you have your envelopes made, run a final check to see that all of the elements of your package fit into the outer envelope you've chosen. Does your lettershop anticipate any problems inserting with the envelope you plan to order? Does your order form fit easily into your Business Reply Envelope? Answering these few questions now will save you grief and expense later.

PAPER FOR PRINTING

Few small and medium-sized direct marketers get involved in buying their own paper directly from a paper manufacturer. They find that the extra effort isn't worthwhile, and prefer to have their printers' price quotes include the cost of the paper they need. But it will pay you to know something about the paper industry and what is available to you as a direct marketer.

When choosing paper for your printing, there are several questions you should ask yourself, as follows:

1. What kind of piece is the paper for? Low-key? Classy? Letter, brochure, order form? The letterhead-type paper appropriate for a letter is probably too lightweight for an order card, especially if you want it to be mailable. For a color brochure you'll want to consider using a coated paper stock, which will bring out the best in your photos. If the idea of choosing papers is new to you, save samples of pieces you like and find out from your printing sales representative the names and weights of the papers used in them.
2. What image do you want to project? Luxury or economy? Jet-setter or homey? The paper you select can help with this.
3. What printing process will be used? How many folds will there be? Some papers are better adapted for sheet-fed than for web presses, and some papers are too thick to fold down well. Ask your printing sales representatives for guidance on this matter.
4. How weighty can the piece be? Remember that you'll want to adhere to postal standards—1 ounce for the lowest first-class rate and 3.87 ounces for the lowest bulk rate. A very heavy stock might put you over this if you're planning a large bro-

264 SELLING BY MAIL

chure or catalog. But when considering a less weighty stock, make sure you don't go overboard. Consider the show-through you'll experience in printing, and try to find a middle ground.

Paper weights are expressed in pounds, with each weight indicating the weight of a 500-sheet ream of paper. There are two sets of designations, one for "bond" stock and one for "book" stock. The standard bond paper stock is 17 by 22 inches and the standard "book" paper stock is 25 by 38 inches. Thus, a 20-pound bond paper is one in which 500 sheets of 17-by-22-inch paper weigh 20 pounds (common bond papers are 16, 20, and 24 pound). A 50-pound book paper is one in which 500 sheets of 25-by-38-inch paper weigh 50 pounds (common book papers range from 30 to 120 pounds, with those in the 50-to-100-pound range the most widely used).

5. How will the piece be used? If it's a read-once-and-throw-away flyer, you won't need to pay as much for paper as you would for a reference catalog that will be used for at least a year. Also, if your piece looks like a throwaway it probably will be thrown away. The weight and quality of your stock contribute to this perception; consider newsprint as opposed to coated paper, for instance. Another hint: If your piece is for business use, don't specify a heavily coated stock, since this is hard on the eyes under fluorescent lights. If your business piece needs a coated stock to emphasize the pictures, talk to your printer about using a varnish in the areas where there are photographs. This can be added as an extra "color" on one of the ink stations of the press.

6. Consider whiteness. Papers are graded by whiteness as well as by weight, flawlessness, texture, and finish. If color fidelity is essential, a very white paper will help you achieve it.

7. Coordination with other pieces. Don't consider your brochure by itself without reference to the paper you're using for your letter, order card, and other elements. Just as colors should be coordinated, so should your paper textures, weights, and types be compatible.

8. How soon do you need the paper? For quick runs, you may have to take what is in stock at your printer or paper supplier. If you're willing to wait, you can specify an exact brand name, weight, and finish to your order.

GENERAL COST-SAVING TIPS

A little vigilance in print production can save you a lot of money. Here are some ideas on reducing your printing costs.

1. Involve your suppliers from the start, and enlist their help in saving you money.
2. Try to form or find a good team of photographers, printers, separators, and other service people who can work together smoothly. Encourage them to work together and explain that you won't tolerate backbiting and assigning blame.
3. Stay on schedule. There is nothing that will destroy a production budget faster than overtime at the color separator's or printer's.
4. Keep checking with everyone. Assign your assistant or other responsible person to expedite the production of your materials and let your suppliers know that you're on top of the job and that they can't put anything over on you.
5. Buy in quantity. Whenever you can plan ahead to buy printing or envelopes or paper, do so. You'll save in the long run, assuming you don't end up with too much inventory.
6. Don't date your materials unless necessary. Try dating only your order cards with a "final date," and referring to "the date on the form" on your other pieces so that they don't become outdated. Or have your lettershop imprint the final date on a standard order form when your labels are being applied.
7. Gang print when you can. If you can do several different brochures at one time, or have a flyer printed on the same paper as your main brochure, you may be able to utilize paper better and save printing time and costs.
8. Use standard sizes. Unless there's a really good reason for using an unusual size paper or envelope, don't use it. Everyone in direct mail is geared to standard sizes, and it will cost you time and money to deviate from them.
9. Check your bills carefully, and expect prior notification of "upcharges." Ask your vendors to send you itemized bills, and let them know that you read every word of fine print. Require them to ask for your approval up front for any overtime, extra charges, and other costs that will be added on to your bill.

APPENDIX I

THE DIRECT MARKETING PLAN

A control marketing plan is essential for any direct marketing program. This overall marketing plan will help all of the departments within a firm to be ''direct marketing oriented'': in other words, to contribute toward the goals of the direct marketing plan and not merely function in a vacuum. Even if you are a one-person operation a marketing plan is invaluable because it will force you to address all relevant issues ahead of time instead of reacting on the spur of the moment when questions arise.

The objective in preparing this plan should be to answer the questions of various departments and personnel, and to put forth performance and profit goals as well as budget figures. The following is a skeleton format that may help you develop your own direct marketing plan.

THE DIRECT MARKETING PLAN

Direct Marketing Review

This first section of the plan will set the scene for your planned direct marketing efforts in terms of competitive forces and your own past results, if any. ''Market'' refers to the market for your chosen product or product category.

- Size of the market
- Trends in the market

- Competitors' shares of the market/your share of market or projected share
- Distribution patterns: Is this product currently sold via direct marketing?
- Competitors' marketing efforts
- Comparison of your product with competitors' in terms of: (1) quality; (2) price; (3) features and benefits.

For general information such as the size of the market and trends in it, you may look to secondary sources such as trade publications, industry associations, and so forth. These sources may also be able to help define share of market, distribution patterns, and other factors. For marketing efforts, observe the marketplace for yourself or engage the help of a consultant who specializes in your product area. For product comparison, "decoy" the competitors' products and compare them with your own in every way, from packaging to collateral materials and price/value ratio.

Problems and Opportunities

On the basis of the above review, you are ready to approach your own marketing program squarely. Address the pluses and minuses of your product and your competitve situation and try to carve out your own market segment, while utilizing your opportunities and handling your problems. For instance, you may have a problem in that your product is considerably more expensive than the competition, but an opportunity in that its benefits become readily apparent in a "long-copy" direct mail brochure format.

A. Problems
B. Opportunities

Marketing Objectives

Moving from general to specific, begin with your objectives in marketing your product. Be as specific as possible. Don't say "increase market share" or "increase sales"; rather, make a statement like "increase market share by 15 percent" or "increase sales from $150,000 to $250,000 in the coming year."

Marketing Strategy

This is the "how to" for the objectives section, zeroing in on how your goals will be accomplished. It should cover the amount of your marketing expenditures, and the media you select (direct mail, newspapers, Sunday supplements, etc.).

Media Objectives

Now focus on the response levels expected in terms of leads, sales, or both. If you are using direct mail lists, for instance, this section of your plan should include a chart with the name of each list, quantity to be mailed, expected orders or leads per thousand names mailed, and any other pertinent information. These estimates may be based on past experience with similar products. If you have no past experience, your list broker may be able to give you "ball park" figures based on his or her experience with similar offers.

Media Strategy

Most specifically of all, this part of your plan should detail your "plan of attack" in a step-by-step manner. For instance, you might discuss a preliminary test of eight lists of 10,000 names each, to be followed up by validations and rollouts of successful lists, the rejection of unsuccessful lists, and more testing of other qualified lists once the offer itself is proven sound. Similar strategy statements should be made for each medium to be tested, such as newspapers, magazines, etc.

Copy Strategy

This portion of your plan will serve as a guide for the creative people working on your promotion. It should list the features and benefits of the product as you wish to see them presented, pointing out your advantages over the competition and disadvantages that must be addressed or soft-pedaled.

If you plan to address a number of different market segments, the copy strategy should be broken down into sections, explaining which product attributes apply to each segment. A set of monogrammed glassware might be sold to the consumer on the basis of style, beauty, versatility, or some other quality. The same set of glassware might be sold as an executive gift because it fits into a typical price range and because it is just personal enough to make a special impression.

Copy Plan

This plan lists the creative assignments for your project, such as a direct mail kit consisting of a letter, brochure, and order form, plus three ads of various sizes, or whatever your strategy calls for. The copy plan will also theorize about the illustrations and tone of the copy to give the creative people a basis for their work. Don't forget to address needed collateral materials which will be included in packages, serve as acknowledgements, or perform some other function.

Instructions for Order-Processing Department

Instructions for Data-Processing Department

Instructions for Fulfillment Department

Depending upon the sophistication of your company and how many different departments are involved, you may have a number of instruction sections as part of your direct marketing plan. These instructions will point out any specific information—codes, methods of processing, drop dates for mailings, packaging information, and other data that the various departments will need to function smoothly.

Rather than addressing each department separately in a memo, it is advisable to include them in the overall marketing plan so that they can see their part in the marketing effort. This helps avoid the ''production orientation'' that may occur in service departments when they operate in a vacuum.

Summary of Budget Information

This chart should put forth projected expenditures for everything from ad and direct mail preparation to list rentals, mailing, and postage. In short, it should cover every cost that is not considered a part of the overhead of the firm doing a promotion.

Special Activities

If any unusual form of research, public relations, or other promotional activity is to be a part of this marketing effort, it should be noted either within the marketing plan or as an addendum.

APPENDIX II

A GLOSSARY OF DIRECT MARKETING TERMS

The terms defined in this glossary will give the beginning direct marketer a good command of the "buzzwords" in the business, and some key definitions that will help in understanding this and other direct marketing books and publications. It is by no means complete. For the most complete glossary available, see the *Direct Mail and Mail Order Handbook* by Richard S. Hodgson. Another good glossary is included by Bob Stone in his book, *Successful Direct Marketing Methods*.

ACTION DEVICE   A tab, sticker, or other item in a mailing package which makes the prospective customer "do something" and leads him or her toward the sale. Example: stickers for books or records that the customer can paste onto an order form to indicate those items that he or she desires.

ADDRESSOGRAPH   A means of addressing a mailing using metal plates with embossed letters which are kept on file. It is the predecessor of computerized mailing lists.

AIDA   Attention, Interest, Desire, Action: the standard formula for the steps through which direct mail copy should take the prospect in order to induce a response.

ALTERATIONS   Changes which a customer or author makes on a typeset manuscript and which are not due to typographer's error, and therefore are chargeable to the customer.

271

ART   The general term for illustrations and photographs used in promotional literature; also the material from which printing plates are made.

BACK END   As opposed to front-end activities, back-end activities are those that take place after an initial order is received. This term may also indicate the customer's buying activities with the firm after his or her initial order.

BANGTAIL ENVELOPE   An envelope which serves a promotional purpose via an extra flap that holds product information, an order form, or both. Often used in credit-card statements, premium notices, and the like, where the "bangtail" promotion rides along free.

BASTARD   A nonstandard size or type of promotional piece which requires special handling and may well cost more than an item of more usual size or folding configuration.

BINDERY   The facility that binds together books, magazines, or pamphlets. "Binding" means wiring with staples, sewing, or plasticizing, depending on the thickness and desired appearance of the bound piece.

BINGO CARD   Deriving its name from its resemblance to this type of game card, the bingo card is a tear-out business reply device inserted in a magazine. The reader simply circles the appropriate numbers on the card to request promotional literature or sales follow-up from advertisers in the publication.

BLACK-AND-WHITE   Another term for one-color printing, where black type or art on white paper is utilized.

BLEED   Where the printing on a piece goes all the way to the edge of the paper. This is accomplished by printing beyond the margins of the piece and then trimming to the margins.

BOLDFACE   A heavy-faced type.

BOUNCE-BACK   An offer to a customer which comes to him or her along with the fulfillment of an order. Also a name for an offer to an "affinity" buyer, e.g., one to whom you would "bounce back" an offer on a second set of western history books after his or her purchase of a first set on that topic.

BROADSIDE   The name for a brochure which folds out to a flat size of 11 by 17 inches or larger. The "broadside" format lends itself to a dramatic product presentation whereby all elements of the offer may be presented on a single reading surface.

BROCHURE Also called a circular, pamphlet, or flyer, this is the general term for a descriptive piece of literature used for promotional purposes.

BULK MAIL Third-class mail which comprises a large quantity of identical pieces, sorted and batched by zip code before they reach the post office. They may also be carrier-route coded if the quantity and savings warrant. Bulk mail privileges require a permit from the post office.

BUSINESS REPLY MAIL A card or envelope with the indicia of the company receiving the order or inquiry. It allows the inquirer or buyer to mail the card or envelope back postage-free. The user must obtain a permit from the post office to utilize business reply.

C/A (change of address).

CARRIER ROUTE PRE-SORT Sorting mail into a nine-digit zip-code sequence so that it is ready to be distributed to individual U.S. Postal Service carriers. This saves additional postage over five-digit zip-code sequencing.

CASH WITH ORDER A request for payment in full when the order is placed.

CATALOG A book or booklet whose purpose is to show merchandise and descriptions, and offer the said merchandise for sale via an order form, telephone, or retail outlets.

CENTER SPREAD The middle two pages of a bound catalog, magazine, or book.

CHARACTER COUNT The number of letters and spaces that will fill a specific area in a printed piece.

CHESHIRE LABELS Mailing labels prepared for use with automatic labeling machines. The machines affix the labels individually to the mailing envelope, letter, or order form.

CLEANING A LIST An updating process which involves removing names to which mail can no longer be sent and changing addresses and other information when possible.

CODE Also known as a key code or source code, this is a number, series of letters, or other identifying device used to determine the source of an order or inquiry. It may appear on the order form or label, or within the return address or coupon on a space ad.

COLD LIST Also called an outside list, this is a list which a mailer rents in order to test a proposal, as opposed to his or her own house list.

COLLATERAL MATERIALS   Printed materials used to support a sale or prospective sale, such as instruction manuals, certificates of authenticity, or warranty information.

COLOR KEY PROOF   Also called a chromalin, this is a proof provided by the color separator which shows the approximate expected result of four-color printing.

COLOR SEPARATION   The translation of an original photograph or other piece of artwork into separate plates for four-color printing.

COLOR TRANSPARENCY   A positive photographic image protected by a transparent cover.

COMPILED LIST   As opposed to a list of buyers of a specific product or service, a compiled list does not promise any sort of past buying activity. Rather, it is a group of names gathered from directories, public records, registrations, and other sources which share something in common (e.g., a compiled list of high school principals).

COMP OR COMPLIMENTARY LIST   A list of advertisers or potential advertisers who receive a publication for free.

COMPREHENSIVE LAYOUT   Also called a "comp," this is a layout for a prospective printed piece which is complete enough to permit the ordering of finished illustrations and photography and the setting of type.

COMPUTER HOUSE   A firm which offers various computer services, including list computerization and maintenance, merge-purge operations, and computer letters.

COMPUTER LETTER   A letter generated by a computer for the purpose of personalizing such things as a name, address, previous buying record, or something else.

CONTINUITY PROGRAM   A promotion which has multiple parts, such as a series of books, records, collector plates, or recipe cards which are shipped on a monthly, semi-monthly, or quarterly basis. The items are unified by a common theme and often by a common price per shipment.

CONTROL   A promotion package or ad that has been proven to perform at a certain level and which is used as the "benchmark" for future testing.

CONTROLLED CIRCULATION   The situation in which a publication distributes some or all of its print run to persons or firms which fit a certain profile pleasing to its advertisers. For instance,

DM News is a controlled circulation publication for persons in the direct marketing field, who are called upon to verify their qualifications by company name and title.

CONVERSION Making a prospect into a lead or buyer, or making a lead into a buyer.

CO-OP MAILING Two or more (usually noncompetitive) offers combined in one envelope and sent to prospects to cut down the individual mailing, postage, and other costs. See the *Standard Rate and Data Service Consumer Lists Book* for a list of organized co-op mailings.

COPY A manuscript, typescript, or other written material to be used in preparing a printed piece such as a letter or brochure.

COPYRIGHT An exclusive right which the law grants to authors and artists, or to the owners of other works.

CORNER CARD The imprint of the sender or the return address on an outer envelope or catalog, which may include the logo or slogan of the mailing firm.

COST PER INQUIRY (CPI) $\dfrac{\text{TOTAL COST OF MAILING OR AD}}{\text{NUMBER INQUIRIES RECEIVED}}$

COST PER ORDER (CPO) $\dfrac{\text{TOTAL COST OF MAILING OR AD}}{\text{NUMBER ORDERS RECEIVED}}$

COST PER THOUSAND (CPM) $\dfrac{\text{TOTAL COST OF MAILING OR AD}}{\text{NUMBER OF THOUSAND MAILED}}$

COUPON The return portion of an ad, which may involve a purchase or a request for more information.

DECK MAILING A group of postcards that contain promotional information and business reply capabilities, sent to a group of people with certain characteristics (e.g., physicians, marketing executives, or some other).

DECOY To inquire or purchase from a company with the intention of learning about its products and methods of promotion.

DECOY NAME A "tipoff" name (a false name at your address, perhaps) inserted in a mailing list. Also known as a "seed name," or "salting the list." This assures the mailer that he or she will know when his or list is being used and how.

DEMOGRAPHICS Social and economic information about people or groups of people, including age, income, educational level, and other data.

DIRECT MAIL   The use of the postal service to send a common message to persons selected by list, zip code, or other means.

DIRECT MARKETING   Also called direct response marketing. Obtaining leads or selling by means of a specific message to a specific prospective buyer or inquirer.

DOWNSCALE   The opposite of upscale, it indicates a market that is relatively low in income and discretionary buying power, and one that is not inclined to respond to luxury offers.

DUMMY   Any "mock-up" of a printed piece which is used to test its appearance, weight, readability, or other properties.

DUOTONE   Two plates are combined to create a piece of art with a darker and a lighter shade of ink.

EXCHANGE   As opposed to a list rental, an exchange takes place when two list owners agree to trade a certain number of names with each other, instead of paying for the mutual usage.

EXPIRE   An expired subscription name, or a person who is no longer an active buyer. This is a separate list classification which usually may be rented at a lower rate.

FILE   Another name for a mailing list.

FILE MAINTENANCE   See LIST MAINTENANCE.

FIRST-CLASS MAIL   Mail that may or may not contain individual messages, but which is afforded the priority treatment.

FOUR-COLOR PROCESS   Also called the full-color process, it indicates the four color plates commonly used in color printing.

FREELANCE   An independent writer, consultant, artist, or other service provider who is not employed by any one firm, but who works with various firms or agencies.

FREE-STANDING INSERT   Also known as free-standing stuffer. A promotional piece which is not constrained by the specifications of a publication, but which is inserted loosely into that publication. It allows an advertiser to "ride along" with the daily newspaper, for instance, while still printing full-color material on a good-quality paper stock.

FREQUENCY   Along with recency and dollars spent, one of the three main criteria for judging the qualification of a buyer or group of buyers on a list. Frequency refers to the number of times the customer has purchased within a given period.

FRONT END   The marketing activities that take place before the entering of an initial sale or lead from a prospect.

FULFILLMENT The processing, servicing, and shipping in response to orders received via direct response marketing.

GANG RUN Running several same or similar print jobs together to save money and time.

GIMMICK A small device which may be tipped into a direct mail letter, order form, or brochure, to call attention to the piece or dramatize the offer. Example: a one-cup packet of coffee tipped into a letter with a heading saying, ''Sit down with a hot cup of coffee and let me tell you about (xyz product).''

GRAPHIC ARTS The general term for the field of printing, and for creative work on promotional materials (including art, layouts and photography).

GUARANTEE The marketer's promise regarding the prospective buyer's satisfaction, and the specific terms of that promise (e.g., replacement guarantee, money-back guarantee, buy-back guarantee, etc.).

HALFTONE A plate, printed piece, or process involving the shooting of artwork through a lined screen which breaks up the art into a dot pattern.

HICKIES Marks on printed material caused by dirt or foreign material during the printing process. They may appear on all pieces or on only a few samples.

HOT-LINE Names on a list which are especially recent and thus command a premium price from the list owner. There are three-month hot-line names and six-month hot-line names, among others.

HOUSE LIST The names owned by a particular firm. These names may be collected through outside solicitation, purchase, or compilation.

IMPRIMATUR Also called an endorsement. An official testimonial for a product or service by an outside organization.

INDICIA Envelope markings substituted for stamps or other regular cancellations in bulk mailings.

INQUIRY A person who has not yet purchased anything from a firm, but who has made him- or herself known via a response to an ad or other solicitation and asked for (usually free) information.

KEY CODE Also sometimes called a key. (See CODE.)

KEYLINE Also called a mechanical. This diagram of copy and art for reproduction is the guide used in making plates and printing a piece.

KROMECOTE   A very glossy, coated paper stock.

LABEL   A piece of paper (it may be pressure-sensitive or not) which carries the name and address (and possibly an identification code) of a prospect or previous buyer. It is affixed to an order form, letter, or outer envelope for mailing purposes.

LAID PAPER STOCK   A paper, often used for letterhead printing, which is not woven but appears to be.

LAYOUT   A rendering of a proposed printed piece, indicating positions for headings, copy, art, and borders. The term may also indicate color treatments.

LEADING   The space that appears between printed lines. Some leading is necessary for readability.

LETTERHEAD   The stationery used by a particular business, which is printed to identify that firm via a logo, name, and address.

LIGHT TABLE   A frosted glass table with lights underneath that make it easy to view transparencies.

LINE DRAWINGS   Solid-black-line artwork that does not require halftone reproduction.

LIST   The names and addresses of prospects, customers, or both who have something in common, whether it be previous buying habits, occupation, or other attributes.

LIST BROKER   A professional counselor to renters of direct mail lists. The broker provides recommendations on list rental for specific propositions, and may be made privy to the results so that he or she can help plan future testing and rollouts. The broker also helps expedite the receipt of lists, merge-purge operations, and other list-related matters.

LIST MAINTENANCE   The regular updating of a list to make sure that addresses are current and buyers are as recent as they should be.

LIST MANAGER   A person or firm appointed to promote and maintain a list for its owner. Rental requests come direct to the manager, who may have the power to grant or refuse the use of a list, or may need to get permission from the owner. The list manager also handles paperwork, collections, and the expediting of rental transactions.

LIST RENTAL   A one-time usage agreement between the owner of a list and an outside source. The owner may be paid a set sum of dollars per thousand names (or net names) rented, or a royalty to be agreed upon between the parties.

LIST SOURCE Origin of the names which appear on a mailing list.

LIST TEST An arrangement whereby a list renter makes his or her offer to a small, randomly-selected segment of a list universe to determine its viability.

LITHOGRAPHY A printing process that involves the use of plates made from photographs. Offset lithography is simply called "offset" in most cases.

LOAD-UP On continuity propositions, a system whereby the customer is sent the bulk of his or her product at once, to save on postage and packaging costs. Generally, he or she is then asked to remit the monthly or semimonthly fee by way of a coupon book until the entire set is paid for.

LOGOTYPE Also called logo. The trademark or signature of a company, which may simply be indicated by a certain typeface, or by artwork.

MAIL DATE The day agreed upon between a list renter and list owner as the "drop date" for a specific mailing at the post office. This mail date must be strictly adhered to, to avoid "dropping mail on top of" another offer and diluting its attention value, although the mailer may request a revised date from the list owner.

MAILER A firm which does direct mailing, or a carton in which products are shipped. Also a term for a direct mail piece.

MAIL HOUSE Also called a lettershop. The firm that handles the labeling of order cards and envelopes and the insertion and mailing of direct mail solicitations.

MAIL-ORDER BUYER A person with a history of frequent and recent purchases by mail, and thus a good prospect for a new mail-order proposition.

MECHANICAL Also called a keyline. The artwork and type ready for printing.

MERGE-PURGE A computer process whereby lists may be merged together to facilitate zip code sequencing and the testing of segments, and can be "purged" of duplicate names, pander names, and other undesirable names, or names which are to be saved for later.

MOONLIGHTER A freelancer who is also employed regularly by a single firm.

MULTIPLE BUYER   Also called a multi-buyer or repeat buyer. A person who has purchased more than once from a firm, on different occasions.

MULTIPLE-REGRESSION ANALYSIS   A technique whereby various characteristics of buyers or prospects are quantified to determine their relative propensity to buy and pay for a certain type of product.

NEGATIVE OPTION   Used by many book and record clubs, this calls for the customer to send back a response and if he or she does not want to purchase a monthly selection. The terms must be approached carefully, under Federal Trade Commission regulations.

NESTING   This is a procedure which may cut costs and time in the mailing/insertion process. One piece of literature is placed inside another before insertion into an envelope, thus cutting the number of positions necessary on the inserting machine. Nesting may also be used to ''nest'' an appropriate order form with selling or other literature.

NET NAME ARRANGEMENT   An agreement with a list owner whereby the renter need pay only for the names left after a merge-purge operation cleans out duplicates, pander names, and others. The term may also indicate a specific percentage or number of names the renter will pay for no matter what the results of the merge-purge operation.

NIXIE   A piece of mail that does not reach its destination, due to a faulty address or name, and is returned by the post office.

NTH NAME   A selection process whereby the user selects only a fraction of the names on a list, randomly, by taking every tenth name, twentieth name, or whatever.

OFFER   The specific buying terms presented to the prospect, including price, payment options, delivery terms, and premiums.

OFFSET PAPER   A type of paper suited to offset lithography. It usually refers to a lower grade of offset lithography paper, as opposed to more expensive or coated stock.

ONE-TIME USE   The usual arrangement for list rental, this is an understanding that the renter will not reproduce the list or use any part of it more than once without getting permission and paying for the privilege.

ORDER BLANK ENVELOPE   A piece which comprises an order form and return envelope all in one.

OUT OF REGISTER   Lack of alignment of colors which are to be printed one right over the other, resulting in "hanging" dot patterns.

PACKAGE   The entire direct mail solicitation, including the outer envelope, letter, brochure, order card, business reply envelope, and whatever other elements are included.

PACKAGE INSERT   A promotional offer that is included in the shipment of a product. It may be from the firm which is shipping the product or from a different firm, via a fee or royalty arrangement. See the *Standard Rate and Data Service Consumer Lists Book* for available package insert arrangements.

PACKAGE TEST   A test of direct mail element or elements within a given package, against the "control" package.

PAGINATION   Determining how type will break from page to page, or how catalog products will appear from page to page.

PANDER NAMES   The names of persons who have indicated that they do not wish to receive direct mail solicitations. These are on file at computer houses so that they can be removed during the merge-purge process.

PASS-ALONG   The factor of additional readers for a direct mail piece or ad, obtained when the recipient passes the piece along to others. In the direct mail process, self-mailers are considered the best means for obtaining pass-along readers.

PASTE-UP   The gluing down of art and type on a keyline in preparation for platemaking.

PENETRATION   The number or percentage of names on a list in relation to the total number of names in a city, state, zip code area, SIC code, or other region.

PERSONALIZATION   The addition of the name or other individual information about a prospect or buyer to a promotion. Often done by computer.

PHOTOSTAT   Also called a stat. A high-quality reproduction of camera-ready art which may be used for offset printing.

PIGGYBACK   An offer that "rides along free" with another offer.

PMS COLORS   Standard, numbered shades and colors which are available to printers in pre-mixed form and may be selected when a specific background or accent color is desired.

POSITIVE OPTION   A system whereby, unlike a negative option, the customer must send back a reply if he/she *does* want merchandise. It is used for some club appeals.

POSTCARD MAILER   A booklet of promotion/reply cards sent out to appeal to a certain market segment, such as physicians, attorneys, or business executives.

PREMIUM   An offer of a free item to the buyer as an incentive to purchase or try a product.

PRESS PROOF   A proof made on a regular press after color separations are complete, and used to check color before the full run is made.

PRESS RELEASE   An announcement sent to newspapers, magazines, or other media with news about a person, product, or service.

PRESSURE-SENSITIVE LABELS   Also called peel-off labels. These are address labels often used where one label needs to serve both the addressing and return function. They may be removed from the outside of a catalog or envelope and placed on the ordering device.

PROGRESSIVES   Also called progs. A set of proofs which can be separated to show each color on its own, and put back together to see how the four colors combine.

PROSPECT   The name of a person who is seen as a potential buyer for a product, but who has not yet inquired or purchased from a firm.

PROTECTION   The time before and after a mail date that is left free of other mailings to assure the mailer a "safe" period during which the prospect will not receive any other mailings based on the same list.

PSYCHOGRAPHICS   Lifestyle or attitude characteristics, as opposed to the merely statistical indicators of demographics.

PUBLICITY   Any form of non-paid promotion in the media.

PUBLISHER'S LETTER   Also called a "Why not?" letter. An auxiliary letter in a mailing which keys in on a specific selling point. The classic publisher's letter has an outer message which says "please do not open unless you have already decided not to respond (or order)."

RATE CARD   A publisher's listing of advertising rates, including volume discounts and other special information.

RECENCY   Along with frequency and dollar volume, one of the three indicators of a customer's propensity to buy. Recency indicates the customer's latest purchase date from a certain company.

REFERRAL   Also called "the buddy system" or "friend of a friend.'' This is a plan whereby the seller asks customers or prospects to identify their friends who are likely to be interested in the same kind of merchandise or offer. The customer may be offered a premium for doing so.

REPLY CARD Also called a "Business Reply Card" or "BRE." An order card or inquiry card which may be dropped right in the mail, since it bears the sender's address and postal indicia.

RESPONSE RATE The percentage of orders per thousand mailed which results from a mailing or ad insertion in a publication.

RETURN POSTAGE GUARANTEED The term that may be printed on outer envelopes in order to receive bulk-rate mail back from the post office if it is undeliverable. The charge for this service is the same as the current single-piece third-class rate. This is the system used for periodic list cleaning.

RETURN REQUESTED A slightly softer version of the above, which indicates that the mailer will reimburse the post office for undeliverable mail which is returned.

ROLLOUT A scheduled mailing of the remaining names in a list universe, if a list test is successful and a subsequent, larger test validates the test results.

ROP A run of paper or run of the press. A newspaper space placement which is within the regular editorial sections of the newspaper, as opposed to a free-standing insert.

RUNNING CHARGES Any fee set by a list owner and paid by the list renter or exchanger to cover the administrative and running costs of lists that are not used or, in the case of exchange, not paid for.

SALTING Same as seed names, decoy, or dummy names. (See DECOY.)

SAMPLE PACKAGE OR MAILING PIECE A piece of copy or a package submitted to a list owner to indicate what will be mailed to the people on his or her list under a proposed list rental or exchange agreement. This allows the list owner to screen out undesirable or overly competitive offers.

SELF-MAILER A one-piece, direct mail item that is not a catalog, but which does not come in an envelope.

SHEET-FED PRESS A press which prints on sheets of paper which are fed into the press one at a time. Usually used for smaller quantity or higher quality printing.

SIGNATURE A section of a catalog or book which may be eight or more pages in length. Catalogs may be repositioned by signature to simulate a new look for re-mailing.

SILVERPRINT   Also called a blueline. A copy of the plate for a printed piece, used as a proof.

SOLO MAILING   A solicitation for a single product or product line.

SOURCE CODE   Same as code or key code. (See CODE.)

SPLIT RUN   Two versions of an ad run in the same publication via a system whereby every other copy of the publication carries one ad and the next in line carries the other. This allows for statistically accurate testing.

STANDARD INDUSTRIAL CLASSIFICATION (SIC)   A code which indicates a business's classification as determined by the U.S. Department of Commerce.

STANDARD RATE AND DATA SERVICE (SRDS)   Chicago-area firm which publishes periodical guides to the users of Business Publications, Canadian Ad Rates, Community Publications, Consumer/Farm Magazines, Direct Mail Lists, TV Network Rates, Newspaper Rates, Print Media, Spot Radio, Spot TV, and other data.

STUFFER   An enclosure in a package, statement, newspaper or other medium for the purpose of selling a product.

SYNDICATOR   A firm that prepares promotions for a list owner to mail to his list or include in statements. The syndicator may also handle fulfillment for the list owner.

TEASER   Also called an envelope teaser. The copy on the outside of an envelope whose purpose is to move the reader to open it and read the offer inside. Also refers to a teaser ad: an enticing ad which encourages the reader to watch for further developments in later-running ads.

TESTING   A preliminary mailing or ad insertion that determines the relative chances of success of a given proposition in a given medium.

THUMBNAILS   Miniature layout sketches used to give a general idea of what a direct mail piece will look like.

TIP-ON   Something glued to a direct mail letter, order card or other printed piece. It may be a gimmick or an action device.

TRADE PUBLICATION   A magazine intended for those involved in a specific trade or profession.

TRAFFIC BUILDER A direct mail piece that does not have the solicitation of a direct order as its main goal, but rather is meant to bring customers into a retail store.

UNIVERSE The total number of people who fit a certain set of characteristics. Also, the total number of people on a specific mailing list.

UPDATE The adding of recently acquired names or buyers to a list so as to assure its accuracy.

UP FRONT Getting the payment for a product or service before it is shipped.

UPSCALE A market which by virtue of its income level, lifestyle, and interests is a good field for luxury or high-income-related offers.

VALIDATION A mailing that takes place after an initial test, to verify the results before a rollout.

VELOX A reproduction of an original piece of art or photo. It may be line art, a half-tone, or a combination of the two.

WEB PRESS A printing press which has a rotary action and uses large rolls of paper. It is used for larger quantity printing (usually 50,000 pieces and up).

WIDE AREA TELEPHONE SERVICE (WATS) A service that provides reduced rates for volume callers within specific areas of the country. This direct-dial service no longer carries a flat rate, but is tied to specific volume levels and to times of day and volumes of calls. WATS service is available on both an incoming and outgoing basis.

WINDOW ENVELOPE An envelope with a see-through area that allows for a labeled reply device and which may also serve as the address mechanism. The window is die-cut, and may remain open or be covered with a see-through material.

ZIP-CODE SEQUENCE The arrangement of names and addresses on a list, beginning with 00000 and progressing through 99999. This provides proper sorting for the third-class postal bulk-mail rate. It may go further, to a nine-digit number, for carrier-route coding and even greater savings at mailing time.

APPENDIX III

PERIODICALS

The following periodicals will be of general or specific interest to the direct marketer. Their addresses and prices are subject to change.

ADVERTISING AGE   Published by Crain Communications, 740 Rush Street, Chicago, IL 60611. Weekly. $50.00 per year.

ADWEEK   Published by ASM Communications, 820 Second Avenue, New York, NY 10017. Weekly; in regional editions for East, Southeast, Midwest, Southwest, and West. $40.00 per year/per edition.

AIS 800 REPORT   Published by Advertising Information Services, 353 Lexington Avenue, New York, NY 10017. Twice monthly. $99.00 per year.

BUSINESS MAILERS REVIEW   Pubblished by Van H. Seagraves, 1813 Sheperd Street, Washington, DC 20011. Twice monthly. $84.00 per year.

BUSINESS PUBLICATION RATES AND DATA   Published by Standard Rate and Data Service, Inc., 5201 Old Orchard Road, Skokie, IL 60076. Monthly. $148.00 per year.

CATALOG MARKETER   Published by Maxwell Sroge Publishing, Inc., 731 North Cascade Avenue, Colorado Springs, CO 80903. Every other week. $115.00 per year.

CONSUMER MAGAZINE AND FARM PUBLICATION RATES AND DATA   Published by Standard Rate and Data Service, Inc., 5201 Old Orchard Road, Skokie, IL 60076. Monthly. $126.00 per year.

DIRECT MAGAZINE Published by Direct Magazine Associations, 60 East 42 Street, New York, NY 10165. Bi-monthly. $12.00 per year.

DIRECT MAIL LIST RATES AND DATA Published by Standard Rate and Data Service, Inc., 5201 Old Orchard Road, Skokie, IL 60076. Twice yearly. $65.00 per year.

DIRECT MARKETING MAGAZINE Published by Hoke Communications, Inc., 224 Seventh Street, Garden City, NY 11530. Monthly. $33.00 per year, or included with membership in the Direct Marketing Association.

DM NEWS Published by DM News Corporation, 19 West 21st, New York, NY 10010. Monthly. Free to qualified direct marketers.

FRIDAY REPORT Published by Hoke Communications, Inc., 224 Seventh Street, Garden City, NY 11530. Monthly. $92.00 per year.

FUND RAISING MANAGEMENT WEEKLY Published by Hoke Communications, 224 Seventh Street, Garden City, NY 11530. Weekly. $72.00 per year.

THE GALLAGHER REPORT Published by The Gallagher Report, Inc., 230 Park Avenue, New York, NY 10017. Weekly. $72.00 per year.

JANUZ DIRECT MARKETING LETTER Incorporating TELEPHONE MARKETING REPORT. Published by Januz Marketing Communications, P.O. Box 1000, Lake Forest, IL 60045. Monthly. $96 per year.

MEMO TO MAILERS Newsletter published by the U.S. Postal Service, P.O. Box 1600, La Plata, MD 20646. Available free to qualified direct marketers.

NEWSPAPER RATES AND DATA Published by Standard Rate and Data Service, Inc., 5201 Old Orchard Road, Skokie, IL 60077. Monthly. $110.00 per year.

NON-STORE MARKETING (NSM) REPORT Published by Maxwell Sroge Publishing Company, Inc., 731 Cascade Avenue, Colorado Springs, CO 80903. Every other week. $135.00 per year.

TELEMARKETING Published by Technology Marketing Corporation, 17 Park Street, Norwalk, CT 06851. Every other month. $39.00 per year.

WHO'S MAILING WHAT!   Publishing by Who's Mailing What! Inc., P.O. Box 8180, Stamford, CT 06905. Monthly. $132.00 per year.

ZIP MAGAZINE   Published by North American Publishing Company, 545 Madison Avenue, New York, NY 10022. Nine times yearly. $24.00 per year.

APPENDIX IV

BOOKS AND MONOGRAPHS

The following is a short list of some of the other books and publications which will help business people to grasp the important concepts of direct marketing, using the information in this volume as a basis. Many of these books are offered for sale through the Direct Marketing Association, 6 East 43 Street, New York, NY 10017. Phone (212) 689-4977. (Major credit cards are accepted.) You can also check for them with your local bookstore or the publisher listed below for each book.

ADVERTISING PURE AND SIMPLE by Hank Seiden. (Television advertising.) Published by AMACOM, Division of American Management Associations, 135 West 50 Street, New York, NY 10020. $12.95.

BUILDING A MAIL ORDER BUSINESS—A COMPLETE MANUAL FOR SUCCESS by William A. Cohen. Published by John Wiley & Sons, 605 Third Avenue, New York, NY 10158. $17.95.

CAREER DEVELOPMENT PROGRAM by George Wiedemann. Published by the Direct Marketing Association, 6 East 43 Street, New York, NY 10017. $375.00

CATALOG MARKETING by Katie Muldoon. Published by R. R. Bowker Company, 205 East 42 Street, New York, NY 10017. $34.95.

DIRECT MAIL ADVERTISING & SELLING FOR RETAIL-

ERS with chapters written by twenty-eight professionals. Published by National Retail Merchants Association, 100 West 31 Street, New York, NY 10001. $19.95.

DIRECT MAIL AND MAIL ORDER HANDBOOK by Richard S. Hodgson. Published by Dartnell, 4660 Ravenswood Avenue, Chicago, IL 60640. $57.50.

DIRECT MARKETING: STRATEGY, PLANNING, EXECUTION by Edward L. Nash. Published by McGraw-Hill, Inc., 1221 Avenue of the Americas, New York, NY 10019. $24.95.

THE DIRECT MARKETING MARKET PLACE by Edward Stern. Published by Hilary House Publishers, 1033 Channel Drive, Hewlett Harbor, NY 11557. $48.00.

DIRECT RESPONSE BROADCAST MONOGRAPH. Published by the Direct Marketing Association, 6 East 43 Street, New York, NY 10017. $24.95.

DIRECT RESPONSE PRINT SPACE MONOGRAPH. Published by Direct Marketing Association, 6 East 43 Street, New York, NY 10017. $24.95.

DMA FACT BOOK ON DIRECT RESPONSE MARKETING. Published by the Direct Marketing Association, 6 East 43 Street, New York, NY 10017. $39.95.

THE DYNAMICS OF MAKING A FORTUNE IN MAIL ORDER by Raymond J. Brandell in collaboration with Raymond E. Brandell. Published by Frederick Fell Publishers, 386 Park Avenue South, New York, NY 10016. $19.95.

ELEPHANTS IN YOUR MAILBOX by Roger Horchow. Published by Times Books, 3 Park Avenue, New York, NY 10016. $12.50.

THE HANDBOOK OF INDUSTRIAL DIRECT MAIL ADVERTISING edited by Edward N. Mayer, Jr., and Roy G. Ljungren. Published by Business/Professional Advertising Association, 205 East 42 Street, New York, NY 10017. $10.00.

HOW TO START AND OPERATE A MAIL ORDER BUSINESS by Julian L. Simon. Published by McGraw-Hill Book Company, 1221 Avenue of the Americas, New York, NY 10020. $24.95.

HOW TO WORK WITH MAILING LISTS by Richard S. Hodgson. Published by the Direct Marketing Association, 6 East 43 Street, New York, NY 10017. $12.00.

INTRODUCTION TO FULFILLMENT OPERATIONS IN DI-

RECT MARKETING MONOGRAPH. Published by the Direct Marketing Association, 6 East 43 Street, New York, NY 10017. $24.95.

JOHN CAPLES: ADMAN by Gordon White. Published by Crain Books, 740 North Rush Street, Chicago, IL 60611. $11.95.

THE LAW AND DIRECT MARKETING. Published by the Direct Marketing Association, 6 East 43 Street, New York, NY 10017. $150.00.

MAILER'S GUIDE TO POSTAL REGULATIONS. Published by Crain Books, 740 North Rush Street, Chicago, IL 60611. $45.00.

NATIONAL SURVEY OF CONSUMERS' ATTITUDES TO-WARD DIRECT MAIL ADVERTISING by Robert A. Hansen. Published by MASA, 7315 Wisconsin Avenue, Washington, DC 20014. Volume I (narrative): $7.50. Volume II (charts): $12.50.

PLANNING AND CREATING BETTER DIRECT MAIL by John D. Yeck and John T. Maguire. Published by McGraw-Hill Book Company, 1221 Avenue of the Americas, New York, NY 10020. $17.25.

PROFITABLE DIRECT MARKETING by Jim Kobs. Published by Crain Books, 740 North Rush Street, Chicago, IL 60611. $22.95.

QUEST FOR THE BEST by Stanley Marcus. Published by Viking Press, 299 Murray Hill Parkway, East Rutherford, NJ 07073. $12.95.

RESPONSE TELEVISION: COMBAT ADVERTISING OF THE 1980's by John Witek. Published by Crain Books, 740 North Rush Street, Chicago, IL 60611. $19.95.

SUCCESS FORCES by Joe Sugarman. Published by Contemporary Books, 180 North Michigan Avenue, Chicago, IL 60601. $9.95.

SUCCESSFUL DIRECT MARKETING METHODS by Bob Stone. Published by Crain Books, 740 North Rush Street, Chicago, IL 60611. $24.95.

TELEMARKETING CAMPAIGNS THAT WORK! by Murray Roman. Published by McGraw-Hill Book Company, 1221 Avenue of the Americas, New York, NY 10020. $29.95.

TELEPHONE MARKETING: HOW TO BUILD YOUR BUSINESS BY TELEPHONE by Murray Roman. Published by McGraw-Hill Book Company, 1221 Avenue of the Americas, New York, NY 10020. $35.95.

TELEPHONE MARKETING MONOGRAPH. Published by the Direct Marketing Association, 6 East 43 Street, New York, NY 10017. $24.95.

TESTED ADVERTISING METHODS by John Caples. Published by Prentice-Hall, Inc., Englewood Cliffs, NJ 07632. $5.95.

APPENDIX V

ASSOCIATIONS AND CLUBS

By joining one or more direct marketing associations, you will come into contact with experienced professionals in the field. Seminars by experts will yield new ideas, and you will be able to meet with people from various agencies, with vendors, and with freelance sources and consultants on an informal basis before inviting them to discuss your propositions in detail. Furthermore, as a member of such an association, you will be on mailing lists that will enable you to receive information about services, seminars, publications, books, and other items pertaining to the direct marketing field.

This is an abridged list of direct marketing associations. There are local clubs in Arizona, California, Colorado, the District of Columbia, Florida, Illinois, Massachusetts, Michigan, Minnesota, Missouri, Nebraska, New York, Ohio, Pennsylvania, and Texas. For a complete list, check the current issue of *Direct Marketing Magazine*.

The Direct Marketing Association, Inc.
6 East 43 Street, New York, NY 10017
(212) 689-4977
Also offices at 1730 K. Street NW, Washington, DC 20006 and 47 Rue de la Chaussée d'Antin, Paris, France 75009.

DMA is the largest and oldest international trade association in the direct marketing field. It represents users, creators, and suppliers of direct mail advertising and other direct marketing techniques. It has nearly 5,000 individual members representing more than 2,800 firms in the United States and thirty-nine other countries. The organization's dues levels are dependent upon the size of the firm and the number of members who will join DMA.

Other national associations and clubs include:

Associated Third Class Mail Users
1725 K Street NW, Washington, DC 20006

Association of Direct Marketing Agencies
111 Presidential Boulevard, Bala Cynwyd, PA 19004

Association of Industrial Advertisers
41 East 42 Street, New York, NY 10036

Australian Direct Marketing Association
32 Buckingham Street, Surrey Hills NSW, 2010, Australia

British Direct Mail Marketing Association
1 New Burlington Street, London W1X 1FD, England

Canadian Direct Mail Association
130 Merton Street, Toronto, M4S 1A4

Direct Marketing Creative Guild, Inc.
516 Fifth Avenue, New York, NY 10036

Fulfillment Management Association
755 Second Avenue, New York, NY 10017

APPENDIX VI

SEMINARS

The following are some of the organizations and firms which offer courses and seminars on direct response-related topics. Some offerings are local only, while larger firms schedule day-long and even week-long seminars at various accessible points nationwide. Contact these organizations directly for course availability, scheduling, and prices.

Business/Industrial Council, Direct Marketing Association
6 East 43 Street, New York, NY 10017

Chicago Association of Direct Marketing
221 North LaSalle Street, Chicago, IL 60601

Direct Marketing Association
6 East 43 Street, New York, NY 10017

Dynamic Graphics Educational Foundation
6000 North Forest Park Drive, P.O. Box 1901, Peoria, IL 61656

International Advertising Association, c/o Mr. Michael Gately
Time International, 303 East Ohio Street, Chicago, IL 60611

New York University, The Management Institute/Department of
    Continuing Education
326 Shimkin Hall, New York, NY 10003

Printing Industries Institute
200 East Ontario Street, Chicago, IL 60611

Response Advertising Seminars/René Gnam
Box 6435, Clearwater, FL 33518

Telephone Marketing Institute, Direct Marketing Association
6 East 43 Street, New York, NY 10017

Third Class Mail Association
1010 Wisconsin Avenue, NW, Suite 630, Washington, DC 20007

University of Missouri-Kansas City, Office of Professional Development
School of Business and Public Administration, Kansas City, MO 64110

APPENDIX VII

A WORD ABOUT ETHICS
AND REGULATION

The stories about the "fly-by-night" direct response marketer are legion and, sad to say, there are unethical operators in the direct response field, just as there are in most lines of endeavor. But direct marketers who are in the business for the "long haul" adhere to the rules of the Federal Trade Commission and their individual industries (such as state regulations on the selling of insurance). What's more, direct marketing organizations have their own sets of ethics and self-regulatory rules. For a very complete list of regulations and ethics, see the Direct Marketing Association's *Fact Book on Direct Response Marketing*.

For an overall view of what is considered accepted business practice, here is the Code of Ethics of the Chicago Association of Direct Marketing (CADM):

We hold that a responsibility of the CADM to its members and to all individuals and firms who use, create, produce or supply material and lists for direct response marketing is to be a constructive and useful force in business and the economy in general.

We further hold that, to discharge this responsibility, they should recognize their obligation to the public, the medium they represent, and to each other.

To this end, CADM requires the observance of this Code of Ethics as being in the best interests of the public, all advertising and of direct response marketing users, creators, producers and suppliers.

The Code is intended to serve as a benchmark for the kind of business conduct which experience has shown to be wise, foresighted, and constructive.

Because we believe dishonest, misleading, immoral, salacious or offensive communications make enemies for all advertising/ marketing, including direct response marketing, we require observance of the Code and standards, by all members of CADM.

1. Direct response marketers should make their offers clear and honest. They should not misrepresent a product, service, publication or program and should not use misleading, partially true or exaggerated statements. All descriptions and promises should be in accordance with actual conditions, situations and circumstances existing at the time a promotion is made. Direct response marketers should operate in accordance with the Better Business Bureau's Basic Principles contained in the BBB Code of Advertising and be cognizant of and adhere to the postal laws and regulations, and all other laws governing advertising and transaction of business by mail, telephone, and the print and broadcast media.

2. Direct response marketers should not disparage any person or group on grounds of sex, race, color, creed, age, or nationality.

3. Solicitations, regardless of the medium used, should not contain vulgar, immoral, profane, or offensive matter nor promote the sale of pornographic material or other matter not acceptable for advertising on moral grounds.

4. Photographs and artwork representing or implying representation of a product, or service or fund-raising program for nonprofit organizations should be faithful reproduc-

tions of the product, service, or aid offered by the fund-raising program. All should be current and truly representative. All descriptions and promises should be in accordance with actual conditions, situations, and circumstances existing at the time of the promotion. Photographs and artwork representing or implying situations related to a product, service, or program should be in accordance with the facts. If models are used, clear disclosure of the fact should be made in immediate conjunction with the portrayal.

5. If laboratory-test data are used in advertising, they should be complete as to source and methodology. Reference to laboratory-test data should not be used in support of claims which distort or fail to disclose the true test results.

6. Direct response marketers should not use unsupported or inaccurate statistical data or testimonials originally given for products or services other than those offered, or testimonials making statements or conclusions known to be incorrect. If testimonials are used, they should contain no misstatement of facts or misleading implications, and should reflect the current opinion of the author.

7. Direct response marketers should not make exaggerated price comparisons, exaggerated claims on discounts or savings, or employ fictitious prices.

8. Direct response marketers should sufficiently identify themselves in every solicitation to enable the consumer to contact them.

9. Solicitations that are likely to be mistaken for bills or invoices should not be used.

10. Products should be distributed only in a manner that will provide reasonable safeguards against possibilities of injury.

11. Direct response marketers should be prepared to make

prompt delivery of orders. Any delay should be promptly reported to the customer, informing him or her of his or her right to consent to the delay or obtain a refund.

12. The terms and conditions of guarantee should be clearly and specifically set forth in immediate conjunction with the guarantee offer. Performance guarantees should be limited to the reasonable capabilities and qualities of the product or service advertised.

13. When products or services are offered on a satisfaction-guaranteed or money-back basis, any refunds requested should be made promptly. In an unqualified offer of refund or replacement, the customer's preference shall prevail.

14. Direct response marketers should not make offers which purport to require a person to return a notice that he or she does not wish to receive further merchandise in order to avoid liability for the purchase price, unless all the conditions are first made clear in an initial offer that is accepted by the purchaser by means of a bona fide order. (For detailed specifications regarding negative option plans, see Federal Trade Communications regulations.)

15. Unordered merchandise should not be sent unless such merchandise is clearly and conspicuously represented to be "free" and the recipient clearly informed of his or her unqualified right to treat it as a gift, and to do with it as he or she sees fit, at no cost or obligation.

16. A product or service which is offered without cost or obligation to the recipient may be unqualifiedly described as "free." "Free" may also be used conditionally where the offer requires the recipient to purchase some other product or service, provided all terms and conditions are accurately and conspicuously disclosed in immediate conjunction with the use of the term "free" and the product or service required to be purchased is not increased in price or decreased in quality or quantity.

17. Direct response marketers should not use or permit to be used unfair, misleading, deceptive, or abusive methods for collecting money owed by delinquent accounts.

18. Direct response marketers who use the telephone to solicit sales or donations should not tape conversations without a beeping device or the consent of the person being called.

19. All telephone contacts should be made during reasonable hours.

20. Direct response marketers should not make telephone calls in the guise of research or a survey when the intent is to sell.

21. Direct response marketers using the telephone should make every effort not to accept orders from minors without the consent of their parents.

22. Conscientious efforts should be made not to call telephone subscribers who have unlisted or unpublished telephone numbers unless a prior relationship exists, and telemarketers should remove such persons' names from their contact lists when requested to do so.

23. Direct response marketers should make no percentage or commission arrangements whereby any person or firm assisting or participating in a fund-raising activity is paid a fee proportionate to the funds raised, nor should they solicit for nonexistent or nonfunctioning organizations.

24. Direct response marketers who sell instructions, catalogs, or merchandise-for-resale, or who sell or rent lists, should not use misleading or deceptive statements with respect to the earning possibilities, lack of risk, or ease of operation.

25. Those who rent, exchange, or purchase lists should make every effort to ascertain the origin, current ownership and market profile of such lists in the interests of directing their promotions only to those segments of the public most

likely to be interested in their causes or to have a use for their products or services.

26. Those who permit the outside use of their lists should at all times be aware that it is not in the best interests of the public or of themselves to allow their lists to be used by organizations that do not observe the CADM Code of Ethics.

27. Direct response marketers who rent or exchange their lists should offer to all those whose names appear on such lists the option to have their names excluded when list rentals or exchanges are made. They should also make conscientious efforts to remove names from their customer or donor lists when requested either directly or in accordance with the DMA Mail Preference Service.

28. No lists should be used in violation of the lawful rights of the list owner; and any such misuse should be brought to the attention of the lawful owner.

INDEX

Accounts payable, 167
Add-ons, 48
  catalog merchandising, 101
Ads, enhancement methods, 230. *See also* Print media
Agencies, 196–204
  choice of, 200–201
  client/agency relationship, 201–2
  collateral services, 200
  commission system, 198
  creative boutique-type firms, 200
  full-service agency, 199
  in-house agency, 202–4
  modular agency, 199–200
  negative aspects of, 197–98
  reasons for use, 196–97
Art direction, 223–27
  information necessary for, 226–27
  sources for, 224
Attrition report, 167

Back-end marketing, 168–87
  business-to-business formats, 187
  collection letters, 182
  computer sales, example, 170–72
  continued sales, front-end approaches, 178–81
  examples of, 176–77

follow-up programs, 169–70
functions of, 168
good-will activities, 173–76
leads, 169
purchase reinforcing material, 172–73
renewals, periodicals/clubs, 182–83
for retail businesses, 183–86
ride-along offers, 182
See also Retail back-end marketing
Bad-debt report, 167
Bangtail envelopes, 185–86
Batch processing, orders, 163
Bleeds, 232
Broadcast media, 140–45
  business-to-business marketing, 145
  radio direct response, 140, 144
  retail business and, 144–45
  television direct response, 141
  See also Television direct response
Brochures, 68–69
  types of, 69
Brokers, mailing lists, 115–17
Buckslip reminders, 76–77
Bulk Rate Mail Permit, 75
Business Reply Envelopes/Cards,

Business Reply Envelopes/Cards
(*Continued*)
73–74, 214–15
sizes of, 74
Business-to-business back-end
marketing, 187
Business-to-business catalogs, 110–
12
aftermarket sales and, 111
creative ideas for, 111–12
Business-to-business formats, 81–84
file folder, 83
how-to booklets, 84
loose-leaf notebook, 83–84
newsletter, 84
special reports/surveys, 84
testimonials, 84
Business-to-business marketing
broadcast media, 145
telephone, 139
Business-to-business offers, 58–59
lead generation, 59
premiums, 59
Business-to-business public relations,
157–60
contacts for, 158–59
materials for, 159–60
objectives of, 157–58
Buyers, 24–31
advantages of mail order, 27
business/industrial buyers, 29–31
mail order, reasons for use, 24–26
profile of, 26
resistances of, 27
retail buyers, 28–29

Cable TV, ad time, 142–143, 145
Cash-management report, 167
Cash on delivery (COD), 45–46
Cash up front, 44
Catalog business, 79, 85–112
allocation of space, 102–4
business-to-business, 110–12
design of catalog, 104–5
market appeal aspect, 92–93
merchandising, 100–109
ordering merchandise, 101–2
positioning of catalogs, 93–100

prime selling spaces, 105–6
retail catalog, 109–10
same catalog/different mailing,
107–8
starting up, 86–89
target market defining, 91–92
Charge accounts
charge card payment option, 44–45
"house" charge, 45
reactivation of, 186
Charge-card option, 44–45
Charge report, 167
Chromalin proofs, 258
Clubs, as products, 37–38
Collections
letters, 182
reports, 167
retailers, 58
Color, separation process, 257–59
Commissions, agencies, 198
Comparative price, 41
Competition, catalog merchandising
and, 100–101
Compiled lists, mailing lists, 114–15
Comprehensive layouts, 228
Computer letters
direct mail, 64
retail direct mail, 80
Computers, order processing, 164–65
Contests, 48
Continuity series, 178–79
Contribution method, 190
Co-op mailings, 186
Copy, 245–52
"call to action" copy, 248
feature/benefit/value format, 247–
48
good copy, characteristics of, 249–
51
headlines, 245–46
length of, 247
P.S. (post script), 248–49
revision of, 251–52
success stories, 248
"you" approach, 246
Copywriters, 239
critique of, 244
information for, 241–44

revising copy, 251–52
samples of work, 240
sources for, 239
Costs. *See* Print production
Coupons, retail direct mail, 81
Customer franchise, 114
Customer lists, mailing lists, 113
Customer service department, 165–67
Customer-status report, 167

Direct mail format, 60–84
brochure, 68–69
Business Reply Envelope, 73–74
business-to-business format, 81–84
critical date schedules, 208–10
inserts, 75–78
lettershops, 215–18
market testing of, 121–22
outer envelope, 74–75
post office, 211–15
reply card, 70–73
retail format, 79–81
seasonality, 205–7
selling letter, 61–67
See also Business-to-business
formats; Retail direct response
format
Direct marketing plan, 266–70
copy strategy, 268–69
marketing objectives/strategy,
267–68
media objectives/strategy, 268
review of market, 266–67
Direct market testing, 121–24
direct mail tests, 121–22
premium testing, 122–23
product/service testing, 123–24
testing in print, 123
Direct response business
acquisition of, 9
catalog business, 85–112
development of, 10–11
mailing lists, 113–20
strategic plan for, 11–12
Direct response marketing
agencies for, 196–204
back-end marketing, 168–87

broadcast media, 140–45
consultants for, 195
criteria for use of, 5–7
direct mail format, 60–84
legal factors, 219–22
offer in, 32–59
public relations, 146–60
telephone marketing, 135–39
See also Financial assessment
Discounts. *See* Pricing strategies

Efforting program, 179–81
800 numbers, 164–65
telephone marketing, 138
Employee-performance reports, 167
Endorsement, in direct mailing, 64–65
Envelopes
outer, direct mail sales ad, 74–75
price quotes, 262–63
Exclusives, catalog merchandising,
101

Feature stories, public relations, 149–51
File folders, business direct response,
83
Financial assessment, 188–89
contribution method, 190
profit-and-loss worksheet, 191–92
profit per response (PPR) method,
189–90
return on investment method, 190
rollout analysis, 191
First-class mail, 212–13
Free trial offer, 42–43
Front-end marketing, 168, 176, 178–81
continuity series, 178–79
efforting program, 179–81
load-up offer, 179
negative option, 181
ship-'til-forbid, 181
Fulfillment, 161–67
customer service, 165–67
forecasting model for, 161
order-processing, 163–65
product production/delivery, 162

Fulfillment (*Continued*)
  reports, types of, 167
  warehouse, functions of, 165
Full-service agency, 199

General-ledger report, 167
Gimmick items, 78
Guarantees, 52
  of acceptance, 52
  of quality, 52
  of repair/replacement, 52

Hard news, public relations, 148
"House" charge, 45
How-to booklets, 84

In-house agency, 202–4
  positive/negative aspects, 203–4
  project manager, 203
Inserts, 75–78
  buckslip reminders, 76–77
  follow-ups, 78
  gimmick items, 78
  premium slips, 76
  product samples, 77–78
  question/answer pieces, 77
  reprints of ads/articles, 77
  self-mailers, 78
  testimonial flyers, 75–76
Interviews, public relations, 152–53
Introductory offers, 40
Inventory-control report, 167

Keylines, 228–29

Layouts, 227–33
  ads, enhancement of, 230
  bleeds/color, 232
  comprehensive, 228
  evaluation of, 229–32
  keylines, 228–29
  pencil roughs, 228
  thumbnail, 228
Lead-generation, 52–53
  back-end marketing, 169, 187
  business-to-business sales, 59

loose leads, 53–54
  offers in "two-step" programs,
    52–53
  television ads, 143
  tight leads, 54
Leads, loose/tight, 53–54
Legal factors, 219–22
  Federal Trade Commission
    requirements, 219
  product liability, 221–22
  promotional copy, 220–21
  trademark search, 221
Lettershops, 215–18
  comparing shops, 216
  relationship with, 216–18
Letters, *See* Selling letter
Load-up offer, 179
Loose leads, 53–54
Loose-leaf notebook, business direct
    response format, 83–84
Loss leaders, 41

Mailgram, direct mail selling, 67
Mailing lists, 113–20
  broker, role of, 115–17
  compiled lists, 114–15
  customer lists, 113–14
  list-rental income, 119–20
  mail-responsive lists, 114
  merge/purge techniques, 119
  response testing, 117–19
Mail-responsive lists, 114
Marketing
  goals of seller, 33
  market segmentation approach, 35
Marketing mix, offer, 32–59
Marketing orientation, 24
Market testing
  direct market, 121–24
  print media, 132–33
  split testing, 133
Merchandising, catalogs, 100–109
Money-back guarantee, 43–44

Negative option, 181
Newsletters, 84
Nonprofit bulk rate, 214

Offer, 32–59
  add-ons, 48
  as lead-generation, 52–53
  business-to-business, 58–59
  conditions of sale in, 49–51
  guarantees, 52
  leads, loose/tight, 53–54
  payment terms, 42–46
  premiums, 46–48
  price in, 39–41
  product in, 33–39
  retail offers, 54–58
  sweepstakes, 48
  See also Retail offer; Sales
    methods
Orders
  order starter, 41
  processing of, 163–65

Package inserts, 186
Paper, choice of, 263–65
Payment terms, 42–46
  cash on delivery (COD), 45–46
  cash up front, 44
  charge-card option, 44–45
  free trial, 42–43
  "house" charge, 45
  money-back guarantee, 43–44
  reservation buying, 42
  split payment, 44
Pencil roughs, 228
Periodicals
  renewals, 182–83
  seasons for mailing, 207
Photography, 236–37
  price quotes, 256–57
Photos, public relations, 153
Pitch letters, 151
Post cards, 213
Post office, 211–15
  Business Reply Envelopes/Cards,
    214–15
  first-class mail, 212–13
  nonprofit bulk rate, 214
  post cards, 213
  third-class mail, 213–14
Premiums, 46–48
  business premiums, 59

market testing of, 122–23
member-get-a-member method,
  47–48
premium slips, 76
Press approvals, 261
Press release, 149–51
Price, 39–41
  pricing factors, 39–40
  See also Pricing strategies
Pricing strategies
  comparative price, 41
  introductory offer, 40
  loss leaders, 41
  order level, discounts for, 41
  order size, discounts for, 41
  quantity price, 41
  refund for catalog, 40
  sale price, 41
  seasonal discounts, 40
Print media, 125–34
  buying space, 132
  control, lack of, 133–34
  decision-making for, 126–27
  directories, use of, 127
  image projection, 128–31
  market testing procedures, 132–33
  remnant space, 131, 132
  R.O.P. (Run of Press) space, 131,
    132
  strategic planning, 125–26
  timing of ads, 134
  See also Copy
Print production, 253–65
  color separation, 257–59
  cost-saving tips, 265
  envelope quotes, 262–63
  paper, choice of, 263–65
  photography quotes, 256–57
  press approvals, 261
  printing quotes, 259–61
  vendors, 253–56
Products, 33–39
  accessories and, 38–39
  all-in-one kits, 35, 37
  assortment concept, 34–35
  club as product, 37–38
  customer choice and, 37
  demonstration of, 33–34

Products (*Continued*)
  differentiation of, 35
  market segmentation approach, 35
  trading-up approach, 37
Profit-and-loss worksheet, 191–92
Profit per response (PPR) method,
  189–90
Public relations, 146–60
  consumer public relations, 153–
    155
  contacts, choice of, 147
  feature stories, 149–51
  follow-up phone calls, 151–52
  hard news, 148
  interviews with media, 152
  photos, 153
  pitch letters, 151
  press release, 149
  reference works for, 147–48
  See also Business-to-business
    public relations; Consumer
    public relations; Retail public
    relations
Publisher's letters, 65, 67

Radio direct response, 140, 144
Remnant space, 131, 132
Renewals, back-end methods for,
  182–83
Reply card, 70–73
  involvement devices, 71–72
  tear-off stub, 71
Reports, types of, 167
Reservation buying, 42
Retail back-end marketing, 183–86
  bangtail envelopes, 185–86
  charge accounts, reactivation of,186
  co-op mailings, 186
  package inserts, 186
  statement stuffers, 185
Retail business
  broadcast media, 144–45
  public relations, 155–57
  telephone marketing, 138–39
Retail catalogs, 109–10
  reasons for use of, 109–10
  vendor-supported programs, 110
Retail direct response formats, 79–81

catalog mailing, 79
computer letters, 80
coupon books, 81
handwritten letters, 80–81
invitation approach, 81
letters for, 79–80
multi-flyer mailing, 79
one-item offer, 79
self-mailers, 81
telegrams, 81
Retailers, 13–23
  direct response divisions, 21–23
  resistance to direct marketing, 13–
    15
  value of direct marketing, 16–21
Retail offers, 54–58
  collections, 58
  direct mail ads, 57–58
  store/mail/phone offers, 57
  traffic builders, 55–57
Retail public relations, 155–57
  contacts for, 156–57
  direct mail supplements, 157
  objectives of, 155–56
Return-goods report, 167
Return on investment method, 190
Ride-along offers, 182
Rollout analysis, 191
R.O.P. (Run of Press) space, 131,
  132

Sale price, 41
Sales methods
  continuity plan, 51
  loading-up, 51
  membership fee, 51
  negative option, 50
  positive option, 50
  ship-'til-forbid, 51
  urgency strategies, 49
Sales report, 167
Sales tax report, 167
Samples, in direct mailing, 77–78
Seasonal factors
  discounts, 40
  months for direct mailings, 205–7
Self-mailers, 78
  retail direct mail, 81

Selling letter, 61–67, 79–81
  attention-getters in, 61, 62–63
  characteristics of, 61–67
  computer letters, 64
  endorsement letters and, 64–65
  inserts, 75–78
  letterhead, 62
  mailgram/telegram as, 67
  outer envelope, 74–75
  P.S. (post script) in, 64
  "publisher's" letter, 65–67
  purposes of, 61
Separation process, 257–59
  price quotes, 257–59
Service companies, order processing,
    163
Ship-'til-forbid, 181
Split payment, 44
Split testing, 133
Standard Rate and Data Service
    (SRDS), 127, 210, 229
Statement stuffers, 185
Support TV ads, 143–144
Sweepstakes, 48

Teasers, on envelopes, 74–75
Telegrams
  direct mail selling, 67
  retail direct mail, 81
Telephone marketing, 135–39

advantages of, 135
business-to-business, 139
incoming, 138
outgoing, 137–38
retail business, 138–39
taped messages, 137
WATS lines, 136
Television direct response, 141–44
  cable ad time, 142–43, 145
  interest level of ads, 141–42
  lead-generating ads, 143
  price of products, 142
  support ads, 143–44
Testimonial flyers, 75–76
Testimonials, 75–76, 84
Third-class mail, 213–14
Thumbnail layouts, 228
Tight leads, 54
Toll-free numbers, 164–65
Trade shows, 101
Type, 233–36
  reading proof, 234–35
  sizes of, 234
  styles of, 233–34
Typesetting, cost-savings, 236

Vendors, 253–56

Warehouse, functions of, 165
WATS lines, 136